Personal Investing
The Missing Manual®

D0711803

Personal Investing: The Missing Manual

BY BONNIE BIAFORE, AMY E. BUTTELL, AND CAROL FABBRI

Published by O'Reilly Media, Inc., 1005 Gravenstein Highway North, Sebastopol, CA 95472.

O'Reilly books may be purchased for educational, business, or sales promotional use. Online editions are also available for most titles (http://my.*safaribooksonline.com*). For more information, contact our corporate/institutional sales department: 800.998.9938 or corporate@*oreilly.com*.

Editor: Peter McKie

Production Editor: Nellie McKesson

Copy Editor: Jan Jue

Indexer: Angela Howard

Cover Designer: Karen Montgomery

Interior Designer: Ron Bilodeau

Print History:

May 2010:	First Edition.

ISBN: 978-1-4493-8178-3

[LSI]   [2013-07-19]

Contents

Part One: Prepare to Invest

Chapter 1
Why Should You Invest?

Chapter 2
Set Your Investment Goals

Chapter 3
Invest with Open Eyes

Part Two: Choose and Buy Your Investments

Chapter 4
How Investments Work

Part Three: Manage Your Investments

The Missing Credits

About the Author

Bonnie Biafore has always been a zealous planner, whether setting up software demos, cooking gourmet meals, or scheduling a vacation to test the waters of spontaneity. Ironically, fate, not planning, turned this obsession into a career as a project manager. When she isn't managing projects for clients, Bonnie writes about personal finance, investing, project management, small business accounting, and technology. She's also branching out into other "dry" topics with a recent article for *Wine Enthusiast*. As an engineer, she's fascinated by how things work and how to make things work better. She has a knack for mincing dry subjects like accounting and project management into easy-to-understand morsels and then spices them to perfection with her warped sense of humor.

Bonnie is the award-wining author of more than a dozen books including *QuickBooks 2010: The Missing Manual*, *Project 2010: The Missing Manual*, *Quicken 2009: The Missing Manual*, the *Better Investing Stock Selection Handbook* (which won an APEX Award of Distinction), *Online Investing Hacks*, and *On Time! On Track! On Target!*. She also writes regularly about financial topics for *Better Investing*, bankrate.com, and interest.com. When unshackled from her computer, she hikes in the mountains, cycles, cooks gourmet food, and tries, mostly unsuccessfully, to say no to additional work assignments. Email: *bonnie.biafore@gmail.com*.

Amy E. Buttell is a journalist who writes about personal finance, investing, healthcare and accounting. She is the author of *The Better Investing Mutual Fund Handbook* and contributed to the book *Online Investing Hacks*. She lives in Erie, PA, with her two sons and two cats in a house near Lake Erie.

Carol Fabbri helps people achieve their financial goals. To accomplish this mission, she writes, speaks, and presents on personal finance to her clients and other audiences. She uses a decade in management consulting and the finance education she got at MIT to teach people how to shed emotional baggage so they make smart investment decisions.

She is the managing partner of Fair Advisors (*http://fair advisors.com*), an independent financial advisory firm, and is the President of Fair Advisors Institute (*http://fairadvisors.org*), a nonprofit dedicated to improving financial literacy in the US. She is frequently quoted in national publications like the *Wall Street Journal*, *Forbes*, and *Smart Money*. Carol's other passions are her husband and her son. Before becoming a mom, she had hobbies. Email: *cfabbri@fairadvisors.com*.

About the Creative Team

Peter McKie (editor) is an editor at Missing Manuals. He has wanted to commission a practical, clear, insightful consumer book on personal investing since he read Peter Lynch's *Beating the Street* a decade ago. Thanks to its authors and their unwavering diligence, this book is everything he envisioned and more. Peter graduated with a master's degree from Boston University's School of Journalism and lives in New York City, where he researches the history of old houses and, every once in a while, sneaks into abandoned buildings. Email: *pmckie@gmail.com*.

Nellie McKesson (production editor) is a graduate of St. John's College in Santa Fe, New Mexico. She lives in Brockton, Mass., and spends her spare time studying graphic design and making t-shirts (*www.endplasticdesigns. com*). Email: *nellie@oreilly.com*.

Jan Jue (copy editor) enjoys freelance copyediting with care and precision, reading a good mystery, and searching for the perfect potsticker. Email: *jjuepub@sbcglobal.net*.

Angela Howard (indexer) has been indexing for more than 10 years, mostly for computer books, but occasionally for books on other topics, such as travel, alternative medicine, and leopard geckos. She lives in California with her husband, daughter, and two cats.

Jason Bowers (technical reviewer) is an independent financial markets consultant and is building a nonprofit hedge fund to support education and independent art projects. He provides confidential analysis, coaching, and economic reporting to wealth managers, traders, and personal investors (*http://21Cconsulting.com*). He has worked with Goldman Sachs and SMB Capital in New York and with other clients worldwide. After market hours, Jason enjoys creating music and playing chess. Email: *jbowers@21Cconsulting.com*

Kristen Tod (technical reviewer) is a freelance technical editor. She was a technology consultant working in the hardware and software industry for more than 10 years.

Acknowledgments

We are deeply indebted to the horde of folks who worked so hard to make this book as good as it is. Special thanks go to Peter McKie for dreaming of this book and then doing the hard work to make it a reality. As always, a huge round of applause goes to the O'Reilly team, including Nellie McKesson, Jan Jue, and Angela Howard for their awesome attention to detail and astonishing productivity. Jason Bowers and Kristen Tod, the technical reviewers, offered valuable insights and suggestions, which taught us some subtleties we didn't know and made this book better.

—*Bonnie Biafore, Amy E. Buttell, and Carol Fabbri*

The Missing Manual Series

Missing Manuals are witty, superbly written guides to computer products that don't come with printed manuals (which is just about all of them). Each book features a handcrafted index; cross-references to specific pages (not just chapters); and RepKover, a detached-spine binding that lets the book lie perfectly flat without the assistance of weights or cinder blocks.

Recent and upcoming titles include:

Access 2007: The Missing Manual by Matthew MacDonald

Access 2010: The Missing Manual by Matthew MacDonald

Buying a Home: The Missing Manual by Nancy Conner

CSS: The Missing Manual, Second Edition, by David Sawyer McFarland

Creating a Web Site: The Missing Manual, Second Edition, by Matthew MacDonald

David Pogue's Digital Photography: The Missing Manual by David Pogue

Dreamweaver CS4: The Missing Manual by David Sawyer McFarland

Dreamweaver CS5: The Missing Manual by David Sawyer McFarland

Excel 2007: The Missing Manual by Matthew MacDonald

Excel 2010: The Missing Manual by Matthew MacDonald

Facebook: The Missing Manual, Second Edition by E.A. Vander Veer

FileMaker Pro 10: The Missing Manual by Susan Prosser and Geoff Coffey

FileMaker Pro 11: The Missing Manual by Susan Prosser and Stuart Gripman

Flash CS4: The Missing Manual by Chris Grover with E.A. Vander Veer

Flash CS5: The Missing Manual by Chris Grover

Google Apps: The Missing Manual by Nancy Conner

The Internet: The Missing Manual by David Pogue and J.D. Biersdorfer

iMovie '08 & iDVD: The Missing Manual by David Pogue

iMovie '09 & iDVD: The Missing Manual by David Pogue and Aaron Miller

iPad: The Missing Manual by J.D. Biersdorfer and David Pogue

iPhone: The Missing Manual, Second Edition by David Pogue

iPhone App Development: The Missing Manual by Craig Hockenberry

iPhoto '08: The Missing Manual by David Pogue

iPhoto '09: The Missing Manual by David Pogue and J.D. Biersdorfer

iPod: The Missing Manual, Eighth Edition by J.D. Biersdorfer and David Pogue

JavaScript: The Missing Manual by David Sawyer McFarland

Living Green: The Missing Manual by Nancy Conner

Mac OS X: The Missing Manual, Leopard Edition by David Pogue

Mac OS X Snow Leopard: The Missing Manual by David Pogue

Microsoft Project 2007: The Missing Manual by Bonnie Biafore

Microsoft Project 2010: The Missing Manual by Bonnie Biafore

Netbooks: The Missing Manual by J.D. Biersdorfer

Office 2007: The Missing Manual by Chris Grover, Matthew MacDonald, and E.A. Vander Veer

Introduction

Why should you pick up a book on personal investing? The answer is simple but stark: Because you have no choice. The sad truth is, you can't save enough money in your lifetime to live comfortably in retirement (even with a Social Security check), send your kids to college, afford long-term health care, or take a dream vacation. Inflation is higher than savings account interest rates, and Social Security benefits go down while the age of eligibility goes up. To live comfortably in the future, you have to create a nest egg and grow it by investing.

Schools typically don't teach personal finance, so unless your parents were savvy investors, you were probably unceremoniously dumped into the working world without much knowledge of financial planning or investing. To make matters worse, investing, like pumping gasoline, has evolved into a self-service industry, with 401(k)s replacing pensions, and discount brokerages standing in for full-service finance houses. If you don't know how to plan and invest for your future, you won't have a very rewarding one. So unless you were born wealthy or hit the Powerball lottery, you need to learn something about investing.

Don't worry. As you'll learn shortly, investing doesn't have to be complicated. You can build a nest egg that meets your needs barely breaking a sweat. However, if you discover that you *enjoy* fiddling with investments, you can add plenty of tricks to your investment tool bag.

Why Investing Is Important

Coughing up the cash to buy a new Mr. Coffee—the one with the timer so your coffee is ready when you wake up—doesn't require investing. Neither, for that matter, does a down payment on a Subaru Outback. For purchases like these, a few months or years of saving gets you the money you need.

Investing comes into play for stuff that costs a fortune—literally. Take retirement, for example. If you get a job right out of college, you might work for 45 years. During that time, your paychecks (not credit card debt!) cover your living expenses. At current life expectancies, if you retire at age 65, you're looking at 35 to 40 years of retirement. Except that you won't be getting a paycheck to cover your cost of living in your golden years. Living on Social Security (if it's even still solvent when you retire) isn't a pretty picture, and greeting customers at Walmart will lose its luster by the time you're 80.

What can you do? At first blush, the answer seems to be to live on half your paycheck and save the other half for retirement. When you're young, making ends meet on your salary is hard enough. Although your paychecks usually increase with time, so do your expenses. In the 1960s, a loaf of white bread cost 25 cents. Today, you eat whole wheat bread, and a loaf runs about $3. That's what inflation does (see page 14 for the full scoop).

With the average inflation rate at 3.4%, the cost of living doubles in about 21 years. By the time a college graduate reaches 100, annual living expenses would cost fourteen times as much, assuming she was still willing to live on pizza and use plastic milk crates as end tables. In addition, retirement isn't the only big goal in your life. College education for your kids isn't cheap, and it's increasing even faster than inflation. You've seen how fast health costs and health care insurance premiums have gone up.

Savings accounts, certificates of deposit, and other savings options rarely beat inflation. Investing turns out to be the answer to this seemingly insurmountable challenge. By investing your money, you can earn 6% to 8% a year on average. That's better than the thin film of mold you get burying your cash in the garden or the interest rates on savings accounts. Most importantly, investment returns are higher than inflation, so your nest egg stays ahead of the increase in prices. The same way inflation makes prices increase at an ever faster pace, investment *returns* help your money grow even faster. The process is called compounding, and page 16 explains how it works. Reinvesting your earnings like dividends and interest is another key to successful investing, as you learn on page 158.

The First Step: Planning

Your next dilemma is figuring out how much you have to invest each month to reach your goals. On one hand, you want to save enough so you don't have to compromise your goals down the road. On the other hand, you don't want to over-save, because you sacrifice unnecessarily only to end up with money left over for your heirs or—heaven forbid—estate taxes.

You have some prep work to do before you start investing. Don't sweat the pop quiz. You won't be graded on your answers. Your assignment: Decide what your goals are. Sit down with a nice cup of tea, coffee, or something stronger, and make a list of what you want in life that costs money (page 21). Be as decadent or as conservative as you want. You can change your mind later (although not decades later). Some goals appear on almost everyone's list: retirement and college educations for your kids for starters. If you pass on procreation, you may opt for a sailboat, a greenhouse full of rare orchids, or climbing the tallest mountain on every continent. It's totally up to you.

With wish list in hand, you don't wait for a fairy godmother to sprinkle pixie dust to make it all come true. You have to come up with a plan to make it happen. How much are your goals going to cost? How much can you earn on your investments? And from there, how much do you have to invest regularly to amass that fortune? Chapter 2 guides you step by step.

Simple Steps to Successful Investing

If you could double your money every year, reaching your financial goals wouldn't be an issue. However, the yin and yang of the financial world are risk and return. The more risk you're willing to take, the higher the potential rewards you can get in investment returns.

With long-term goals like retirement 30 years from now, higher levels of risk aren't unreasonable. The higher returns make it easier to reach your financial goals, and your investments have time to recover from short-term drops. Those short-term drops are where a lot of people get into trouble, though. If you get nauseous when your investments go down, you may overreact and sell when you shouldn't, or make other emotional decisions that are bad for your bottom line. (Page 45 explains several of the psychological mistakes investors make and how you can avoid them.)

By understanding the different types of investments at your disposal, you can invest at a level of risk your stomach can handle. For long-term growth, you can't beat stocks (Chapter 6). Their higher returns are great for growing your nest egg, but they go hand in hand with the occasional bad year (1929, 2008, and a few others in between). To smooth out stocks' wild ride, you can also invest in bonds (Chapter 7) and real estate (Chapter 8).

 Tip Investing smaller amounts on a regular schedule (page 178) improves your results and helps you stop worrying about whether you're buying at the right time. The technique is called *dollar cost averaging,* because you automatically buy more shares when the price is lower and fewer shares when the price is higher. The result: a lower average purchase price, which means a higher total return. If you contribute to a 401(k), you've been doing it without knowing it.

The key to balancing risk and return is something called *asset allocation* (page 159)—how you divvy up your money among different types of investments. More money in stocks means higher risk and higher long-term returns. More in bonds provides less risk and lower returns.

A lot of your investment performance stems from the asset allocation you pick. That means you don't have to train to be the next Warren Buffett. In fact, once you settle on your asset allocation, your investments don't need a lot of hand-holding. A handful of index mutual funds apportioned to your asset allocation is all it takes to get started (page 166).

At the same time, you don't just plop your money into investments and forget about them until it's time to withdraw some cash. Because stocks, bonds, and other investments grow at different rates, your asset allocation goes out of whack over time. From time to time, you have to rebalance your portfolio to bring your asset allocation back on target (page 170). For long-term goals, checking your allocation once a year is usually enough. If the percentages are within 1% or 2%, you can leave things alone until another year passes. When your goals fall in the 5- to 10-year range, a quarterly or semiannual tune-up may be in order.

Sometimes, investments don't turn out as you hoped. If that happens, it's time to do some weeding and feeding. Getting rid of "dogs" not only improves your portfolio; it's another opportunity to bring your asset allocation back on track.

 Note You have to adjust your asset allocation to reduce risk as you get closer to needing money from your investments. That way, your portfolio doesn't take a big hit just when you plan to take out cash. Page 188 tells you how.

One thing that's impossible to simplify is taxes. The government offers a plethora of tax-advantaged options for retirement, college, and health-care saving. This book helps you decide which types of tax-advantaged accounts (tax-deferred, tax-free, and so on) make sense for you. You'll also learn which types of investment to put in which types of accounts if you use a combination of taxable and tax-advantaged accounts.

About This Book

These days, bookstores, libraries, and the Web are chock-a-block with financial and investment information. The problem is they're like a dictionary. How do you find the word you want to spell correctly if you don't know how to spell it? If you're trying to learn about investing, how do you sort through thousands of books and web pages to find what you really need to know about your money?

This book takes the place of the manual that should have accompanied your first paycheck (or the first allowance your parents paid you). In these pages, you'll learn the basics of investing and find step-by-step instructions for using websites to choose the right funds (page 71), stocks (page 103), bonds (page 127), and so on. If you're just starting out with investing, you can read the first few chapters to learn how to keep investing as simple as possible. After that, you can jump from topic to topic depending on what you want to invest in and the investing task at hand. The book helps you figure out which investments are right for you and the best way to use them.

 Tip Although every year seems to introduce new investment options and tax regulations, this book is a good primer for setting up and managing your investment portfolio. Of course, it's a good idea to check for changes in government regulations before you make new investments or change the ones you already own.

Personal Investing: The Missing Manual is designed to accommodate readers at several levels of investment knowledge. The primary discussions are written for people with beginner or intermediate investment skills. But if you're reading about investing for the first time, special boxes with the title "Up To Speed" provide the introductory information you need to understand the topic at hand. On the other hand, people with advanced skills should watch for similar boxes called "Power Users' Clinic," which give more technical tips and tricks for more savvy investors.

About the Outline

Personal Investing: The Missing Manual is divided into three parts, each containing several chapters:

- **Part One: Prepare to Invest** gets you started with what you have to do *before* you get into the nitty-gritty of investing. First, you learn how investing helps you achieve your long-term goals. Before you start investing, you need to know what those goals are. You'll learn how to identify your goals and then estimate what they're going to cost. The last chapter explains how to build an investment plan to reach those goals. You'll also learn to sidestep the psychological mistakes people often make when they invest, so your investments can truly shine.

- **Part Two: Choose and Buy Your Investments** starts with a quick overview of what you can invest in. These chapters then take you through each type of investment, including funds, stocks, bonds, and real estate investment trusts (REITs). The last chapter in this section explains how to keep your investment portfolio in tip-top condition.

- **Part Three: Manage Your Investments** gives you the full scoop on investing for big life goals: retirement, college education, and health care. These chapters start by explaining the special challenges you'll face. Then, they take you through how to pick the right investments and the right types of accounts. Finally, they explain how to spend the money you've worked so hard to put together.

The Very Basics

These days, the Web is a treasure trove of investment information. So, to use this book, you need to know a few computer basics. Web pages and programs like Microsoft Excel respond when you click mouse buttons to choose commands from menus, or press combinations of keys for keyboard shortcuts. Here's a quick overview of a few terms and concepts this book uses:

- **Clicking.** This book gives you three kinds of instructions that require you to use your computer's mouse, trackball, or track pad. To **click** means to point the arrow pointer at something on the screen, and then—without moving the pointer at all—press and release the left button on the mouse (or trackball or laptop track pad). To **right-click** means the same thing, but using the right mouse button. To **double-click,** of course, means to click the left button twice in rapid succession, again without moving the pointer at all. And to **drag** means to move the pointer while holding down the left button the entire time.

When you're told to **Shift+click** something, you click while pressing the Shift key. Related procedures, such as **Ctrl+clicking,** work the same way—just click while pressing the corresponding key.

- **Menus.** The **menus** are the words across the top of your screen: File, Edit, and so on. Click one to make a list of commands appear, as though they're written on a window shade you've just pulled down. Some people click to open a menu, and then release the mouse button; after reading the menu command choices, they click the command they want. Other people like to press the mouse button continuously as they click the menu title and drag down the list to the desired command; only then do they release the mouse button. Either method works, so choose the one you prefer.

- **Keyboard shortcuts.** Nothing is faster than keeping your fingers on your keyboard, entering data, choosing names, triggering commands—without losing time by grabbing the mouse, carefully positioning it, and then choosing a command or list entry. That's why many experienced Excel fans prefer to trigger commands by pressing combinations of keys on the keyboard. For example, in most word processors, pressing Ctrl+B produces a **boldface** word. When you read an instruction like "Press Ctrl+C to copy the selection to the Clipboard," start by pressing the Ctrl key; while it's down, type the letter C, and then release both keys.

About→These→Arrows

Throughout this book, and throughout the Missing Manual series, you'll find sentences like this one: Choose Data→Filter→AutoFilter. That's shorthand for a much longer instruction that directs you to navigate three nested menus in sequence, like this: "Choose Data. On the Data menu, point to the Filter menu entry. On the submenu that appears, choose AutoFilter."

Programs like Word 2007, Excel 2007, and PowerPoint 2007 use a ribbon instead of a menu bar. The arrow shorthand applies to the ribbon as well. For example, Data→Sort & Filter→Filter is shorthand for selecting the Data tab on the Office ribbon, navigating to the Sort & Filter section, and then clicking Filter, as you can see below.

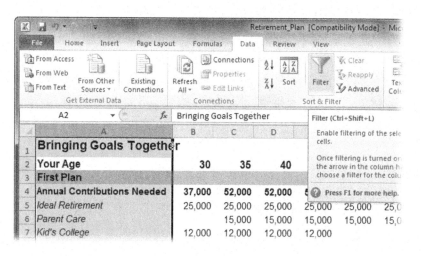

Similarly, this arrow shorthand also simplifies the instructions for opening nested folders, such as Program Files→Microsoft Office→Office12→1033.

About MissingManuals.com

At *http://www.missingmanuals.com*, you'll find news, articles, and updates to the books in this series.

But the website also offers corrections and updates to this book (to see them, click the book's title, and then click Errata). In fact, you're invited and encouraged to submit such corrections and updates yourself. In an effort to keep the book as up-to-date and accurate as possible, each time we print more copies of this book, we'll make any confirmed corrections you suggest. We'll also note such changes on the website, so that you can mark important corrections into your own copy of the book if you like.

In the meantime, we'd love to hear your suggestions for new books in the Missing Manual line. There's a place for that on the website, too, as well as a place to sign up for free email notification of new titles in the series.

About the Missing CD

This book helps you invest. As you read through it, you'll find references to websites that offer additional resources. Each reference includes the site's URL, but you can save yourself some typing by going to this book's Missing CD page—it gives you clickable links to all the sites mentioned here. To get to the Missing CD page, go to the Missing Manuals home page (*www.missingmanuals.com*), click the Missing CD link, scroll down to **Personal Investing: The Missing Manual,** and then click the link labeled "Missing CD".

Safari® Books Online

 Safari® Books Online is an on-demand digital library that lets you easily search over 7,500 technology and creative reference books and videos to find the answers you need quickly.

With a subscription, you can read any page and watch any video from our library online. Read books on your cellphone and mobile devices. Access new titles before they're available for print, and get exclusive access to manuscripts in development and post feedback for the authors. Copy and paste code samples, organize your favorites, download chapters, bookmark key sections, create notes, print out pages, and benefit from tons of other time-saving features.

O'Reilly Media has uploaded this book to the Safari Books Online service. To have full digital access to this book and others on similar topics from O'Reilly and other publishers, sign up for free at *http://my.safaribooksonline.com*.

Part 1
Prepare to Invest

1 Why Should You Invest?

Buying this week's groceries might set you back $50 or more. As long as you live within your means, you can pay not only for your groceries, but also for your rent, utilities, and other expenses out of your paycheck. But how do you pay for living expenses when you aren't *getting* a paycheck—when you retire, in other words? (If you think you can live on Social Security, think again.) And what about your dream of seeing the lights of your life, Pooter and Scooter, graduate from top-notch universities? And don't forget that 20th-anniversary around-the-world cruise you and your partner fantasize about. All this is gonna take some moola—and probably a lot more than you expect.

For example, say you spend $40,000 a year on living expenses and you expect to enjoy 30 years of retirement spending at that same level. You do the math and reel in horror when you realize that you need $1,200,000 for your retirement. If you earn $50,000 a year, spend $40,000 on expenses, and save the remaining $10,000 in your mattress for 30 years, you'll have, er, $300,000. You're a whopping $900,000 short.

But it turns out that you're a lot further from your goal than that. You've probably heard of inflation, that nasty tendency of prices to go up a little bit each year—on average about 3.4%. That doesn't sound like much, but it adds up over time, as you'll learn in this chapter. For example, by the end of your 30-year retirement, with 3.4% inflation, your $40,000 in living expenses will actually cost about $105,476, and the price tag for your 30 years of retirement is more like $2,030,000.

Lottery tickets don't cut it. The returns from savings accounts, certificates of deposit, and other savings options rarely beat inflation, so you simply can't save enough to pay for everything you need or want. What can you do? Fight back by investing your money instead of stashing it in your mattress.

When you invest your money, your savings work harder. The return on a diversified portfolio of stocks and bonds averages about 7%. That not only beats inflation, it shoots growth hormones (all organic) into your nest egg. Invest that $10,000 savings per year and earn 7%, and you'll have almost a million dollars after 30 years, instead of $300,000. Still not as much as you need, but you'll learn how to make ends meet by the time you finish reading this book.

 Tip As you'll learn in this chapter, investing isn't necessary to meet the demands of short-term goals—say those within the next 5 years (a vacation, sprucing up the bathroom, or buying a new sofa). That's because inflation doesn't have a chance to bloat the prices you pay. For these goals, savings options are fine. Just find a money market account, savings account, or certificate of deposit that pays a generous rate of interest. You can see a list of online resources on the web page for this book at *www.missingmanuals.com/cds*.

How Inflation Hurts

Forty years ago, mailing a letter cost 6 cents and a loaf of bread ran about 25 cents. Today that stamp costs 44 cents, and a loaf of whole wheat bread fetches almost $3. Big deal, that's only 38 cents extra for the stamp and a couple of bucks more for the bread. But that steady and seemingly trivial increase in prices, called *inflation* (as if price tags slowly inflate like balloons), *is* a big deal. Here's why.

You can find links to all the websites mentioned in this book on the book's Missing CD page. To get there, go to the Missing Manuals home page (*www.missingmanuals.com*), click the Missing CD link, scroll down to *Personal Investing: The Missing Manual*, and then click the link labeled "Missing CD."

Inflation in the United States runs, on long-term average, 3.41% a year (*http://tinyurl.com/5m2snb*). That means that the prices you pay go up about 3.41% each year. This year's weekly $100 grocery bill will cost you $103.41 next year.

 It's good for a laugh with the bean-counter crowd, but economists go on a shopping spree to figure out the inflation rate. Their shopping list, aka the *Consumer Price Index* (CPI), includes everything the average person spends money on— housing, transportation, groceries, clothes, medical care, education, utilities, fun, and so on. They gather prices from 50,000 households and 23,000 stores around the country. They tweak the list based on the importance of the items. (People can't cut back much on housing and heat, even if the prices go up, but they might rein in their spending on entertainment.) Finally, the economists compare each price to what they paid the year before, average all the price changes, and calculate the percentage that the total bill went up or down. (It almost always goes up.)

But inflation's small increases recur year after year. And each year's increase expands the previous year's increase (a process known as *compounding*, explained in detail on page 16), so the increases get bigger and bigger over time. Those groceries that went up $3.41 the first year, increase by $3.53 the second year, $3.65 the third year, and so on. After several decades, inflation adds up to serious money, especially for big-ticket items like annual living expenses in retirement, as you'll soon see.

With each year of inflation, a dollar's *buying power* (what one dollar can buy) decreases, so you need more dollars to pay your bills. But the salary increases you get might not keep up with inflation, in which case your buying power falls further behind year after year. If you struggle to make ends meet now, it just gets harder as time passes.

The average wage increase from 1998 to 2008 was 4%, according to the Social Security Administration. Their Wage Index web page (*http://tiny.cc/gaqx0*) shows historical wage increases by year. But lots of people receive wage increases that are lower than the inflation rate.

What's really scary is that many things you save for go up even faster than inflation, like the ones shown below. Even big-ticket items that increase at the same rate as inflation, like your retirement living expenses, can expand to really scary numbers, like $184,192 for 1 year's expenses in the year 2050 (see the table below).

Goal	Average cost in 2009	Rate of price increase	Cost in 20 years	Cost in 40 years
Stamp	$0.44	4.85%	$1.13	$2.93
Assisted living facility for a year	$33,900	4.72%	$85,269	$214,479
Private room in a nursing home for a year	$74,000	4.27%	$170,772	$394,100
Public college	$30,500	6%	$97,817	$313,714
One year's retirement living expenses	$50,000	3.41% (average inflation rate)	$94,376	$184,192

Why Scary Numbers Aren't That Scary

There's no question that more than $300,000 for a college education and almost $400,000 for a year at a geriatric resort are scary numbers. It turns out that time and compounding, your enemies when it comes to inflation, are your best friends when you invest to achieve long-term goals. With timeframes like 18 years until your newborn heads to college or 40 years until you retire, investing your money to take advantage of compounding returns can cut scary numbers down to size. You don't have to save a bazillion dollars. You squirrel away a much smaller amount and let your investment returns do the heavy lifting over the decades.

I Need More Time

What if I don't have 40 years to invest?

Sure, time is a big help when you invest for big financial goals, but it isn't the only answer. You can still reach your goals if you have less time to prepare: It just takes a little more discipline. Here's how you can get where you want to go in less time:

- **Save more money and use it to invest.** What if you saved $1 each day and invested it in your retirement account? Earning a 7% return on an annual contribution of $365 gets you to $5,043 after 10 years, $14,963 after 20 years, and $34,478 after 30 years. So, if you invest the $4 you spend on a latte for your morning commute, you could have $137,913 more in your nest egg 30 years from now. The government allows people 55 and older to contribute more to IRAs, Roth IRAs, and other retirement investment accounts to help them catch up (pages 178 and 181).

- **Keep money in your investment accounts longer.** Postponing your retirement helps in a lot of ways. You contribute for several more years, your investments have more time to grow, and your Social Security benefits increase (page 192). If you use a Roth IRA, you don't have to start withdrawing when you turn 70 1/2, as you do with a regular IRA (page 183).

- **Reset your objectives.** If your retirement plan still doesn't work, you can notch down your annual living expenses in retirement (page 31).

How Investing Makes Your Money Work Harder

With inflation's 3.41% price increases compounding year after year, figuring your expenses produces some galactic numbers. Sadly, you can't choose whether to accept the compounding of inflation. But what if you could use compounding to *inflate* the money you save? It turns out that you can, by investing your money and reinvesting all your earnings. You can choose the compounding of the returns you earn on your money, so it's important to understand just how powerful this strategy is.

True, investment returns aren't as steady as the inflation rate. (Page 190 tells you how to reduce the risk of varying investment returns.) Some years are better than others, and some years are downright dogs. But for now, assume that your investments increase 7% each year (that's the return most financial planners tell their clients they can expect on a diversified investment portfolio). Say you seed a retirement account with $10,000, as the table below shows. If you earn 7% the first year, you'll have $10,700 at the end of the year.

The second year, you earn $749 (7% on $10,700) and end up with $11,449. If you earn 7% each year for 40 years (from the time you start working until you retire), you'd have almost $150,000! That's $140,000 of earnings on a single $10,000 investment.

Year	Ending balance	Annual return	Cumulative return
1	$10,000	$700	$700
2	$10,700	$749	$1,449
3	$11,449	$801	$2,250
4	$12,250	$858	$3,108
5	$13,108	$918	$4,026
39	$139,948	$9,796	$139,745
40	$149,745	$10,482	$150,227

On the other hand, what if you invested $10,000 and earned 7%, but withdrew each year's earnings? (That return is called *simple interest*, because you earn the same amount on your original investment each year.) You'd earn $700 each year for 40 years, for total earnings of $28,000 on your original $10,000 investment. By letting your investment returns compound, your total earnings are five times what you'd earn with simple interest. The graph below shows how your nest egg grows like wildfire when you compound your earnings.

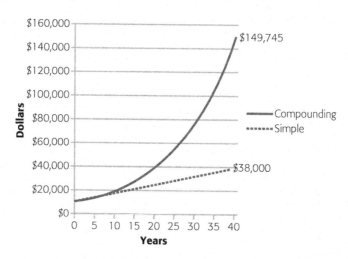

As you've seen with inflation, compounding is a powerful force, even when the rate is small. But this technique really shines when you earn higher returns, like the 7% from a diversified portfolio, and give your portfolio time to mature. The graph below shows how a $10,000 nest egg grows when you put your money in diversified investments, bonds, money market funds, and savings accounts. Compare the line for inflation to see how investing can help you beat the steady rise in prices.

You can see below how investments start to take off after 15 years. That's compounding at work, and that's why it's important to start investing for long-term goals as early as you can.

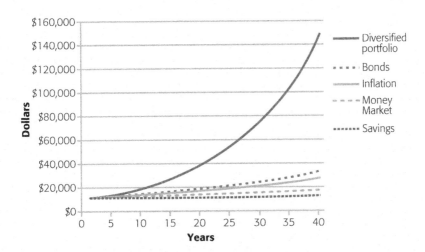

Investing for the Long Term

Although well-diversified investing works like magic when you give it time, it doesn't make sense for short-term goals. That's because you have to accept some risk to earn higher returns. Investments in the stock market can decrease during a single year—and do so every several years. The good news is that the risk of losing money decreases the longer you keep your money invested (think decades).

During recessions, the stock market can really tank, like the almost 50% drop it suffered in 2001. You wouldn't want to see half your nest egg go away the year before you retire. However, since 1929, the average annual return on stocks is more than 10% despite battering from the Great Depression and several recessions.

Besides, a diversified portfolio isn't invested solely in the stock market, as you'll learn in Chapter 9. By investing in stocks, bonds, and real estate, you won't see drops as big as the ones for stocks alone. Chapters 9, 10, and 11 also tell you how to move money that you need in the next few years into ultra-safe savings so it's around when you need it.

Lots of folks would rather be certain of having a small amount of money than worry about whether a large nest egg might falter right when they need it. You might think that putting money into a guaranteed money market account means you won't lose money. Think again. If your money doesn't keep up with inflation, you lose buying power, which is the same as losing money.

2 Set Your Investment Goals

According to Yogi Berra, "If you don't know where you are going, you might wind up someplace else." Planning for long-term goals seems overwhelming to a lot of people, tedious to many others. Whatever the reason, plenty of folks forego planning and hope for the best—or claim they'll make do with whatever they end up with. However, by not planning, chances are good that you end up in one of two situations, neither one desirable. You may save *too much* and sacrifice your lifestyle today needlessly. Far more likely, you'll save *too little* and turn your golden years into something much less satisfying.

A financial plan means you have a shot at getting the lifestyle you want now *and* in the future. The good news: Creating a plan isn't tough.

This chapter starts with the fun part—building your bucket list. Do you want to own the Red Sox, live on a sailboat, or sit on your porch swing drinking lemonade? The first step is making a list of everything you want to achieve in life. Planning for retirement may seem like a job in itself. For sure it's one of the toughest and most important goals you plan for. If you're like most people, it isn't your *only* long-term financial plan. Whether you have kids to put through college, parents to care for, or just a bunch of fun you want to have before you kick the bucket, you have to think about several goals all at the same time.

All of them are gonna take money. So the next step is figuring out how much your dreams are going to cost and how much you have to invest to get there. This chapter shows you how to plan for the most common goals people have and how to put everything together to come up with an overall plan.

 The ins and outs of planning for specific goals are described in other chapters in this book: Investing for retirement is covered in Chapter 10; Chapter 11 talks about investing for college education; and Chapter 12 discusses paying for health care.

Building Your Bucket List

Dreams give you something to reach for, something to keep you going. They don't have to be pie in the sky. All you need to make your dreams come true is the desire to do so and a plan. Dream + Plan = Achievable Goal.

Like the advice for brainstorming sessions, don't hold back. Your first pass at a bucket list can contain every dream you have a hankering for—no matter how far-fetched. If you dream of owning an island, add it to the list. Sure, chances are the whole enchilada may be out of reach financially. If it is, you can do what professional financial planners do and come up with an optimistic list, a pessimistic one, and the one that's most likely to pan out. By coming up with alternatives for each of your goals, you can build a list that's within your means—even if it doesn't have everything you want. If the island scenario has to be beached, you can add a bungalow in the Florida Keys as a backup. Your pessimistic goal could be a week with Aunt Birdy at her condo in Boca.

 Your list (and the plan you build around it) also doesn't have to be perfect *or* set in stone. Plans almost always change. You can fine-tune your list as you go or as your circumstances change. For example, page 208 explains how you can adjust your college-savings goals if your kid ends up with a jaw-dropping scholarship.

Multiple versions of each of your goals take some of the pressure off. If you begin to chafe at the sacrifices you have to make to reach all your ideal goals, switch some goals out for those on your B list. Dream versions also make it easier to prioritize multiple goals. If you don't see a way to get your first picks, you can keep your highest priority ideal goals and back off on the ones that aren't as important.

To build your plan, your goals need to include rough time constraints and estimated price tags. Describe your goals in as much detail as you can envision. If you can practically see them, feel them, and taste them, you're more likely to stick to your plan to reach them. The rest of this chapter shows you how.

If you have trouble getting the ball rolling, ask yourself some of the following questions:

- Where do you want to live? Do you want to be near family or as far away as possible?
- What's an ideal day in retirement look like? How about an average day?
- Do you want to work or volunteer with a charity?
- Do you want to travel?
- Do you want to pursue your current hobbies in retirement?
- What new hobbies do you want to take up?
- What do you wish you had time for now?

Retirement, College, or Other Goals

Retirement is something that everyone has to plan for. But if you're like most people, you have goals other than how to spend your time and money during your golden years. Maybe you have kids to get through college; or your parents didn't plan like you're planning, and you have to help care for them; or you're angling for a vacation home, boat, or Viking six-burner stove.

No matter what you dream of, goals can cost a bundle. If your dreamy price tag sends a jolt of reality through your system, no worries. The key to success is prioritizing your goals so you ensure that you reach the most important ones.

First up: Your retirement comes before your kids' college fund. That's right: Your little darlings should not be the most important thing in your life. Your kids can get scholarships, financial aid, and loans. When it comes to your retirement, you're on your own. Putting your retirement first doesn't deny your child a future. You aren't doing something selfish. Besides, they have to learn to take care of themselves at some point, so why not now? Explain that you're saving for your retirement so they won't have to take care of you. They're likely to thank you.

Your retirement should also come before helping your parents with their bills. It's tough because they're the folks who raised you. But if you don't save for your own retirement, you end up propagating a family tradition. If you start the conversation with your parents early on (page 34), you may not have to do as much to help them.

The Big Kahuna: Retirement

Sometimes, you wish retirement was next week. Other times, you wish you had more time to prepare for it. Planning for retirement is tough for two reasons: It's so far off that it doesn't seem real, and then, because you spend decades in it, the price tag is enormous.

Before you can start planning for retirement, you have to flesh out your retirement goal with the following details:

- **When you're going to retire.** As you'll learn shortly, when you retire affects your plan in several ways.

- **What your life will be like then.** Your lifestyle says a lot about how much money you'll need each year during retirement. Those annual expenses are the key to how big your retirement nest egg has to be.

After you have your target in sight, you're ready to figure out how to pay for it. This section guides you through retirement planning step by step. (Chapter 10 helps you navigate the maze of retirement saving options.)

When You Retire

When the Social Security program started in 1935, benefits began at age 65. Ironically, life expectancy at the time was only 61. People didn't have to plan for retirement because they weren't likely to have one. Today that's different. Although full Social Security benefits start a little later, life expectancies are a lot longer, so most people spend decades in retirement.

When you retire affects your plan in several ways:

- **The number of years you have to save.** Retiring later means you have more time to contribute money to your retirement accounts and more time for your retirement investments to grow. (Page 18 shows how compounding grows stronger with time.)

- **The number of retirement years you have to pay for.** Unless your family is renowned for short lives, plan on living to be 100. If you're married, one of you is likely to live *past* 100. Subtract the age you plan to retire from 100, and you have the number of retirement years you have to pay for. For example, if you're eyeing 65 for retirement, that's 35 years in retirement, and that means you need to sock away a lot of cash.

- **How much you get in Social Security benefits.** Retiring later increases your Social Security benefits. The amount you receive is based on your 35 highest-earning years. With luck, the years just before retirement are some of your highest paid. If you were born in 1937 or earlier, the age of full retirement is 65. If you were born between 1938 and 1960, full retirement gradually increases to age 67. If you were born in 1960 or later, full retirement is age 67. Each month that you postpone retirement beyond your full retirement age increases your benefits. If you were born after 1942, your benefits increase 8% per year. If you were born before that, benefits increase gradually from 3% to 8%.

What's Retirement Going to Cost?

Another big factor in your retirement plan is how much you plan to spend each year in retirement. Some expenses like food, utilities, and insurance, don't change (except for inflation). But maybe you exchange your work wardrobe for jammies and flip-flops. Maybe you drive fewer miles because you no longer commute to work. Maybe you pay off your mortgage. On the other hand, you may travel more, drive an RV around the country, take up hobbies, or pay more for health care and medicine.

 Living on your own? According to census data, more than half of the women and a quarter of the men retiring today enter retirement alone. Sadly, your annual expenses are almost the same as those for a couple, without the benefit of a second income or second Social Security check.

Starting from scratch is never easy, but you don't have to when you estimate annual living expenses in retirement. You can start with what you spend now. To estimate what you'll spend in retirement from your current spending, just answer the following nine questions. (You can download the planning spreadsheet, Retirement_Plan.xls, from *http://www.missing-manuals.com*; see the Tip in this chapter's introduction for details.) Start with rough guesses and then fine-tune your answers to build a more accurate plan.

Note When you use the planning spreadsheet, you don't have to figure out how much things will cost in the future. Answer the questions based on what things cost today.

		Your answers	Annual amount
1	Estimating Your Retirement Needs		
2	Fill in your answers to these questions:		
3	How much do you spend in a year now?	$ 70,000	$ 70,000
4	Will you pay off your mortgage before retirement? If so, enter your **monthly** mortgage payment.	$ 1,200	$ (14,400)
5	Will other debts be paid off before you retire? If so, enter your current monthly debt payment.	$ 800	$ (9,600)
6	Will college savings or tuition end before you retire? If so, enter the **monthly** payment.	$ -	$ -
7	How much are you saving for retirement today? If you're already saving for retirement, you may not have to when you retire. Enter the **annual** amount you contribute to retirement accounts.	$ 10,500	$ (10,500)
8	Do you expect your taxes to go down significantly? Becaue most people pay fewer taxes in retirement, enter the amount you expect your tax bill to decrease during retirement.	$ 4,000	$ (4,000)
9	Are there other expenses you won't have in retirement? Enter the estimated **annual** decrease in expenses.	$ 2,000	$ (2,000)
10	What are you going to pay for healthcare in retirement? Enter what you expect to pay **annually** for healthcare in retirement (at least $4,000 for the minimum Medicare benefits).	$ 7,500	$ 7,500
11	What additional expenses will you have in retirement? Enter your estimated **additional annual** cost for vacations, travel, memberships, dinners out, and so on.	$ 10,000	$ 10,000
12			
	Your annual living expenses in retirement		$ 47,000

Estimating Expenses / How Much You Have to Save / Bringing It All Together / Calculat

- **How much do you spend in a year now?** The easy way to calculate this number is to take your income and subtract any money you aren't using. The other way is to add up all your expenses for a 12-month period.

- **Will you pay off your mortgage before retirement?** Many people don't want mortgage payments when their income is lower. If you're one of them, subtract what you pay on your mortgage. (In the worksheet, enter your monthly mortgage payment.)

- **Will other debts be paid off before you retire?** If you plan to pay off other debts, like student loans or credit card balances, before you retire, subtract these payments. (In the worksheet, enter the amount you pay toward these debts each month.)

- **Will college savings or tuition end before you retire?** If tuition expenses or college savings contributions will end before you retire, sigh with relief and subtract them. (In the worksheet, enter the amount you pay toward these debts each month.)

- **How much are you saving for retirement today?** If you're contributing to retirement savings, you may not have to save more during retirement. Subtract this amount. (In the worksheet, enter the annual amount you contribute.)

- **Do you expect your taxes to go down significantly?** Most people have less income in retirement and qualify for a lower tax rate, which often means a much lower tax bill. If you expect your taxes to decrease, see what you paid last year. Then, use your annual taxable retirement income and the IRS tax bracket (*http://tinyurl.com/tax-brackets*) for that amount to estimate how much you'll pay in retirement. Subtract the difference between the two numbers from your annual living expenses. (In the worksheet, enter the annual decrease you expect.)

- **Are there other expenses you won't have in retirement?** If you expect other expenses to decrease in retirement, for instance, auto expenses because you no longer commute two hours a day, subtract the annual amount from your current living expenses.

- **What are you going to pay for health care in retirement?** The minimum you should enter is $4,000 for bare-bones Medicare benefits. You can find more information on estimating health-care expenses in Chapter 12 and in *Your Money: The Missing Manual.*

- **What additional expenses will you have in retirement?** You may have additional expenses in retirement depending on how you spend your free time. Add your estimate of how much more you'll spend in retirement for travel, vacations, hobbies, memberships, dinners out, and so on.

Sources of Retirement Income

Money for your living expenses during retirement may come from several sources. However, if you're like most people, *you* are the primary retirement breadwinner. You pay your retirement bills from your retirement portfolio: from its income (dividends and interest) and a small bit from its principal, often enhanced with earnings from a part-time job. You also get some money from Social Security, but it's rarely enough to live on. If you're *really* lucky, you get some money from your company's pension plan.

Social Security and pension payments reduce the retirement expenses you have to pay for out of your own pocket. So, start by figuring out how much you'll get from those two sources. Then you can see how much you'll need from part-time work and your retirement nest egg.

Thanks, gov!

On average, Americans have less than $25,000 in savings when they retire. That measly amount provides about $1,400 per year to live on during a 30-year retirement. Not good. Luckily for those folks, the government has a safety net: Social Security. You won't live in "luxury" on the benefits it pays and its coffers are drying up at a frightening pace, but most retired Americans rely on it.

 Note You're usually eligible for Social Security if you've worked for 10 years or more. If you're married or were married for 10 years and haven't remarried, you're eligible for half of your spouse's Social Security payment.

Each year around your birthday, the Social Security Administration sends you a letter showing your estimated Social Security benefits. When you're close to retirement age, the estimates are fairly accurate. If you still have some years until retirement and you expect to earn more in the future, your Social Security payment will probably be higher than the estimate.

Social Security payments depend on your salary. Salaries above $54,000 in 2009 increase payments a piddling amount. If you make more than $54,000, the estimate you get is relatively accurate. If your salary is below that threshold but you expect it to increase, use the Social Security benefits calculator (*http://tinyurl.com/SSA-Benefits*) to estimate your benefits more accurately.

What About Social Security?

Whether you count on Social Security or think it'll be bankrupt before you see a dime, here are some questions to ask to figure out whether Social Security will help you pay for retirement:

1. **What's the full retirement age?** If you were born after 1959, it's 67. From 1938 to 1959, it increases gradually from 65 to 67.

2. **How much does my payment go down if I retire early?** Retiring early puts a crimp in Social Security benefits. For example, if you were born in 1960 or later and retire at 62, your payment drops by 30%. In addition, if you retire early, you may miss out on your highest earning years, as you learn on page 193.

3. **How is my payment calculated?** Your highest 35 years of earnings are adjusted for inflation and put through a formula that gives you partial credit for different bands of your total earnings: 90% for the first $9,000, 32% from $9,000 to $54,000, and 15% for $54,000 to the maximum salary of $106,800.

4. **What's the most I can get?** If you earned the maximum salary from 1974 to 2008, the maximum annual payment is $31,016.

5. **Will Social Security be around when I retire?** The Social Security Trust Fund is projected to run out of money in 2037. (It was 2041 until the recent recession.) Politicians swear they will never let the fund run out. Although Social Security is unlikely to disappear, you may see the full retirement age increase or other changes that reduce the benefits you receive.

Pension plans

More than half of all Americans have an employer-sponsored pension plan. The problem is that what you think of as a pension—a steady stream of income that your company pays you during retirement—is called a *defined-benefit* plan, and that's only half of what the government considers a pension. Defined-contribution benefits like 401(k) plans and 403(b) plans are also officially pensions, but *you* contribute most, if not all, of the money to those.

Defined-benefit plans are great for employees, because the employer is on the hook to amass enough money to pay pension benefits to covered employees. If you have one of these plans, congratulations! You'll have a steady stream of income for the rest of your life. However, the number of defined-benefit programs dropped by almost 70% between 1965 and 1997, and the decline hasn't stopped. They're expensive for employers and are considered outdated because most employees don't stay with the same employer for long.

On the other hand, the number of *defined-contribution* plans continues to increase. With these plans, employers get tax incentives, but don't have to invest much in the plan. As an employee, a defined-contribution plan is less desirable than a defined-benefit plan (but it's still a valuable savings tool):

- **You have to contribute the bulk of the money to the plan.** Yes, large companies often match your contributions, up to a total of 6% of your salary. You want to take advantage of company matching, but what the employer contributes is nothing compared to what you'd get from a defined-benefit plan.

- **The maximum 401(k) contribution may not be as much as you need to save each year for retirement.** In 2010, the maximum 401(k) contribution is $16,500. If you got a late start or have lavish retirement goals, you'll have to save more in other types of accounts (see page 177 for your options).

- **Your returns aren't guaranteed.** You're in charge of choosing the investments you make in your 401(k) or 403(b). If you choose safe options or your investments don't do well, your account isn't likely to satisfy your retirement needs.

Work during retirement

Gone are the days of golfing away your golden days. Many retirees choose to continue working during retirement. They opt for reduced hours or working at something they enjoy more. With the recent recession, many Baby Boomers have no choice but to work during retirement. If part-time work is part of your plan, estimate how much money you'll earn and how long you plan to work.

 Tip You may want to keep working, but that doesn't mean you'll find a job. You have to be realistic about your ability to continue working, especially if robust old age doesn't run in your family. Don't plan on part-time income just to make your numbers work.

Nest egg income and principal

If you build a big enough nest egg, you can live off the income. Your heirs and charities will be pleased. However, most people have to dip into principal to make ends meet. The common rule of thumb with retirement nest eggs is to take out no more than 4% of your principal each year (page 194).

 Note Because your retirement accounts continue to grow, withdrawing 4% may not decrease the balance you have in your retirement coffers.

Building Your Retirement Plan

Now that you know when you're going to retire, how much money you need each year, and how much income you're likely to receive, you can create a retirement plan. Put your calculator away. You can download the spreadsheet file, Retirement_Plan.xls, from *www. missingmanuals.com/cds*, and let it do the math for you. You fill in the answers you came up with in the previous sections, and the spreadsheet spits out how much you need to save for both your ideal and Plan B retirement. It takes care of calculating increased costs due to inflation as well as the increases in your retirement nest egg based on your investment return.

 Tip You can find links to all the websites and spreadsheet files mentioned in this book on the book's Missing CD page. To get there, go to the Missing Manuals home page (*www.missingmanuals.com*), click the Missing CD link, scroll down to *Personal Investing: The Missing Manual*, and then click the link labeled "Missing CD."

Here's how you use the How Much You Have to Save worksheet to figure out how much you have to contribute each year toward retirement:

 Note The worksheet assumes that inflation will be 3.4%, the historical average, and that investment return is 7%, a conservative value. The age for the end of the plan is 100. It's high, but you don't want to run out of money before you run out of heartbeats.

1. **Fill in your current age and the age at which you plan to retire.**

   The worksheet subtracts your current age from your retirement age to figure out how many years you have in which to accumulate your nest egg. The age you retire also determines how many years of retirement you have to pay for, as you learned on page 25.

 Note Fill in values in today's dollars. The worksheet takes care of calculating increases due to inflation.

2. Fill in your annual retirement living expenses for your Plan B retirement and your ideal retirement.

The worksheet uses these numbers to calculate how much you have to contribute each year for both alternatives, in case you can't afford your ideal retirement.

	A	B	C
1			
2	**Your Retirement Numbers**		
3			
4	Your current age	40	
5	Age you plan to retire	67	
6	Annual living expenses for Plan B retirement	$ 47,000	
7	Annual living expenses for ideal retirement	$ 65,000	
8	Social Security at full retirement	$ 35,000	
9	Part-time income during retirement	$ 15,000	
10	Number of years of part-time income	5	
11	Amount you have saved so far	$ 150,000	
12			
13			
14	**Your Numbers:**		
15	Amount to save per year for Plan B retirement	$ 726	
16	Amount to save per year for ideal retirement	$ 11,931	
17			
18			

Estimating Expenses | How Much You Have to Save | Bringing It All Together

Ready

3. Fill in the annual amount you expect to receive from Social Security the first year you qualify for full retirement.

The worksheet takes care of calculating increases in Social Security each year. If you qualify for a defined-benefit pension program (page 29), you can add your pension payment to the Social Security value. Look at your latest statement to see how much you can expect to receive from your employer after retirement. Your HR department can provide estimated benefits for additional years of service.

4. Fill in the amount of money you expect to earn from working during retirement. Fill in the number of years you plan to work during retirement.

The worksheet uses that income to offset your retirement expenses during the years you plan to work.

5. Fill in the amount of retirement savings you already have.

The more retirement money you already have, the less you have to save going forward.

6. Look at the results for your Plan B and ideal retirement.

If you can't afford either one, see page 38 for steps you can take to come up with a plan that does fit within your current budget.

 Note You may hear a pitch for adding a whole-life or universal-life insurance policy to your retirement plan. These types of insurance are like a combination of term-life insurance, which pays the policy amount when the person insured dies, and investment of your premiums. They build cash values that you can borrow against. But they're a lot more expensive than plain term-life insurance. See *Your Money: The Missing Manual* to learn more about these insurance options.

Other Long-Term Goals

College costs, health care, long-term care for you, care for your elderly parents, and fun may be on your list of goals. Figuring out how to achieve these goals is similar to the process you used for retirement:

- **How long do you have to save for the goal?** Whether you have 5, 10, or 20 years to make your dream a reality makes a huge difference in how much you have to contribute.

- **How many years must you pay for the goal?** With college, you plan for 4 years, but helping your folks may last 10 years or more.

- **How much will the goal cost?** Estimate the total cost for your goal (see page 198 for advice on estimating college costs). Don't forget to subtract any reductions in expenses the goal creates. For example, if you live in Tuscany for 5 years, you may rent out your house and cover your mortgage payment.

To figure out how much you need to save for a long-term goal, download the spreadsheet, LongtermGoal_Plan.xls, from *www. missingmanuals.com/ cds*, fill in a few answers about the goal, and let it do the math for you.

Health Care and Long-Term Care

Health care and long-term care (LTC) are a fact of retirement life. The price tag for a year in a nursing home 30 years from now is enough to give you a heart attack today. You have to decide whether you're going to count on your kids (not the best plan), save enough to pay the bill (almost impossible), or pay for long-term care insurance (it's expensive). You got it: There's no good answer.

These days, the best guess for annual health-care costs during retirement starts at $7,500. At $7,500 for the first year, you'll need $250,000 or more in retirement funds just for health care! If your health isn't great to begin with, bump that number up. Chapter 12 tells you how to save for health care and how to pick a health insurance policy. (You can also learn more about health-care costs and LTC in *Your Money: The Missing Manual*.)

LTC includes nursing homes, assisted living, and in-home care when you can't take care of yourself. These costs can wipe out a lifetime of savings in no time, so LTC insurance is one way to protect your financial plan. LTC policies make sense for people between the ages of 45 and 60. If you're younger than 45, the lower premium doesn't make up for paying for all those extra years of coverage. Over 60, your premiums skyrocket.

Tip The reality of LTC expenses is dawning on most insurance companies. They're getting fussier about whom they insure, and preexisting conditions can make you uninsurable. If you wait to get insurance and start to forget stuff in the meantime, you may not be able to get a policy.

If you're thinking about LTC insurance, look at how long it pays for care, how much of your care it pays for (and whether that increases with inflation), and the type of care it covers. For example, if you want to stay at home, make sure that the policy covers home care.

College Savings

Just like on an airplane, put *your* oxygen mask on first, before your child's. Once you have your retirement in place, you can figure out what you can do for your kids. Saving for college has its own special challenges, as Chapter 11 explains in detail. In short, the price tag is scary, and you have fewer than 20 years to save. Still, you can choose from plenty of options that help you save for college. And asking your kids to pitch in isn't the worst thing in the world.

Caring for Aging Parents

Many parents and children end up spending several years in retirement at the same time. Whether you consider that a blessing or a curse, one thing is certain: Paying your parents' bills is never fun, and it can eat away your savings. Talk to your parents *now* about their plans. If push comes to shove, add their care to your own planning.

The conversation may be awkward, but it's better than working things out during a health crisis or being blind-sided by expenses that change your retirement standard of living.

 Tip Address the topic at a low-stress time. December holidays aren't ideal, even if everyone is together. If you get anxious just thinking about it, bring an estate attorney or specialized financial planner into the conversation; they walk people through these discussions every day. They can impartially help you through the entire discussion.

The big things to discuss include:

- **Health care costs.** Find out about your parents' health care, long-term care, and disability insurance policies. If they don't have insurance, ask how they plan to pay for those expenses.

- **Handling life-threatening situations.** Find out how they want to be cared for in a life-threatening situation, for example, if one is in a coma or requires life support. An attorney can help you prepare a living will or health-care power of attorney.

- **Plans for their estate and care for a surviving spouse.** Find out about their wills, investment accounts, insurance policies, and any trusts. Be sure to find out where they keep their documents and how you can get them if you need them.

A Second Home

Maybe you have your eye on a vacation home or want to buy a house as an investment or a rental property. If you're thinking about a vacation home, the big question is whether you can afford it.

For investment or rental properties, you need to think about risk. You're betting that a single building within a single geographic area will increase in value or produce net income. (If a rental is empty, you still have to pay the mortgage and other expenses.) For a less risky way to diversify into real estate, see Chapter 8 on real estate investment trusts and *Your Money: The Missing Manual.*

Leaving a Legacy

Many people want to be remembered after they die, and leaving money is one way to do that. If you want to leave an inheritance to your heirs or to charities, that is another long-term goal. If you plan on leaving money to charity or someone other than your spouse, get the advice of an experienced estate attorney, or the government may end up the recipient of your generosity.

Fun Stuff

Whether you dream of starting a business in a few years or taking a year off to live in Tuscany, the planning process is the same as for other long-term goals. Timeframe is often the key to these goals, because you may sprinkle your goals throughout your life. The amount of time you have before your goal comes to fruition affects how much you can contribute. If you're planning a romantic 20th-anniversary vacation for 5 years from now, you have to save more money to reach your goal. First, you need to put your money in safer investments, so a last-minute stock market dive doesn't squelch your plans. Safer investments tend to deliver lower returns, so they don't grow your money as much as stocks. In addition, the short timeframe means compounding (page 16) doesn't have a chance to do its magic. When you have more time to reach a goal, you can invest in higher-return investments and let their value compound.

Putting It All Together

Each of your goals has a different timeframe and a different investing plan. You may have 30 years until retirement, while your kid heads to college in 10. Seeing the big picture of your goals is your first step in building a comprehensive plan. That high-level perspective includes each of your goals, their priority, investment plan, and timing. If your try at a plan doesn't work, you can make adjustments until you find a mix that works within your budget, as you can see below.

	Your Age	30	35	40	45	50	55	60	65	70	75
1	Bringing Goals Together										
2	Your Age	30	35	40	45	50	55	60	65	70	75
3	First Plan										
4	Annual Contributions Needed	37,000	52,000	52,000	52,000	40,000	40,000	25,000	25,000	25,000	25,000
5	Ideal Retirement	25,000	25,000	25,000	25,000	25,000	25,000	25,000	25,000	25,000	25,000
6	Parent Care		15,000	15,000	15,000	15,000	15,000				
7	Kid's College	12,000	12,000	12,000	12,000						
8											
9	Plan B Scenario										
10	Annual Contributions Needed	16,500	26,500	28,500	28,500	22,500	22,500	12,500	12,500		
11	Plan B Retirement	10,500	10,500	12,500	12,500	12,500	12,500	12,500	12,500		
12	Parents		10,000	10,000	10,000	10,000	10,000				
13	Kid's College	6,000	6,000	6,000	6,000						
14											
15	Achievable Scenario										
16	Annual Contributions Needed	13,500	21,500	23,500	23,500	20,500	20,500	12,500	12,500		
17	Plan B Retirement	10,500	10,500	12,500	12,500	12,500	12,500	12,500	12,500		
18	Parents		8,000	8,000	8,000	8,000	8,000				
19	Kid's College	3,000	3,000	3,000	3,000						
20											

Estimating Expenses | How Much You Have to Save | Bringing It All Togeth...

Major life goals like retirement and college education have special tax-advantaged accounts (see pages 64–67) to help you save. That makes it easy to segregate the money you're contributing toward those goals. Setting up separate accounts for other goals based on their timeframe is like separating lights and darks in the laundry. That way, you can invest the entire balance based on when you need the money (page 188). In addition, you can avoid the three-aspirin headache of trying to keep track of depositing money for one goal while withdrawing for another.

To figure out how much you need to save each year for all your goals, use the Bringing It All Together worksheet in Retirement_Plan.xls:

1. **For one long-term goal, take the annual contribution amount you calculated, and copy (Ctrl+C [⌘-C]) that value into the cells for all the years you have to save that amount.**

   For example, if you have to save for your kid's college education from the time you're 30 until you reach 49, paste (Ctrl+V [⌘-V]) the value into the 30 to 45 columns.

2. **Repeat step 1 for each long-term goal you have.**

   The worksheet includes rows for retirement, parent care, and college. You can change what each of these rows represents, or add additional rows for other goals.

3. **Look at the number in the Annual Contributions Needed row.**

   If you can't afford the amount you have to save, you can use the Plan B Scenario and Achievable Scenario rows to adjust your plan.

What If I Can't Save Enough?

If the plan you came up with requires a higher annual contribution than you earn in a year, something's gotta give. You have a few options:

- **Prioritize.** As you learn on page 209, your retirement comes before your kids' college. If you can't meet the annual contribution, knock off some of the lower priority goals.

- **Go with Plan B goals.** When you built your list of goals, you came up with second- and third-tier options, just in case the numbers didn't pan out. If you can't contribute enough, now's the time to replace some of your first-pick goals with less extravagant ones.

- **Reassess how much you can save.** Maybe your annual contributions are out of reach right now, but that could change in a few years as your salary increases or you get a bonus or inheritance.

- **Save what you can.** If you can't stash the magic annual amount every year, don't give up completely. Contribute what you can. Each dollar you invest gets you part of the way there.

Say you finish your plan and discover you need to save between $37,000 and $52,000 per year until retirement to cover your retirement, your new-born's college fund, and to care for your aging parents, as you can see in the first scenario above. You earn $70,000 a year, so that plan simply isn't going to work.

You can make a few changes:

- After talking to your parents, you decide to cut the amount you save for them.

- You decide to save for part of a public school education instead of a private school.

- You switch to your Plan B retirement plan.

Saving more than $28,000 a year still isn't doable. Based on your budget, you decide that you can save no more than $15,000 a year right now. You postpone saving for your son's college for five years. If your salary raises don't come, you can revise your plan to reduce college savings, and then to reduce the money to help your parents.

3 Invest with Open Eyes

W hat's the biggest obstacle to reaching your financial goals? You. Because you're human, you have hard-wired idiosyncrasies that push you to make mistakes with your money. This chapter explains those traps and helps you avoid them.

First, you'll learn how to clean up your finances so you're ready to invest. Debt has become more of an American habit than eating hotdogs, so you'll learn which debt is good and which is loaded with nitrates. Then, you'll find some quick fixes to investment choices you've already made. Next, you'll learn how to control Americans' second passion, overspending. Finally, this chapter identifies common psychological pitfalls that many people fall into when they invest and shows you how to avoid them—whether that means writing in an investment journal or simply turning off the TV. Consider it your "12-step program" to smart investing.

Clean Up Your Finances

How you borrow money is as important to financial success as how you save and invest it. Debt is good when you borrow money to achieve an important goal, like buying a house, going to college, starting a business, or buying a car to get to work. Borrowing to buy lots of goods you want but don't truly have the money for isn't good money management. And if you pay a high interest rate on that debt (like the rates credit cards typically charge), you're on your way to financial ruin.

Borrowing for a Good Reason

Borrowing money to buy a house is usually a good reason to assume debt. Mortgages typically come with reasonable rates, you can deduct mortgage interest from your taxes, and you build equity in your home over time. In addition, houses usually increase in value over the long term, so you may also realize a capital gain (profit). However, a mortgage represents good debt only if you understand its terms—the mortgage rate, whether that rate remains constant (or the loan has a balloon payment you have to pay in full in a few years), whether you pay interest and principal (or interest only), and so on—*and* you can afford the payments. If you're confused by your financial obligations when you take out a mortgage, call a Housing and Urban Development (HUD) counseling center (1-800-569-4287) to sort things out (or pick up a copy of *Buying a Home: The Missing Manual*).

Borrowing to improve your quality of life is another good reason for debt. However, you must always evaluate the financial pros and cons to see whether the benefits you get are worth the interest you pay:

- If you need a car to get to work, a car loan makes sense. An auto loan is also a good way to start building your credit score. (See *Your Money: The Missing Manual* for more about credit scores.)

- The cost of 4 years at a private college averaged about $120,000 in 2010. With a college degree almost mandatory for many careers, borrowing to get your degree is relatively easy to justify. Still, you have to compare how much you plan to spend on your degree to the financial benefits it will bring to your career. Fortunately, student loans typically come with low interest rates and let you pay off your loans over long periods.

- Borrowing to start a business can be risky, but can also be a tremendous opportunity to change your life.

Get Rid of High-Interest Debt

You *know* you're being ripped off if you borrow from "payday" lenders who cash your paycheck and charge the equivalent of 485% interest per year (nice work if you can get it) or from anyone who loans you money in a back alley at 25%. But credit cards, which charge loan rates of up to 23.99%, are just as guilty of gouging borrowers. And if you borrow big and then make minimum or close-to-minimum payments each month, your borrowed balance (principal) and interest pile up. Say your car breaks down and you charge the $1,000 repair on a credit card with an 18% interest rate. If you pay only the minimum amount each month, it will take you more than 9 years to pay off the balance—and you'll have paid $923 in interest, almost a 100% premium over the original bill.

If you need more proof that high-interest debt is bad, go to the Bankrate Credit Card calculator (*http://tinyurl.com/kuctqp*), enter all your credit card debt, and see how long it will take you to pay off that debt and how much you'll pay in interest.

A loan's interest rate is key to taking on manageable debt. As a rule of thumb, look for a rate that's no more than 1% to 2% higher than the return on a safe investment, like Treasury bonds. For example, in March 2010, a 30-year Treasury bond paid 4.64% interest, so you'd look for an interest rate no higher than 6.64%. During the same period, someone with good credit could get a 30-year mortgage for 4.75% to 5.25% interest, which is well within the 1% to 2% rule of thumb. If you borrow the same $1,000 in the repair example above at 5%, it takes 6 years to pay off the balance, and you fork over only $174 in interest.

If you're paying high interest rates on debt, shift that debt to lower rates. Here's how:

1. **If you have more than one credit card or loan, make a list of your balances and the interest rates you pay on each.**

   List your cards and loans in order, from highest rate to lowest.

2. **Call each of your card companies and try to negotiate a lower fixed rate for your balance so you can consolidate your debt to one or two lower-rate cards.**

   Be sure to ask whether the rate on the card will increase in the near future and what the fee is to transfer in money (usually 2% or 3% of the balance you transfer). As long as the rate is fixed and the transfer fee is reasonable, moving your balance can help you pay off your debt faster by reducing how much you pay in interest. If you always pay at least the minimum balance on time, you're in a strong position to negotiate, because you're a dependable and profitable customer. If you ask them for a lower card interest rate, like 7% to 9%, and you tell them you're negotiating with other lenders, they may accept your proposal.

3. **If your credit card companies won't reduce your card rate to a reasonable level, another option may be to ask your bank or another lender about a *home equity line of credit* (HELOC).**

   A HELOC is a line of credit against the equity you've built up in your house from your down payment, paying off the balance on your mortgage, or because the value of your home has increased. The interest rate on a HELOC is about the same as a mortgage rate, so it's a great way to consolidate high-interest debt to one low-interest-rate source.

   A HELOC is a line of credit, which means you can borrow the amount you need up to the credit limit the lender sets when you apply for the loan. Similar to a credit card, you must pay a minimum amount each month, but you can pay off the balance as quickly as you like. (If you use the money you're no longer paying on high-interest-rate cards to pay off the HELOC balance, your debt balance will go down more quickly, as you see in the next step.)

   It's essential to remember that a HELOC uses your house as *collateral* (the asset that guarantees the money you borrow). If you run up your HELOC balance and then can't pay it off, you're likely to lose your house. For that reason, you must use a HELOC wisely. If you use one to consolidate high-interest-rate debt to lower-cost debt, then dutifully pay down your balance to get out of debt more quickly. Once you pay off your debt, use the HELOC only in emergencies.

4. **After you lower your interest rates as much as you can, start using the money you're saving in interest to pay extra on your highest-rate debt until that balance is zero.**

   Say you owe $1,000 on a card with an 18% interest rate, and you pay the $25 minimum each month. As you saw above, it takes 113 months to pay off the balance, and you pay $923.12 in interest. If you move your balance to a card with a 9% rate, your minimum payment drops to $17.50. If you continue to pay $25 each month, you'll pay off your bill in 48 months and pay only $193.39 in interest.

5. **When the highest-rate debt is gone, repeat step 4 with the next-highest-rate debt.**

   For a while, it'll be tough to change your bad debt habits. You have to make a conscious decision to not charge more to your credit cards and to be disciplined about paying down the balance on your credit card debt. By doing so, slowly but surely, you'll learn not only to live within your means, but also to save and invest money to reach your financial goals.

Tip Borrowing money to invest (buying on *margin*) can get you into trouble—fast. When you buy stock on margin, you put in half the cash value of the stock. For example, if you buy 100 shares of stock at $10 per share ($1,000 total), you can use $500 of your own money and borrow the other $500 from your brokerage. If the stock goes up to $15 per share, you sell the stock for $1,500. After you pay back the $500 you borrowed, you make a profit of $500 (minus interest). If you used your $500 to buy the stock outright (without borrowing), you'd buy 50 shares. When you sold those 50 shares for $15 per share, you'd make $250, half the amount you made on margin.

But if the stock goes down, you *lose* twice as much as you put in *and* you pay interest on the money you borrowed. So, if the stock went down to $5, you'd lose $500 on the stock itself. Because you borrowed $500 and have to pay that back, you'd lose the $500 that you put in, too. In addition, if the margin rate on your account is 10% per year, you'd also pay $50 per year in interest on the money you borrowed. If you don't have enough cash in your account to pay these debts, your brokerage can sell your *other* investments to pay back your loan and interest without telling you. A similar concept brought down major financial institutions during the financial crisis of 2007–2009, so you should probably steer clear.

Spend Money Wisely

If you spend all the money you earn, your retirement won't be pretty. On average, Americans save only 1% to 4% of their disposable income each year. Although the average U.S. savings rate has gone up, it isn't enough to help people pay for things like college and retirement.

Historical data shows that if you save money instead of spending it, you could have almost three times as much money in 20 years. So, before you spend $20 on Chinese takeout, ask whether it's worth $60. To help you save more, try some of these tactics:

- **Keep a written record of what you spend.** Keep track of how you spend every dollar using categories like food, utilities, rent, dining out, auto repair, and so on. After a few months, add up your expenses in each category. When you realize how much you spend in some categories, for example, $400 a month dining out, you can start thinking about ways to cut back, like bringing lunch to work or cooking at home more often. Learn more about tracking what you spend and creating a budget plan at *http://tinyurl.com/ybe3n6y*.

- **Don't give up everything.** Just as a diet is more successful if you allow yourself the occasional treat, a savings plan works better if you let yourself spend some money on fun stuff. If you and your spouse have date nights, don't give them up, but consider less expensive entertainment. Spending $50 each week adds up to more than $50,000 over 20 years, so cutting that weekly expense to $30 saves you $20,000.

- **Prioritize your spending.** Ask yourself what *really* matters: paying your mortgage, feeding the kids, commuting to work. Set aside money for that and then economize. A $500 birthday present each year for 20 years means $14,000 less when you retire. Bankrate.com has a calculator to help you calculate the impact of your spending changes (*http://tinyurl.com/ykxevho*).

- **Get rid of the fat in your spending.** Buy a latte but skip the pastry. Over 10 years, if you give up the $2.95 blueberry muffin (with 360 calories), you'll save $12,824 (and over a million calories).

- **When you invest, don't forget the fees.** Investments come with expenses, which reduce the return you earn. Be as frugal with investment expenses as you are with day-to-day spending. Page 90 gives you the full scoop on fund expenses and how to control them.

Expect Base Hits, Not Home Runs

The pounds you lose the first week of a diet don't fall away at the same rate forever. Likewise, double-digit gains on investments can't continue year after year. The path to investment success is slow and steady. There are no shortcuts. When you invest, be realistic about your expectations for returns. Then, use that realistic perspective to figure out how much you have to contribute each month to achieve your financial goal in the timeframe you have. The reason? If you do your figuring using unrealistic returns, you won't have enough money when you need it. For example, if your long-term goal for college tuition is to have $250,000 in 10 years and you plan for a 14% return on your investments, your financial calculations tell you to contribute $1,595 each month. If that investment earns a more real-world 7%, however, you'd have only $178,000. To reach your goal with a realistic 7% return, you have to contribute $2,232 each month.

You may luck out with an investment that returns an impressively high number—like the 14% in the example above. You remember an experience like that, because that one great success makes you feel smart and happy. The problem is, you can come to expect such unrealistically high returns every time, even though it was a phenomenon you're unlikely to see again anytime soon. This tendency, called *anchoring,* can make a good return seem average and a realistic return seem poor.

If your expectations are off base, you may start hunting for higher returns in bad places, like in overly risky investments, last year's big thing, or what someone forecasts as next year's sure bet. For example, many fund managers have good quarters and a few even have good years, but none have consistently beaten the market, year over year. Some funds try to show how they would have succeeded based on what worked in the past. But past successes don't guarantee future returns.

The fact is, investment returns go up and down. But a medium-risk diversified portfolio historically averages a 7% return. Asset allocation, where you divide your portfolio among different types of investments to manage risk, is a key investment strategy (you'll learn all about it in Chapter 9). For example, in a typical portfolio, you invest in stocks for long-term higher returns (with higher risk), bonds to reduce that risk and earn income, and cash as a safety net to handle upcoming expenses.

Sidestepping Pitfalls in Investor Psychology

In theory, investors are rational people, but you're an investor and you know you're not completely rational all the time. When you're outside your comfort zone, as many people are when they invest, you may act irrationally. It turns out that some of your bad habits are hardwired into your brain—after all, those habits helped early humans survive in the wild (long before they started investing). For example, early humans who were part of a community survived, while individualists often became someone's lunch.

Even today, people experience pain when they go their own way. The result is herd behavior, that is, doing what everyone else is doing. For investors, herd behavior often means buying because everyone else is. Unfortunately, by the time you buy, the people who bought before you have inflated the investment's price, so you may end up buying at a higher price than the investment is worth. If you sell after everyone else has sold, you sell at a price that's often below the true value of the investment.

Our brains have evolved to seek immediate pleasure. Short-term successes, like killing your dinner or watching an investment go up in value, both release chemicals in the brain that give you pleasure and instill confidence. This quirk of evolution worked well for hunters, but isn't so good for long term investors.

To be a successful investor, you have to recalibrate your brain. You *can* teach an old dog new tricks—behavioral research shows that you can adopt better habits, and as you do, you build new neural pathways that strengthen that behavior. Each success reinforces your new *good* habits, and they grow stronger until they eventually become second nature. Honest. This section describes the different types of bad habits you may have as an investor and how to retrain yourself to be more successful.

Which Type of Investor Are You?

Researchers studying investors have categorized their behavior by risk tolerance, psychology, gender, and a gazillion other factors. However, all this research boils down to four investor types, based on the level of risk they're willing to tolerate and on their confidence level, as the table below shows. If you recognize yourself in any of these descriptions, you can learn how to improve your investing habits. Most people see a little bit of themselves in a couple of the categories. This overlap is normal, so read all the descriptions and develop a plan that works for your personality.

	Lower risk	Higher risk
Insecure	**Protectors** have low risk tolerance and are very insecure about money. They want to keep every nickel, even if it'll be worth a penny in a few years. They're emotional about their money, so rational arguments don't persuade them.	**Followers** have a slightly higher risk tolerance, but are frightened by money. They don't want to make bad decisions and they regret past decisions, so they want someone else to make decisions for them.
Confident	**Leaders** are confident and willing to take risks to obtain higher returns. They're analytical, independent thinkers.	**Power players** have confidence and high risk tolerance, so they're willing to take unnecessary risks just to play a hunch.

 Studies have shown that women are typically less confident and that men trade 45% more often than women. However, overall, men's investment returns are 1.4% lower than women's.

Protectors

Protectors hate change and they worry. If you're a protector, you may work for the same company your whole life and keep your money in a savings account. You're insecure about what you know about money and have a very low tolerance for risk. You're emotional about investments and have trouble listening to logical arguments.

The finance industry has built an illusion of complexity around money over the years. Lots of careers and salaries depend on your being intimidated by money. In reality, a bunch of fancy words just cover up straightforward ideas. Investing doesn't have to be complicated.

Protectors' bad habits

Here are the bad habits that protectors exhibit:

- **Attachment to investments you already own.** Whether you invest in your employer's stock or an ETF, you treat every investment in your portfolio as sacrosanct. Sadly, this habit means that you keep poor investments you should sell. Protectors prefer the status quo and avoid change. But portfolios benefit from rebalancing (see page 170 for details).

- **Dislike of losses.** The "flight" part of your fight or flight instinct kicks in with any kind of loss, including loss on investments. In fact, people instinctively find losing much more painful than they find winning pleasurable. If you don't want to admit to an investment loss, you hold onto a loser because the loss won't feel real if you don't sell. In addition, you may hold onto an investment until its price returns to your purchase price (or a high value that you remember), so you don't feel like you lost money. In reality, you would have done better by selling the loser investment and buying a new one with better prospects.

Tip Protectors often stay out of the market after a loss or hold cash because they think it's safe, while they disregard the dangers of inflation (page 14).

- **Fear of the unknown.** If you're afraid of the unknown and haven't learned to invest, you *won't* invest. Unfortunately, without investing, you aren't likely to achieve your financial goals (page 13).

Tip Many employees stick with buying their employer's stock, because they know the company, which may be why some companies that offer employer stock as a retirement-plan option see more than 90% of employee contributions invested in their stock. Betting your retirement on your employer's stock is risky. If the company runs into trouble, you could be out of both a job and a good chunk of your retirement savings at the same time.

- **Fear of mistakes.** Protectors would rather do nothing than make a mistake. Many employees review their 401(k) investments and do nothing else, because they're afraid of change. But inaction has a huge downside. Even if you set up your portfolio perfectly at the beginning, it needs regular tweaking to stay in tiptop shape (see page 168).

Protectors' new habits

It's tough to overcome your protector emotions, even if reason, like the examples in this book, tells you to change your ways. Try the following:

- Focus your emotions on your goals, and remind yourself how much you want to achieve them.
- Make small, gradual changes to your investments. Once you set up your investments, continue to make small changes to keep your portfolio on track (page 170).
- If you don't think you can do either of these steps or you have an incredible urge to put this book away right now, consider having someone, like a financial adviser, help you with your investments.

Followers

If you're a follower, you do just that: Follow the herd, because that makes you feel safe. Your risk tolerance is low, although you may think it's higher. You're insecure about your knowledge of investments. However, because you follow the herd, you buy when everyone else buys, so you buy at the peak. You sell when everyone else sells, so you sell at the bottom. That's 180 degrees from what you should do to make money in investments.

Followers' bad habits

Here are some of followers' bad investing habits:

- **Ignoring losses.** As a follower, you tend to ignore losses. If you acknowledge a loss, you often throw caution to the wind, and jump on the next trend. You're affected by news in the media and place excessive emphasis on the short term instead of the big picture.
- **Not learning from your mistakes.** Because you take other people's advice instead of making your own decisions, it's tough to learn from your mistakes. You don't analyze your needs, develop your own plan, or evaluate investments to select those that are right for you. So, if your investments don't work out, you have no information to help you understand why.

- **Believing information that's familiar.** Hearing about something a lot doesn't make it true. But many people think an event is more likely to happen if they hear about it often. For example, you may remember the movie *Jaws* when you swim in the ocean, but only one or two fatal shark attacks occur each year in the United States. You may start to believe that stock prices are too high, too low, and so on, if you hear that every hour on TV.

  A similar bad habit is recalling recent events instead of historic trends, which is a great way to pick last year's winners, but doesn't help you invest for the future. If you buy stocks based on recent events, you're likely to buy high and sell low. For example, in summer 2008, articles about the price of oil came out daily. But oil prices hit their peak shortly after the quantity of articles about them peaked, so investing based on that news meant buying when prices were at their highest.

- **Opinions change.** Do you know someone whose opinion depends on who they talk to? They like country music if they're talking to a cowboy and hip-hop if they're talking to a teenager. Followers do the same thing with investments. If you're a follower, your opinion changes depending on the last piece of investment advice you heard. This wavering is especially true when you talk about losses and may make you feel more risk-tolerant than you really are.

Followers' new habits

The good news is that you have great potential. You can think logically about your investments and benefit from a few changes:

- **Learn.** Education is the best tool for a follower. Because you think logically, you can learn about investing and put your knowledge to work making good investment decisions.

- **Think for yourself.** Once you learn how to invest, research your investments before you make decisions. That makes it easier to stop following trends and listening to so-called experts.

Leaders

Leaders are confident, aggressive, and contrarian. They're strong thinkers, analytical, and want evidence before making a decision. But they still have a few bad habits.

Leaders' bad habits

Here are some pitfalls that leaders tend to fall into:

- **Taking credit for wins,** while discounting losses as out of their control. If you're a leader, you may confuse randomness and skill, which keeps you from learning from your mistakes, because you don't think you make any.

- **Ignoring information that contradicts beliefs.** Leaders value their opinions more than new information that doesn't match their beliefs.

- **Believing information that's familiar.** Surprisingly, leaders are just as likely to believe what they hear frequently as followers are. In addition, receiving more information boosts your confidence but not your knowledge. As you learn more about a subject or a stock, your confidence increases. Unfortunately, your knowledge hits a plateau near the beginning, so you think you know a lot more than you do.

 Studies show that most people believe they're smarter than average. Leaders are convinced of it. If you're a leader, you have so much confidence you lose sight of your real track record.

- **Buy and sell frequently.** Leaders like to be in control, and one way they prove their superiority is by constantly buying and selling investments. But buying and selling in the short term doesn't produce better results in the long term. Most day traders don't succeed.

Leaders' new habits

If you're a leader, you need to accept a new definition of success. Instead of making changes frequently or trying to prove your success, learn to love a slow and steady approach to investing:

- **Learn.** Education is a great tool for leaders. You can learn about investing and have the confidence to put your knowledge to work.

- **Keep an investment journal.** Document all your investment decisions, why you make them, and what your expectations are. Documenting your thoughts keeps you grounded and helps control your urge to take credit when credit isn't due. When you review your investments, look at your journal to remind yourself why you bought them and whether you'd purchase the same things again.

- **Commit to future decisions.** People are bad at estimating how they'll behave in the future. As a leader, your overconfidence could lead you to make spur-of-the-moment decisions that don't match your original plan. When you decide on an investment, commit to that decision while your analysis is fresh in your mind. For example, if you're going to reallocate when your asset allocation is off by 3%, automate the decision by setting up transactions with your broker or advisor (page 167).

- **Play devil's advocate.** You instinctively look for evidence that your decisions are right. While making an investment decision, try to argue why you're wrong instead. Doing so helps counteract your tendency for overconfidence.

Power Players

Power players are aggressive and entrepreneurial, strong-willed and confident. Typically, they earn their own wealth and are very emotional about building it.

Power players' bad habits

Power players are like leaders without the benefit of analytical thinking. Their emotions drive them to extremes. In addition to the pitfalls listed for leaders, power players have additional bad habits:

- **Excessive ego.** If you think you're a whiz at investing, you may put off saving because you believe you can make money quickly. When you're successful, you lose your fear and may overreact, because you trust your gut, not analysis. Because long-term investing success comes from analysis and not instinct, power players can buy and sell investments frequently and on a whim, which can lead to frequent losses as well as high fees.

- **Forgetting about losses.** Power players forget losses, but believe they control random events if they win. When something good happens, you believe you knew it all along.

Power players' new habits

To succeed as long-term investors, power players need to ignore some of the strengths that helped them succeed in other areas of their life. Here are some ways you can do that:

- **Focus on the big picture.** Power players are emotional, so you aren't going to be persuaded to change your behavior with numbers. Instead, like protectors, you need to focus on the big picture. Investing can turn your greatest strengths in business into weaknesses. Your confidence won't benefit your long-term investments, so you need to rise above your instincts and make wise investment choices based on analysis.

- **Consider delegating finances to a trusted advisor.** If you can't overcome your emotions, work with someone who handles finances rationally. As a successful businessperson, you know that visionaries often need to hand the reins of a business over to others to move forward. As a power player, consider whether you can rise above your pitfalls and help yourself.

- **Set aside 10% to play with.** A true power player doesn't want to hand everything over to someone else or have decisions made solely on analysis, so give yourself a play fund. Take 10% of your long-term investing money, and do what you will with it. But leave the other 90% to the time-proven analytical approach.

Part 2
Choose and Buy Your Investments

4 How Investments Work

During your lifetime, you invest in a lot of things: a college education, financial investments, or a long-term relationship. In every case, you expect some kind of payback in return, whether it's a good paycheck, savings to support you during retirement, or someone to hold your hand at the movies.

You know that life can be a bit of a gamble. The higher you aim, the higher the risk of failure. The same holds true for investments; the ones with the highest returns also come with the greatest risk that you may lose money. Investments with lower average returns tend to be safer, but don't help your portfolio grow as much. So, when you invest, you perform a balancing act between earning high enough returns to reach your financial goals and limiting the risk you face.

This chapter starts with an introduction to the four main types of investments. You'll learn how each one works, why they produce the returns they do, and the level of risk each one presents. Because investment returns are so important, you don't want to give them up needlessly. That's why this chapter also talks about how the government taxes your investments, and how you can keep those taxes from eating up your returns.

The Big Four: Typical Investments

Although the financial world is as rife with exotic investments as a cafe is with fancy coffees, most people do just fine choosing from four basic types of investments (funds, stocks, bonds, and real estate). In fact, with the right fund, you can purchase one investment (the fund) and let the fund manager take care of purchasing the other types of investments (because some funds put money into a smorgasbord of investments). Even so, to make sure you're getting the combination of returns and risk you've decided on (page 156), you need to understand the four investment types.

 Note When you know which types of investment you're interested in, you can jump to one of the other chapters in this book to learn more:

- Chapter 5 gives you the full scoop on the type of investment almost everyone owns: funds. You'll learn about index funds, actively managed funds, exchange-traded funds, and more.
- Chapter 6 talks about how to evaluate stocks.
- You can learn about how to invest in bonds and the difference between bonds and bond funds in Chapter 7.
- Chapter 8 shows you how to dive into real estate with real estate investment trusts.

Stock: Owning Part of a Company

A *share* of stock is just that—a share of ownership in a business, whether it's your own, a friend's, or a publicly traded corporation's, like Google. (You may see these investments referred to as stocks, common stocks, equities, or shares.) The business's performance has a lot to do with whether its share price goes up or down. So does investors' opinion of the company's prospects; it determines whether they'll pay more or less for the stock.

You make money when the share price goes up (the increase in value is called a *capital gain*)—although the money doesn't land in your hot little hands until you actually sell your share. You can also earn money on stock through *dividends,* a payment of part of the company's profits to shareholders, which you'll learn about shortly.

If a company's products or services are on everyone's must-have list, sales and earnings usually rise. Investors want a piece of the action, so they bid more for shares, which sends the share price higher. For example, when Google went public, one share of its stock sold for about $108. In February 2010, the share price was around $540, about five times the original price.

Although Google's stock looks like a tremendous success story, you can see below that the trip Google's share price took wasn't a straight line. Owning stock has the potential to deliver attractive returns, as Google's stock shows. Between 1926 and 2009, stocks returned about 11% a year on average (assuming dividends were reinvested in stock).

However, higher stock returns come with higher risk. In any 1 year, the overall return for stocks could be just about anything. The highest 1-year increase—of 54%—occurred in 1933. The largest 1-year drop, 43.3%, was 2 years earlier, in 1931. This potential for wild gyrations is the reason you invest in stocks for long-term, not short-term, goals, as you'll learn on page 156.

On the other hand, Enron, an electric and natural gas utility company, shows the worst case when investing in stocks. The company saw its stock go from $90 per share to $0 when the company went bankrupt. Although Enron is an extreme example, if investors suspect trouble (like products becoming obsolete, increased competition, decreasing earnings, losses, and so on), they bid less for shares, lowering the stock price.

 If a company goes bankrupt, it pays off its debts and other liabilities first. If there's any money left over, it goes to shareholders. (Page 131 explains the hierarchy of payouts when a company goes out of business.)

Many companies reinvest their profits back into the company. That way, they grow their businesses without borrowing or issuing more shares. But at some point, a company might run out of productive uses for its profits. Then it might pay out some of those profits as dividends to shareholders. Most investors view regularly increasing dividends as a sign of a company's financial strength. (On the other hand, if a company reduces its dividend payment, the share price usually drops as well, because investors worry that the company is struggling.)

 Cash dividends often add a bit of stability to share price, because the dividend acts like a foundation for the price. A dividend paid by a stock is similar to a yield earned on a savings account. (You calculate the yield by dividing the dividend payout by the share price.) Unlike a savings account, the dividend yield increases as the stock price goes down. If the dividend yield goes high enough, the stock becomes an attractive investment for the yield alone.

Bonds: Lending Money

A bond is like a loan you make to a company or to the government (both known as the bond *issuer*). In return for the use of your money, the issuer pays you interest on a regular schedule. Then, when the bond *matures* (that is, when the loan comes due, usually between 1 and 30 years), the issuer gives you your original investment (your *principal*) back.

Many investors buy bonds for the interest they pay. For example, retirees often use bond income to cover part of their living expenses. The interest rate a bond pays doesn't change once the bond is issued. Even if the company that issues the bond does spectacularly well, you still earn the original interest rate. For example, a $1,000 bond with a 6% interest rate pays $60 in interest each year until the bond matures. That's one attraction of buying and holding a bond: Your return may be lower than what you'd earn from investing in stock, but you know what your return will be all along.

Although most investors stick with bonds purely as income investments, you can make money with bonds in another way. Although a bond's interest rate doesn't change, its price can. For example, if market interest rates go up, the bond price goes down. (Page 136 explains why this happens.) But if interest rates go down, the bond price goes up. If you sell a bond before it matures for more than you paid for it, you earn a capital gain, just as you do when you sell a share of stock for more than you paid.

The reason bond prices change in response to market interest rates is competition, plain and simple. If you buy a $1,000 bond that pays 4% interest, you get $40 a year in interest. If a new bond comes out that pays 5% interest ($50 a year), why would anyone want to pay full price for your bond? To make your bond competitive, you have to drop its price so the new owner earns 5% interest. In this example, you'd have to sell your $1,000 bond for $800. (There's more to bond prices than that, as you'll learn starting on page 136.)

Bonds are much less risky than stocks if you hold them until they mature, because you get back their face value regardless of the state of the market. In fact, bonds aren't as risky as stocks even if the issuer gets into trouble. As you see on page 131, bondholders get repaid before stock shareholders if a company goes out of business. Credit quality is one way to gauge how much risk you take investing in a bond (based on the risk of the issuer missing interest payments or not paying back principal). You'll learn how to evaluate bonds and their risks in Chapter 7.

Investing with Others: Funds

If you don't have a lot of money to invest, it's tough to build a diversified portfolio of individual stocks and bonds. There's also the issue of time spent figuring out which stocks and bonds to buy and keeping an eye on them to make sure they perform the way you expect. Finally, you may simply worry that you don't know enough to get everything right (page 46). The solution for many people is funds, whether they're mutual funds, exchange-traded funds, or more exotic varieties.

When you buy shares in a fund, the fund company tosses your cash in the same pot with the money from other people and then uses that money to buy a bunch of stocks, bonds, other types of investments, or some combination of different types of investments.

Funds have become the odds-on favorite with lots of investors for several reasons:

- **Diversification.** In many cases, as little as $1,000 gets you the diversification you need to keep your risk at a level you can live with.

- **Ease of use.** Choosing a fund doesn't take as much time or effort as picking a stock or bond, as Chapter 5 explains. In addition, the fund's managers do the heavy lifting in research and investment decisions, so you don't have to spend as much time making sure your investments are performing up to your expectations.

- **Market focus.** Once you decide what part of the market you want to invest in (page 160), you can find funds that cover it. Stocks? Bonds? Tiny companies? Asian companies? Companies that are socially responsible? You can find a fund that focuses on each of those investments. Among the thousands of funds in the United States, you can find funds that cover the entire investment world or funds that invest in only a few dozen stocks.

Index funds are so named because they mimic a *market index* (a collection of investments that represents a market segment; the S&P 500, for example, is an index of the stocks of the country's biggest companies, while the Barclays Aggregate Bond Index is a broad bond market index). They're the easiest and most cost-effective way to invest in funds. Although index funds still have fund managers, the funds practically run themselves, because they invest in whatever the index is made up of. If the S&P 500 drops a company from its list, an S&P 500 index fund does, too.

Because of the way they invest, index funds don't have to pay fund managers big salaries, and they don't have to buy and sell holdings often. For both those reasons, index fund expenses are some of the lowest you'll find (on average, about 0.25% per year).

In contrast to index funds, *actively managed* funds mean someone's actively making investment decisions about what to buy, sell, or hold onto. Actively managed funds try all sorts of strategies to earn above-market-average returns: picking stocks, investing in specific industries, and so on. However, over the long term, most actively managed funds end up nose to nose with the market average. That matching performance, combined with higher fund expenses for actively managed funds, is the reason index funds usually make more sense, as you'll see shortly.

A relative newcomer to the investment scene is the *exchange-traded fund* (ETF). An ETF can be an index fund or an actively managed fund. It pools investors' money like a mutual fund does, but you can buy or sell shares in an ETF anytime you want, just as you can with a stock. Page 75 gives you the full scoop.

It's no surprise that you have to pay someone else to do mutual fund investment work, like researching investments and making buy and sell decisions. Unlike with stocks and bonds, where you pay commission only when you buy or sell, mutual funds charge ongoing fees and expenses.

Just like inflation, mutual fund expenses might not sound like much, but those expenses directly affect your investment returns. Whether the fees are out of this world, like 2% per year for some actively managed funds, or the frugal 0.2% some index funds charge, those expenses reduce the return you receive. For example, say you have $10,000 in a mutual fund and the fund returns 6% in 1 year ($600). However, the fund has a 1% *expense ratio* (the annual cost for managing and running the fund). You pay $100 per year in expenses, so your fund investment nets only $500, or 5%, that year.

As you learned on page 16, a 1% difference in return (say from 6% to 5%) over decades makes a ginormous difference in the size of your portfolio. Because actively managed funds charge higher expense ratios, they have to deliver higher returns just to stay even with the market average. And because they typically don't manage to do that over time, most actively managed funds can't keep up with their index fund counterparts.

 Page 90 tells you all about the different types of expenses that mutual funds charge, how much they charge, and how to decide when enough is too much.

Real Estate Investment Trusts (REITs)

If you want to diversify your portfolio beyond stocks and bonds, real estate is another option. Because most people can't afford to invest in individual properties, real estate investment trusts (REITs) are the answer. These companies invest in the real estate market, so you can buy shares in a REIT on a stock exchange and immediately own a slice of hundreds of properties. You don't have to play landlord or wait months to sell a building you own directly. Some REITs invest in real estate mortgages, which means they lend money to companies to buy real estate. Chapter 8 tells you how to invest in REITs.

Note REIT mutual funds or REIT ETFs purchase several individual REITs, which gives you even more diversification.

By law, REITs pay out 90% of their income to shareholders, so their dividends (5%, 6%, or more per year) are attractive to income investors. However, REIT dividends are taxed as ordinary income, which is a higher tax rate than what you pay on stock dividends, so REITs are best held in a non-taxed account (page 142).

A REIT's share price can increase, too, if its earnings or the value of its properties increases. Of course, what goes up can also come down, which was true of many REITs during the recent real estate market debacle.

Putting all your eggs in one basket is never a good idea. REITs let you diversify by owning many properties. With REITs, you can also diversify by geographic location or by type of property, such as shopping malls, apartment buildings, condos, office buildings, hotels, resorts, storage facilities, industrial parks, and health-related facilities.

Taxing Decisions

Every tax season, the federal and state governments wait impatiently for their tax fix from the money you make, whether it comes from your salary, poker winnings, or earnings from your investments. Paying taxes on investment gains and income hurts, because you're handing over money that would otherwise be compounding like crazy to help you reach your financial goals (page 16).

Because retirement, college education, and health care are so important, you can get some tax relief by putting money for those goals into several types of government-sponsored tax-advantaged accounts (a fancy name for accounts that give you some kind of tax break). Even if you invest in taxable investments, you can minimize your tax bill by allocating those investments carefully between taxable and *tax-advantaged* accounts. In other words, put your most taxable investments in tax-advantaged accounts, and put investments with the smallest tax bills in your taxable accounts.

 Note The following chapters give you the full scoop on tax-advantaged accounts for long-term goals:

- Chapter 10 covers retirement investment accounts.
- Chapter 11 discusses options for saving for college.
- Chapter 12 talks about how to save for health care.

You'll see why paying attention to taxes is important below. Then you'll get an introduction to the different types of tax-advantaged accounts available. And finally, you'll learn the pros and cons of putting specific types of investments in tax-advantaged and taxable accounts.

The Big Tax Bite

In Chapter 1, you learned why you need the higher returns that investing provides to beat inflation and reach your financial goals. But just when you thought you had the inflation problem licked, you realize that taxes nibble away at your nest egg like money-eating piranhas.

Bonds and REITs deliver lower long-term returns than stocks do (page 156), and then, to make matters worse, returns from them get taxed as ordinary income—at the highest tax rate you pay, in other words. Long-term capital gains (like those you get when you sell a stock after holding it for more than a year) and stock dividends deliver higher long-term returns and have the additional advantage of a lower tax rate.

The table below summarizes tax rates for different types of investment returns for someone in the 25% tax bracket (with a taxable income of between $33,950 and $82,250).

Investment return	Tax rate
Bond interest	Ordinary income: 25%
REIT dividends	Ordinary income: 25%
Stock dividends	15% (5% for people in the 10% or 15% tax bracket)
Short-term capital gains (held less than 1 year)	Ordinary income: 25%
Long-term capital gains (held longer than 1 year)	15% (0% for people in the 10% or 15% tax bracket)

 Note Mutual funds distribute interest, dividends, and capital gains that their underlying investments produce during a year. If you hold mutual funds in a taxable account, you have to pay taxes on those distributions as if you owned the individual securities. Mutual funds that don't buy and sell frequently, such as index funds, don't generate as much in capital gains, which reduces the capital gains taxes you owe (page 63).

Although 2010 tax rates are as low as rates have been in years, even relatively benign tax rates dramatically reduce your investment results. Here's an example:

- Say you're single and make $50,000 a year, which puts you in the 25% tax bracket.

- You invest $50,000 in one lump sum, allocated to 60% stocks, 20% bonds, and 20% REITs.

- Assume that stock dividends and capital gains provide a total return of 10%; your bonds pay 5%; and your REITs return 6%.

- Other than rebalancing your portfolio to maintain the percentages in each type of investment, you let your portfolio grow for 40 years.

The table below shows that taxes reduce your overall return from 8.2% to 6.75% per year. That doesn't sound like much, but over 40 years, that smaller return cuts your retirement portfolio by about 40%, from $1,169,662 to $681,845.

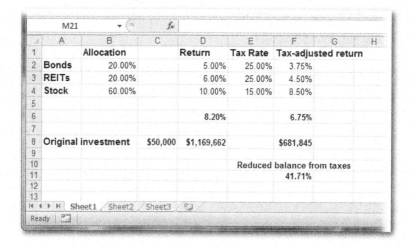

	A	B	C	D	E	F	G	H
1		Allocation		Return	Tax Rate	Tax-adjusted return		
2	Bonds	20.00%		5.00%	25.00%	3.75%		
3	REITs	20.00%		6.00%	25.00%	4.50%		
4	Stock	60.00%		10.00%	15.00%	8.50%		
5								
6				8.20%		6.75%		
7								
8	Original investment		$50,000	$1,169,662		$681,845		
9								
10						Reduced balance from taxes		
11						41.71%		
12								
13								

Making the Most of Tax-Advantaged Accounts

Tax-advantaged accounts come with a variety of features, but the most common characteristic is delaying the time when you have to pay taxes. *Tax-deferred* means your money can grow unfettered by taxes, which come due only when you ***withdraw*** from the account. You can reinvest the full amount of interest, dividends, and capital gains you earn to compound for years without a dollar going to taxes. Only when you withdraw money during retirement do you pay taxes; at that time, your tax rate might be lower.

Chapters 10, 11, and 12 give you the full rundown on different types of tax-advantaged accounts, but here's a quick introduction:

- **401(k) and 403(b).** These tax-deferred accounts (page 178) have become the mainstay for employer-sponsored retirement savings, with the majority of employers choosing to offer them over traditional pension plans. You contribute a percentage of your paycheck before paying taxes on it, so your tax savings reduce how much you pay out of pocket for your contribution. For example, if you're in the 25% tax bracket and contribute $10,000 to your 401(k) or 403(b), you save $2,500 in taxes, so your net out of pocket is only $7,500.

  In 2010, the maximum annual contribution is $16,500. (If you're over 50, you can add a catch-up contribution of up to $5,500.) You must start withdrawing from your account when you're 70 ½.

Tip If your company matches a portion of what you contribute, that match is like an immediate 100% return on the portion the company matches. It's unlikely you'll find a return that good elsewhere, so if you can't afford to contribute the maximum amount to your 401(k), at the least, contribute enough to get the full company match.

- **Traditional IRA.** Anyone with earned income (salary, wages, tips, bonuses, and so on) can contribute to a traditional IRA, another tax-deferred account option. If you've contributed the maximum to your 401(k) or 403(b), a traditional IRA is one way to get more money into retirement savings. In 2010, you can contribute up to $5,000 (plus an additional $1,000 catch-up contribution if you're over 50). Your contributions might be tax-deductible depending on your income. For example, if you're single and your adjusted gross income is less than $56,000, your entire contribution is tax deductible.

  You must be younger than 70 ½ and have earned income to contribute to a traditional IRA. As with 401(k) plans, you must start withdrawing when you reach age 70 ½.

 Note If you switch jobs and don't want to keep your retirement funds in your employer-sponsored retirement plan, you can move your money into a *rollover IRA* to continue the tax deferral.

- **Roth IRA.** Similar to traditional IRAs, 401(k)s, and 403(b)s, you don't pay taxes on interest, dividends, and capital gains in a Roth IRA (page 182). What gets everyone's attention is that you withdraw from these accounts *tax-free* after the age of 59 ½. The catch is that contributions to a Roth IRA aren't tax deductible. That is, you pay taxes on the money before you contribute to the account. With some income limitations, Roths have the same contribution and catch-up limits as traditional IRAs.

  Roth IRAs have other features that make them attractive for saving for your later retirement years. You can continue to contribute after you reach 70 ½, and there's no mandatory annual distribution at any time. Because you contribute after-tax money, you can withdraw your contributions at any time without paying taxes or penalties.

 Note Because you contribute after-tax, you can withdraw your contributions without paying taxes or penalties. Before you can withdraw earnings tax-free , you must be 59 ½ and have converted or contributed to the Roth at least 5 years earlier.

- **Roth conversion.** If you convert a traditional or rollover IRA to a Roth IRA, you have to pay taxes on the tax-deferred contributions you made to the original account. Page 183 helps you decide whether a conversion makes sense for you.

- **Inherited IRA.** A beneficiary of an IRA can transfer the money into an inherited IRA to keep the tax-deferral going until the IRS requires distribution. The tax rules for inherited IRAs make Einstein's theory of relativity look like a piece of cake, so consulting a tax advisor is a good idea if you inherit an IRA.

- **SEP-IRA.** For small businesses or self-employed individuals, the simplified employee pension IRA (SEP-IRA) is the easiest pension plan option. You can contribute up to 25% of your income each year (to a maximum $49,000 in 2010). You can set up a SEP-IRA for a side business even if you already have a 401(k) at your day job.

 Note See page 187 to learn about other retirement account options for small businesses, such as Keogh and SIMPLE plans.

- **Section 529 college savings plan.** Investments grow tax-deferred in these popular college savings plans. Withdrawals are tax-free as long as you use them for qualified educational expenses (page 200). The contribution limits are high, sometimes as much as $300,000. Whoever contributes to the account is the owner, who can then name a family member as the beneficiary. That's good news for two reasons. First, colleges don't take the 529 investment into account when they calculate a student's financial aid, because the account isn't in the student's name. Second, if the current 529 beneficiary ends up getting a big scholarship, you can change the beneficiary.

- **Section 529 college prepaid plan.** Prepaid plans lock in future tuition costs at today's rates (page 202). They aren't as popular as 529 savings plans, because they make it harder to roll over into another plan or switch to another beneficiary.

- **Coverdell education savings account.** Investments in these accounts grow tax-deferred, and withdrawals are tax-free if you use them for qualified educational expenses. The big drawback to these accounts is the $2,000 annual contribution limit, a drop in the bucket for college costs.

- **Health savings account.** If you have a high-deductible health insurance plan, you can set up a health savings account (HSA), described in detail on page 218. In 2010, an individual can contribute up to $3,050 pre-tax with a $1,000 catch-up if you're 55 or older. Unlike with flexible spending accounts, you don't have to use the money you contribute during a specific year. You can invest the money in the same kinds of options you have with an IRA. Withdrawals for health care are tax-free.

 Note Medical savings accounts (MSA) work like health savings accounts, except that only self-employed people or employers with 50 or fewer employees qualify for them.

Tax-Advantaged or Taxable: Where to Put Investments

Tax-advantaged accounts limit how much you can contribute each year. If you're saving for a goal that has tax-advantaged account options (retirement, college, and health care), rule number one is to contribute as much as you can to these accounts before you contribute to taxable accounts.

After that, you have some decisions to make about which investments to keep in tax-advantaged and taxable accounts. In short, keep investments with the highest tax bills in your tax-advantaged accounts and those with lower tax bills in taxable accounts.

 Note The ultimate investment savings comes, sadly, when you die. Your beneficiaries inherit the stock you owned on a *stepped-up basis,* which means that they inherit it as though they paid market value for the investment on the date of your death. That means your beneficiaries don't have to pay capital gains on the increase in the stock's value that occurred during your lifetime.

As you learned on page 63, the tax rates on interest income, dividends, and capital gains vary and depend on the type of investment and how long you hold it. The table below shows you which types of investments are better in tax-advantaged and taxable accounts from a tax perspective—if you have a choice of accounts.

Investment type	Investments to hold in a tax-advantaged account	Investments to hold in a taxable account
Stock Mutual Funds or ETFs	Stock funds that pay high dividends (because the dividends are taxable). High-turnover (page 90) funds (they produce capital gains, and short-term capital gains in particular), as fund managers trade investments. The gains are taxed at ordinary income rates. Mutual funds, because their managers have to sell shares to meet redemption requests, generating capital-gains taxes.	Stock funds that pay low or no dividends. Low-turnover stock funds, such as index funds. ETFs, which don't have to sell investments to meet redemption requests the way mutual funds do. Tax-managed funds, which invest with an eye toward reducing taxes.
Individual Stocks	Stocks that pay high-dividends, which are taxable. Stocks you trade frequently, which results in capital gains.	Stocks with low or no dividends. Stocks you tend to buy and hold onto, because you don't pay capital gains until you sell, and then they're long-term capital gains.

Investment type	Investments to hold in a tax-advantaged account	Investments to hold in a taxable account
Bonds and Bond Funds	Regular bonds and high-yield bonds, because they produce current income taxed at ordinary income-tax rates.	Municipal bonds and bond funds; the federal government doesn't tax income (nor does the state tax bonds if you buy state-issued bonds in the state where you live).
REITs and REIT Funds	REITs tend to pay attractive dividend rates, and their income is taxed at ordinary income tax rates.	

 Tip Stock dividends are taxed at a lower rate than bond income, so you're better off holding stocks that pay high dividends in taxable accounts rather than bonds or bond funds in those accounts.

Managing Taxes in Taxable Accounts

Sometimes, you have to put higher-taxed investments into taxable accounts. For example, if you're saving for a short-term goal, stocks may be too risky, so you put your money in bonds or bond funds, or in a savings account. Or you may be saving for a goal that doesn't have a tax-advantaged account option. Don't worry. Although you shouldn't make investment decisions purely to avoid paying taxes, you can keep your investment taxes low with the following tactics:

- **Buy and hold individual stocks and bonds instead of stock or bond funds.** You don't pay capital gains on individual stocks and bonds until you sell them; fund managers may trade within stock or bond funds frequently, and you pay taxes on any gains from those trades. Sell individual securities in taxable accounts only to rebalance your asset allocation or because an investment hasn't panned out as you hoped.

- **Buy municipal-bond funds or municipal bonds.** If you want more bonds in a taxable account, purchase municipal bond funds. The federal government doesn't tax municipal bond income. In addition, you don't pay state taxes on municipal bond income if you buy municipal bonds issued by your state.

- **Delay selling until the capital gains are long term.** If you sell an investment before you own it for a year, you earn a short-term capital gain, which is taxed at ordinary income rates (for someone in the 25% tax bracket, that rate is 25%, versus the 15% for long-term capital gains). If you're close to the 1-year mark and the investment isn't in mortal danger, hold off on the sale until you pass the 1-year mark.

- **Wait until the next calendar year to sell.** If the end of the year is close, delay a sale until January. That way, you don't pay tax on the capital gain until the following year, which means you have a full year to use that money, for example, to earn interest on savings or invest in something else.

- **Offset capital gains with capital losses.** If you have capital gains and also have some losers you want to unload, sell the losers in the same tax year as the winners. Your capital losses offset your capital gains. This tactic is particularly effective for short-term capital gains, taxed at higher, ordinary income rates.

 If you have more than $3,000 in long-term capital losses, you can use those losses to offset long-term capital gains. However, if you don't have enough long-term capital gains to offset all of your long-term capital losses, you can deduct no more than $3,000 of a long-term capital loss in one tax year and must carry the remaining loss over to future tax years.

5 Funds

S hort on time or investing experience? Simply want an easy way to invest your nest egg? You aren't alone. Company-sponsored retirement accounts and college savings accounts have introduced tons of folks to the joy of mutual funds. By the end of 2008, almost half the households in the United States owned shares in mutual funds, according to the Investment Company Institute. Why? Because they're easy to use and they work well, as you'll learn shortly.

This chapter begins with the three main flavors of funds: index funds, mutual funds, and exchange-traded funds (ETFs). Index funds are a bit like funds on automatic pilot: They're set on a course to replicate the performance of an index, like the Dow Jones Industrial Average, and off they go. Under their skin, index funds are either mutual funds or exchange-traded funds, but they're so helpful in setting up an investment portfolio (page 166) that they earn a separate designation as a type of fund.

Mutual funds, which many people own through retirement and college savings accounts, are available directly from the companies that manage the funds or through a broker or financial advisor. They pool your money with other people's money and then invest it. You can find mutual funds that track indexes or that are actively managed, which means there's someone at the helm of the mutual fund ship.

Exchange-traded funds, a relative newcomer to the investment scene, work akin to mutual funds, except that they give you more flexibility in buying and selling their shares. You'll find more detail on them below.

But choosing a fund isn't a slam-dunk. This chapter tells you what to look for, whether you're in the market for an index fund, an actively managed fund, a mutual fund, or an ETF. In addition, you'll learn what you can do when your fund choices are limited—when your company's 401(k) plan offers only a handful of funds, for example.

The Vanilla, Chocolate, and Strawberry of Funds

Funds come in three basic flavors and each has its pros and cons. Here's a quick introduction:

- **Index funds.** These funds get their name because they replicate a particular index in the financial market, like the S&P 500 or the Dow Jones Industrial Average. As you learn in detail on page 166, index funds are the perfect solution for *asset allocation,* where you dole out your nest-egg dollars to different types of investments to achieve a comfortable balance between good returns and an acceptable amount of risk.

- **Mutual funds.** To invest in a mutual fund, you buy shares of the fund directly from the company that manages it (like Fidelity Investments or Vanguard) or through a broker or financial advisor. The fund adds your money to other people's money and then invests it, usually in a variety of stocks, bonds, and so on. Voilà! That one purchase gives you instant diversification with a lot less effort than buying individual stocks, bonds, or other investment thingamabobs. Mutual funds can be index funds or actively managed, which means they have one or more managers who make decisions about what investments to buy, sell, or hold.

- **Exchange-traded funds (ETFs).** This type of fund pools investors' money just as mutual funds do, but unlike with mutual funds, which process purchases and sales at the end of each day, you can buy or sell shares in ETFs anytime you want, just as you can with a stock. ETFs often replicate market indexes, but some simply purchase a basket of investments to achieve their goals.

 With mutual funds, the value of the fund is calculated from the prices of the securities in the fund's portfolio. This valuation occurs once a day, when the market close. On the other hand, the prices of ETFs change all day long, just like the price of stocks.

Index Funds: Taste Great, Less Filling

In the financial world, an index represents all or some part of the investment market. For example, the S&P 500, a well-known index, reflects the value of the stock of the 500 largest publicly traded companies in the United States. The higher the index value, the better the stocks of the represented companies are performing. That's why you hear news reports like, "The S&P 500 rose two points today."

An index can represent just about any part of the financial market: U.S. stocks, foreign stocks, global stocks, bonds, the Asian market, and so on. An *index fund* buys the investments that its corresponding index owns (or, at the very least, a representative sampling) to replicate the performance of the index. An index fund of the S&P 500, for example, is made up of stocks from the 500 largest U.S. corporations. However, an index fund's return is usually slightly lower than that of its index doppelganger, because the index fund has to pay fund-management expenses.

Index funds are an easy and effective way to build a diversified investment portfolio. (Page 166 shows you just how easy it is.) In addition, over longer periods of time (5 to 10 years or more), index funds usually outperform actively managed mutual funds, primarily because their expenses are usually much lower than those of actively managed funds, as you learned on page 60. What index funds buy or sell is determined solely by their corresponding market indexes, so they don't have to pay fund managers big bucks to make investment decisions.

The table below shows several of the indexes that index funds commonly mimic.

Index name	Index type	Represents
MSCI U.S. Broad Market Index	Stock	3,900 companies representing 99.5% of the U.S. market capitalization.
Wilshire 5000 Total Market Index	Stock	The broadest index of the U.S. stock market, representing all U.S. stocks with readily available price quotes.
Dow Jones Industrial Average	Stock	An arbitrary but widely followed collection of 30 large U.S. companies.
S&P 500	Stock	500 largest publicly traded companies in the United States.
Russell 2000	Stock	The 2,000 smallest companies in the Russell 3000 Index (the 3,000 largest U.S. companies that make up 98% of the investable U.S. stock market).

MSCI EAFE	Stock	Stock markets in developed countries, excluding the United States.
MSCI Emerging Markets Index	Stock	Stock markets in 22 developing countries.
Barclay's Capital U.S. Aggregate Bond Index	Bond	The U.S. investment-grade (high-quality) bond market.

You can often find more than one index fund that tracks each part of the market. For example, the S&P 500, the MSCI Broad Market Index, the Wilshire 5000, the Dow Jones U.S. Total Stock Market Index, and the Russell 3000 all cover the portion of the market called "large-cap blend," a mix of stocks from growth and value companies valued at more than $5 billion apiece, as described on page 80. Although each index covers the same broad category—large-growth stocks, for example—each index represents a unique assemblage of companies or investments. Although there may be some overlap of companies among different indexes, you won't find two indexes with an identical collection of investments. Then, each index usually has several index funds (from different fund companies) mimicking the index. Even so, picking an index fund is much simpler than choosing an actively managed fund, as you'll learn on page 94.

Mutual Fund Basics

In October 2009, a total of 7,758 mutual funds jockeyed for investors' attention. Just like when you buy a used car, you don't want to buy a fund based on how it looks on the outside. You have to look under the hood to find out what it's designed to do, how well it performs, how much it's going to cost to operate, and whether gotchas are waiting to getcha.

You can narrow the field initially by looking at what prospective funds invest in. Another measure is how well a fund performs. Truth be told, you can weed out most of the funds within a category with one simple test—did the fund outperform its benchmark market index over the long term (10 or more years)? Fund expenses (management fees, marketing fees, trading expenses) come out of the money a fund makes on its investments, so every penny of expenses reduces the return you get. Finding funds with good track records and below-average expenses can bring your list of fund candidates down to a handful. Once you understand what to look for (which starts on page 76), you learn how to find the best funds for you.

Aptly named, an actively managed fund has one or more managers (usually backed by a team of analysts), who actively choose which stocks, bonds, or other securities to buy or sell. The fund may, for example, concentrate on small but promising companies in Latin America. The manager of this type of fund would probably travel to Latin America, visit potential companies, analyze their finances, and then invest in the ones with the most potential. Actively managed mutual funds don't have to mimic an index, so they can concoct any kind of fund strategy—from one that focuses on a few dozen stocks to others that invest in anything the manager thinks will make money.

The management team earns a fee for its research, analysis, and resulting investment performance. *Some* years, *some* actively managed traditional funds put in truly spectacular performances. Other years, they totally miss the boat. Although actively managed traditional funds are supposed to beat the returns of stocks in their part of the market, most don't do so over the long term. The culprit? The double whammy of high expenses and so-so management.

You really have to do your homework if you want to consider an actively managed fund. Page 94 tells you how.

Exchange-Traded Funds

Exchange-traded funds (ETFs) came on the scene in the 1990s, but by the end of 2009, more than 900 publicly traded ETFs held $790 billion of investors' money. ETFs cover many sections of the market, like emerging market stocks and real estate investment trusts, just as mutual funds do.

An ETF acts partly like a stock, partly like a mutual fund. It owns a portfolio of securities like a mutual fund does, but you can buy or sell its shares anytime the market is open, just as you can with a stock. Unlike a mutual fund, where the fund value is calculated at the end of the day based on the value of the securities it owns, an ETF's price is determined by what investors are willing to pay for each of its shares, which is sometimes higher and sometimes lower than the value of its portfolio.

ETFs have grown popular because they offer several advantages over mutual funds:

- **Flexibility.** You can buy or sell whenever you want.
- **Choice.** Many ETFs track broad segments of the market. Some cover extremely narrow slices of the market, not available through actively managed or index funds.

- **Rock-bottom expenses.** ETFs usually have expenses even lower than those of index mutual funds. However, you do pay a brokerage commission every time you buy or sell. They're great if you plan to buy and hold, but if you use a typical online trading account, commissions can eat up your investment gains if you buy and sell ETFs often. Even $5 commissions, a low rate for the average investor, can add up, especially if you don't invest much money at one time. For example, if you put $1,000 in an ETF and then sell it, paying a $5 commission for each transaction, you've spent 1% of your investment.

Gem in the Rough

Closed-End Funds

Closed-end funds trade on stock exchanges like ETFs do, but they aren't nearly as popular. A closed-end fund sells a specific number of shares in an *initial public offering*, similar to an IPO for a stock. Because a closed-end fund doesn't issue more shares if more people want to invest in it, supply and demand affect the share price—even more than they do for ETFs. While an ETF's price may be a few percentage points higher or lower than the value of its holdings, a closed-end fund's discount or premium can be as much as 10% or 20%. (ETFs trade more closely to the value of their underlying stock because they're more liquid than closed-end funds in most cases. Some types of ETFs—Merrill Lynch's HOLDRs, for example—let institutional investors swap their shares in the fund for the underlying securities.)

The key to a good closed-end fund investment is finding a fund with strong management and a good track record, a fund that's also trading at a decent discount to its underlying value. The average investor doesn't buy shares in a closed-end fund's IPO. The commissions are outrageous. Instead, wait until it's trading on the market, and then place an order with your discount broker.

What a Fund Invests In

Each mutual fund or ETF you buy plays a part in your overall investment plan (page 162), so you need to cast the right funds in the roles you have to fill. For example, if you set your asset allocation target for 70% stocks and 30% bonds, you want to buy one or more funds that deliver those percentages. Your comfort level with investment risk is another important factor in choosing funds. If you're a nervous Nellie, you don't want funds that skyrocket one day only to plummet the next. The first step to finding the right fund is figuring out what the fund or ETF invests in.

Mutual funds and ETFs cover all kinds of investments and all sorts of investing styles. Whether you want investments that are supersafe or heartstoppingly aggressive, broad-based or narrowly focused, or something in between, the *investment objective* is the first place you look. Simply put, it's what the fund tries to achieve: producing income, increasing the value of your investment (called capital appreciation), high total returns, or some combination of objectives. To find a fund's investment objectives, look near the front of the fund's *prospectus* (which you can usually download from the fund company's website).

One Size Fits All

If you don't want to build your own retirement savings plan, a *target date* fund may be the answer. If you plan to retire in 2025, you can look for a target date 2025 fund. These funds invest more aggressively when the retirement date is further in the future and gradually switch to more conservative investments as you get closer to the gold watch. Major fund companies like Vanguard, Fidelity, and T. Rowe Price offer them, but they come with different levels of expenses (usually very high), strategies, and portfolios.

Although target date funds handle the heavy lifting, you still have to check them out to find the one that's right for you. The most important characteristic is the fund's make-up (its allocation of stocks, bonds, international investments, and so on, as described on page 76) and how that make-up changes over time. If the asset allocation is close enough to your target, you can buy that one fund and let it take care of reallocating your money.

You can figure out the fund's asset allocation by reviewing the investment objectives and strategies in its prospectus and by seeing what underlying funds the target date fund owns. If you find more than one target date fund that meets your needs, choose the one with the most experienced manager and lowest costs.

But what if you're more risk-tolerant or risk-averse than the average investor your age? Because target date funds are one size fits all, each target date fund follows a plan for moving to more conservative investments as you get closer to retirement. But you don't have to pick the target date fund based on the year you plan to retire—you can choose it based on how much risk you're willing to accept in exchange for potentially higher returns. For example, if you want a plan that's more daring, invest in a fund whose target date is later than your retirement date. That way, the investment plan is less conservative than the norm.

Asset Allocation Categories

Because asset allocation is one of the most powerful tools in your investment toolbox (page 160), it's also the first step in deciding which types of funds to buy. Once you have *your* asset allocation percentages figured out (page 162), you can start looking for funds in the asset type categories you chose. Morningstar shows high-level asset allocation for funds, as you can see on page 80. Here are the main asset categories you'll find in mutual funds and ETFs:

- **Stock funds** invest in publicly traded stocks issued by companies based in the United States or overseas. They're great for growing your nest egg for long-term goals (page 156).

- **Bond funds** buy bonds (page 156) issued by state, local, federal, or even foreign governments, or national or international corporations. They're good when you want to reduce your risk or to receive income to live on (page 128). Funds that invest in municipal bonds come with tax advantages (page 130).

- **Money market funds** invest either in very short-term bonds or in a collection of investments that simulate the returns of short-term fixed-income investments. If you're looking for a place to stash your savings, a money market fund makes sense because they're reasonably safe, but pay more interest than bank accounts.

 Money market funds are safe, but they aren't bulletproof. In 2008, the nation's oldest mutual money market fund *broke the buck*—its net asset value fell below $1 a share. The federal government guaranteed the value of all money market funds to prevent a panic, but that guarantee ended early in 2010. Today, federal deposit insurance protects only money market deposit accounts (not money market funds) in banks, savings and loans, and credit unions. There are ETF money market funds, but because their value fluctuates, they won't trade at a steady $1 per share.

- **Blend funds** invest in a mix of stocks and bonds. They're great when you want to buy one fund to play multiple roles in your financial plan.

- **Real estate funds** invest in REITs. (See Chapter 8 for the skinny on REITs.)

- **Commodity funds** invest in futures contracts on commodities like wheat, gold, or oil. Futures contracts? Commodities? If you don't know what they are, don't invest in them.

Tip If you get queasy watching wild swings in your portfolio value, stick to more conservative funds. Otherwise, you may overreact and sell when you should be buying, or vice versa, as page 45 explains.

Stock, real estate, commodity, and currency funds sit at the aggressive end of the investment spectrum. They shoot up quickly when times are good, but can drop just as fast during recessions. Blend, bond, and money market funds are more conservative.

Investment Style and Size Categories

As you gain investment experience, chances are you'll want to focus on different slices of the overall investment market. For example, if you're a gardener at heart, you may develop a penchant for growth companies. For diehard shoppers, value companies that are a great deal at the price may sound appealing. You can also carve up stocks by the size of the company. Morningstar, an independent provider of investment data and research, makes it easy to find the fund you're looking for. You can search for funds by style or size by using the site's Fund Screening tool (*http://tinyurl.com/ yypeg7*). Many of Morningstar's features are free simply by registering with the site. Some of its advanced features are subscription based, but they offer a 14-day free trial.

Morningstar's style box is like one side of a Rubik's cube. The columns show investment style, while the rows show company size. Each box in the style box is a combination of an investment style and company size.

Here are the three investment styles Morningstar shows in its style box:

- **Growth,** as the name implies, invests in growing companies, whose stock prices increase in value as the company sales and earnings increase. These companies have higher sales and earnings growth rates. They typically have higher price-earnings ratios (PE ratios, described on page 120) because investors expect more from these companies in the future.

- **Value** investing makes money for you because they're selling at a low price compared to their value. In effect, they're on sale, and you earn your reward when their prices return to a fair value.

- **Blend** represents a style that buys companies in both growth and value categories.

Company size can affect how much stock prices can go up, but also how much they jump around. Depending on your tolerance for excitement, you may decide to focus on larger or smaller companies. Here's how the Morningstar style box divides up company size:

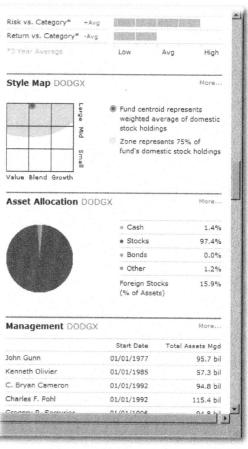

- **Large** is for *large-cap companies,* by Morningstar's definition, the largest 250 U.S. stocks. Large-cap stocks are sometimes defined as companies whose stock is valued at more than $5 billion (and sometimes $10 billion). Large companies tend to be more stable. They don't grow as fast, but their stock prices don't bounce around as much.

- **Mid** is for *mid-cap stocks,* by Morningstar's definition, the next-largest 750 U.S. companies. Mid-cap stocks are sometimes defined as companies whose stock is valued between $1 billion and $5 billion to $10 billion. These stocks are usually a trade-off between stability and growth.

- **Small** represents *small-cap stocks,* the smallest remaining companies, usually those with total stock value of less than $1 billion. These companies can grow faster, which means their stock prices can increase faster. But the companies can run into trouble just as easily, so they're riskier investments.

Bond Fund Characteristics

With bond funds, average maturity and credit quality (page 131) are the keys to finding the right fund. *Maturity* affects how sensitive bonds and bond funds are to changes in interest rates. *Credit quality* is a measure of the risk of default. The Morningstar style box for bond funds slices and dices by these two measures. To see a bond fund style box as shown below, view a bond fund on the Morningstar website, and then click Portfolio in the horizontal navigation bar.

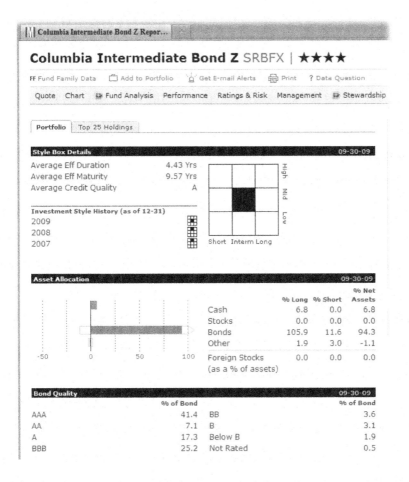

Morningstar's creditworthiness categories are:

- **Low** is for the most risky bond funds (which come with the highest yields to compensate for their risk).

- **Mid** includes funds that are investment grade, but aren't top-of-the-line safe.

- **High** includes the safest funds (which also come with the lowest yields), such as most U.S. government and top-rated corporate bonds.

Individual bonds mature on a specific date, and their maturity affects how sensitive their prices are to interest rate changes (page 136). Unlike an individual bond, a bond fund doesn't have a specific maturity date. That's because bond funds own lots of bonds, and the portfolio changes constantly as bonds mature and get replaced.

A quick-and-dirty gauge of how sensitive a bond fund is to changes in interest rates is bond fund *average effective duration,* which is the average duration of all the bonds in the portfolio—basically, the overall maturity of the fund. The shorter the duration, the less sensitive a bond fund is to changes in interest rates. Longer durations mean the price will drop more when interest rates rise. For bond funds that are otherwise equal, choose the one with the lowest average effective duration.

Morningstar divides bond funds into three duration categories:

- **Short.** Bond funds with an average effective duration of 3.5 years or less.

- **Intermediate.** Bonds with an average effective duration of 3.5 to 6 years.

- **Long.** Bonds with an average effective duration of 6 years or more.

Does the Fund Do What It Says?

Too many funds claim to invest one way, but actually invest another. Federal regulations aim to prevent that. They require funds whose name indicates an investment style, like Fidelity Large-Cap Growth Fund, to invest 80% or more of their assets in large-cap growth companies. But funds with more generic names aren't required to invest in a specific way. The only control on what they do comes from the fund's investment objective and strategy. A fund prospectus spells that out, but you still have to see whether the fund actually delivers on what it says. Sometimes, results are enough; with growth funds, for example, you can simply look at their long-term returns. But digging deeper into a fund's portfolio tells all.

The Morningstar Portfolio tab dishes out the skinny on a fund's portfolio so you can tell if it invests in what you're looking for:

- **Company size.** Look at the percentages in different-sized companies. If a fund bills itself as large-cap fund, you want the majority of its investments in large companies.

- **Foreign or domestic.** Check the fund's percentage of foreign and domestic investments. For funds that invest in foreign markets, the Morningstar Portfolio tab also shows percentages by region or country.

- **Number of holdings.** The number of securities in a fund is more important for stock funds, because a small number of stocks (fewer than 30) can mean erratic fund performance. If you're hoping to make oodles of dough in small-cap companies, a focused fund may be just what you want. Keep in mind, a focused fund can nose-dive if the manager doesn't pick the right investments. On the Morningstar Portfolio page, click the Top 25 Holdings tab to see individual holdings and the total number of holdings.

When a fund spreads its assets among more companies (200 or more, say), fund performance tends toward that of a market index, because no one holding makes much of an impact. Be sure to compare a widely diversified fund's performance to the closest index. You may be able to get the same performance for less cost in management fees with an index fund.

Click to see the number of holdings   % by company size

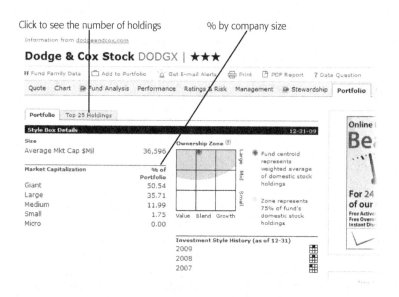

Information from doddandcox.com

Dodge & Cox Stock DODGX | ★★★

FF Fund Family Data   □ Add to Portfolio   🔔 Get E-mail Alerts   🖶 Print   📄 PDF Report   ? Data Question

Quote   Chart   📊 Fund Analysis   Performance   Ratings & Risk   Management   📊 Stewardship   **Portfolio**

Portfolio   Top 25 Holdings

Style Box Details   12-31-09

Size
Average Mkt Cap $Mil   36,596

Market Capitalization	% of Portfolio
Giant	50.54
Large	35.71
Medium	11.99
Small	1.75
Micro	0.00

Ownership Zone ⓘ

● Fund centroid represents weighted average of domestic stock holdings

Zone represents 75% of fund's domestic stock holdings

Value Blend Growth

Investment Style History (as of 12-31)
2009
2008
2007

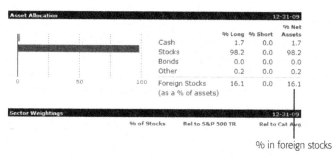

Asset Allocation   12-31-09

	% Long	% Short	% Net Assets
Cash	1.7	0.0	1.7
Stocks	98.2	0.0	98.2
Bonds	0.0	0.0	0.0
Other	0.2	0.0	0.2
Foreign Stocks (as a % of assets)	16.1	0.0	16.1

0   50   100

Sector Weightings   12-31-09

% of Stocks   Rel to S&P 500 TR   Rel to Cat Avg

% in foreign stocks

 Note A fund that holds too much cash undermines any investment objective. When you invest in a stock or bond fund, you pay expenses to get returns appropriate for stock and bond funds. You don't want a manager to babysit your money by sticking it in cash. You can do that for yourself. Avoid funds that routinely stick more than 10% to 15% in cash.

Evaluating Fund Performance

If a fund's performance tops the charts for 1 month, 3 months, or the most recent year, the fund company advertises like crazy. Excited, greedy investors send money in by the boatload, hungry for a piece of the action. In reality, by the time the cash pours in, the fund has usually passed its peak. All those new investors watch the fund go down, taking their money with it. Resist the temptation to chase short-term hot returns. Instead, choose funds with above-average long-term performance—ones that beat the competition and, more importantly, the market indexes, over 3, 5, or 10 years or more.

Troubleshooting Moment

Watch for Closet Index Funds

When you invest in stock funds, avoid closet index funds. They charge the high fees of actively managed mutual funds, but invest much like a market index. All they do is charge you fees for performance you could get cheaper from a genuine index fund, whether a mutual fund or ETF.

Spotting a closet index fund is simple. You compare the fund's average P/E ratio, sector weightings, and average earnings per share to the values for the fund's comparable index. The Morningstar fund Portfolio tab makes this easy, because it shows the ratio of a fund's numbers to its comparable index, as you can see below. The closer the ratios are to 1 (which represents an exact match), the more likely the fund is a closet index fund.

Here's how you do it using the Portfolio tab on a fund's Morningstar web page:

1. Find the fund's Price/Prospective Earnings value (the P/E ratio, based on forecast earnings), Long-Term Earnings (average earnings per share), and Sector Weightings (the percentage invested in different market sectors).

2. Look at the values in the columns labeled "Rel to <comparable index>". For example, in the figure, the column is "Rel to S&P 500 TR" because Dodge & Cox Stock Fund is in the same portion of the market as the S&P 500 index. If the numbers are all very close to 1, the fund could be a closet index fund.

3. Look at the values in the columns labeled "Rel to Cat Avg", which compares the fund to all other funds in the same category. If the numbers are all very close to 1, the fund could be a closet index fund.

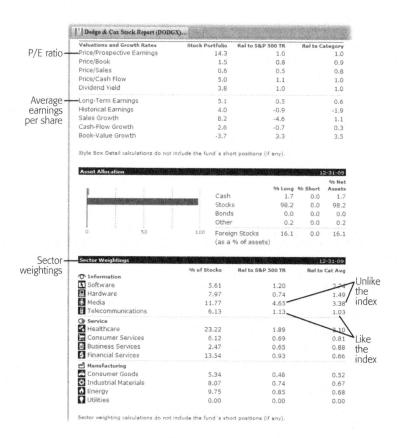

Dodge & Cox Stock Report (DODGX)...

P/E ratio →

Average earnings per share →

Valuations and Growth Rates	Stock Portfolio	Rel to S&P 500 TR	Rel to Category
Price/Prospective Earnings	14.3	1.0	1.0
Price/Book	1.5	0.8	0.9
Price/Sales	0.6	0.5	0.8
Price/Cash Flow	5.0	1.1	1.0
Dividend Yield	3.8	1.0	1.0
Long-Term Earnings	5.1	0.5	0.6
Historical Earnings	4.0	-0.9	-1.9
Sales Growth	8.2	-4.6	1.1
Cash-Flow Growth	2.6	-0.7	0.3
Book-Value Growth	-3.7	3.3	3.5

Style Box Detail calculations do not include the fund's short positions (if any).

Asset Allocation   12-31-09

	% Long	% Short	% Net Assets
Cash	1.7	0.0	1.7
Stocks	98.2	0.0	98.2
Bonds	0.0	0.0	0.0
Other	0.2	0.0	0.2
Foreign Stocks (as a % of assets)	16.1	0.0	16.1

Sector weightings →

Sector Weightings   12-31-09

	% of Stocks	Rel to S&P 500 TR	Rel to Cat Avg
Information			
Software	5.61	1.20	2.24
Hardware	7.97	0.74	1.49
Media	11.77	4.65	3.38
Telecommunications	6.13	1.13	1.03
Service			
Healthcare	23.22	1.89	2.10
Consumer Services	6.12	0.69	0.81
Business Services	2.47	0.65	0.88
Financial Services	13.54	0.93	0.66
Manufacturing			
Consumer Goods	5.34	0.48	0.52
Industrial Materials	8.07	0.74	0.67
Energy	9.75	0.85	0.68
Utilities	0.00	0.00	0.00

Unlike the index

Like the index

Sector weighting calculations do not include the fund's short positions (if any).

The funds you want to add to your portfolio have to beat two types of competition:

- **Comparable market index.** The first competitor is the index for the part of the investment universe that the mutual fund covers. Finding the right index is as easy as checking a fund's annual or semiannual report, because the SEC makes them show market index comparisons. (Morningstar, too, shows the comparable index for funds, as you can see on page 88.) For actively managed mutual funds, you want one that outperforms the comparable index, because you're paying higher expenses for that performance. Usually, index funds deliver performance slightly below that of the comparable index, because of the bite that expenses take out of fund returns. If you're buying an index fund, you want a fund whose performance is as close to its comparable market index as possible.

- **Peer group.** You also want to compare a fund's performance to that of other funds with similar investment objectives to make sure you're getting the best of the bunch. Financial data-tracking companies like Morningstar and Lipper show the competition (page 88). You can access subscription-based Lipper data through sites such as The Wall Street Journal Online (*http://www.onlinewsj.com*), which provides a free 14-day trial.

Morningstar (*www.morningstar.com*) makes it easy to evaluate a fund's long-term performance:

1. **In the Quote box (front and center at the top of the page), type the fund's name or ticker symbol, for example, DODGX or Dodge & Cox Stock.**

   As you type the name or ticker symbol, a drop-down list shows you all the funds that match what you've typed so far. When you see the fund you want, click its name in the drop-down list.

2. **When the fund information appears, on the horizontal navigation bar below the fund name, click Performance.**

   The first thing on the performance page is a chart of the growth of $10,000 over the past 10 years compared to the growth of the comparable index and the fund's peer group. The legend above the chart not only shows the colors for the lines, but also the Category label identifies the fund's peer group, and the Index entry tells you which index the fund is trying to beat. A quick way to check whether a fund beats the competition is to make sure that the line for the fund is above the lines for the comparable index and the fund's peer group, as you can see below.

3. **In the Trailing Total Returns section, check the longer-term comparisons to the peer group and comparable index.**

   The Total Return % column shows the fund's total return for each timeframe. Positive numbers mean the fund increased in value. Negative numbers show a decrease for the period. The second column, +/– S&P500 TR in the figure below, shows how much the fund exceeded or fell behind the return of its comparable index. The negative numbers for the 3- and 5-year periods (not visible in the figure on page 88) show that Dodge & Cox Stock Fund lagged the S&P 500 index. But it outperformed the index in the most recent year and over 10 years.

   The last column, "% Rank in Category", shows how the fund did compared to its peer group. The fund was near the top of its class in the most recent year and over 10 years. It didn't do nearly so well for the 3- and 5-year periods, which included the severe down market in 2007–2008.

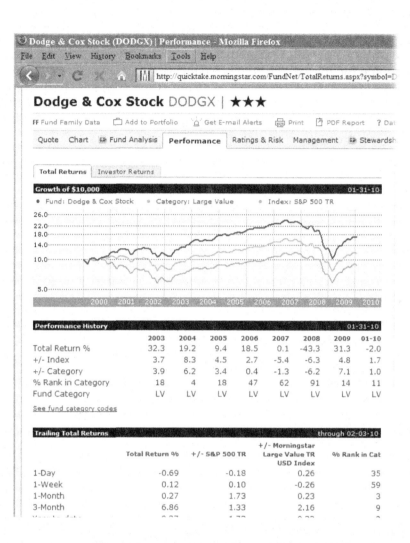

Dodge & Cox Stock DODGX | ★★★

FF Fund Family Data   ☐ Add to Portfolio   🔔 Get E-mail Alerts   🖶 Print   🗐 PDF Report   ? Dat

Quote   Chart   ☒ Fund Analysis   **Performance**   Ratings & Risk   Management   ☒ Stewardsh

Total Returns   Investor Returns

Growth of $10,000   01-31-10

● Fund: Dodge & Cox Stock   ○ Category: Large Value   ● Index: S&P 500 TR

Performance History   01-31-10

	2003	2004	2005	2006	2007	2008	2009	01-10
Total Return %	32.3	19.2	9.4	18.5	0.1	-43.3	31.3	-2.0
+/- Index	3.7	8.3	4.5	2.7	-5.4	-6.3	4.8	1.7
+/- Category	3.9	6.2	3.4	0.4	-1.3	-6.2	7.1	1.0
% Rank in Category	18	4	18	47	62	91	14	11
Fund Category	LV	LV	LV	LV	LV	LV	LV	LV

See fund category codes

Trailing Total Returns   through 02-03-10

	Total Return %	+/- S&P 500 TR	+/- Morningstar Large Value TR USD Index	% Rank in Cat
1-Day	-0.69	-0.18	0.26	35
1-Week	0.12	0.10	-0.26	59
1-Month	0.27	1.73	0.23	3
3-Month	6.86	1.33	2.16	9

![Microsoft Excel - Plum_05_rollingreturns]

	A	B	C	D	E	F	G	H
1		2003	2004	2005	2006	2007	2008	2009
2	DODGX annual return	32.3	19.2	9.4	18.5	0.1	-43.3	31.3
3								
4								
5	Sum of 5 previous years					79.5	3.9	16
6	5-year rolling return					15.9	0.78	3.2
7								
8								

The return that a fund produces isn't necessarily the return you see in your portfolio. If you pay a sales *load* (commission) to buy the fund or have to pay taxes on your capital gains and dividends, those payments chew off a hunk of your fund return. Fund companies have to report returns adjusted for sales loads and taxes in the prospectus:

- **Load-adjusted return** is the return you would actually receive taking into account the sales load you pay. Page 90 dishes out the full scoop on fund fees. In a fund prospectus, the load-adjusted return is usually called "Investment Results (with maximum sales charges)". The prospectus also compares the load-adjusted return to the returns of similar market indexes, so you can tell whether the load fund overcame the load handicap to outperform the index.

- **Tax-adjusted return** is the return a hypothetical taxpayer would see if the fund were in a taxable account. The return takes into account the taxes the investor has to pay on capital gains, dividends, and interest the fund distributes. When you pay taxes on distributions, you have less money to reinvest (and reinvesting is what you want to do, as page 158 explains). On the Morningstar website, click Tax in the horizontal navigation bar on the fund's web page and look for "Tax-adjusted Return".

Tip Because you want your money to grow, even if you want safe investments, you still want them to beat inflation. Fund companies don't have to report inflation-adjusted returns. The easiest way to see if your fund beats inflation is to look for a long-term return above the average inflation rate (about 3.4% per year).

Watch Out for Turnover

Portfolio *turnover* reflects how many investments a fund manager buys and sells in the fund portfolio during a year. For example, 100% turnover is equivalent to selling every security in the portfolio during 1 year. Turnover cuts into your returns in two ways:

- The fund pays a brokerage commission for every trade. Those commissions aren't included in a fund's expense ratio, so high turnover can take another big chunk out of your investment return.
- If you own funds in a taxable account, you have to pay taxes on capital gains that the fund distributes (whether you reinvest the distributions or not).

A good guideline for stock funds is 50% turnover or less. Turnover of 20% or less is even better. Bond funds can have higher turnover because bonds mature, and the fund managers have to replace them.

One way to find low-turnover funds is to look for funds that bill themselves as tax managed. Index funds have low turnover by definition, because the managers buy or sell only when the underlying index changes (no more than once or twice a year). Morningstar shows a fund's turnover rate on the Chart page (on the horizontal navigation bar below the fund name, click Chart).

Keeping a Lid on Fund Expenses

Every dime you pay in fund expenses is one less dime you get in returns, so high fund expenses can turn hot fund returns into dogs. For that reason, lower fund expenses are almost always better. The one exception to that rule is an actively managed fund that has trounced similar funds for 5 to 10 years. (Page 91 tells you how to see a fund's true performance after deducting its expenses.) Knowing your enemy is the first step to keeping fund expenses under control. This section describes the different types of fund fees and what you can do about them.

You usually see fund expenses as an *expense ratio,* that is, the fund expenses expressed as a percentage of the money you have invested in the fund. Say you have $10,000 in a fund with a 1% expense ratio. You pay $100 in expenses per year. Because the expense ratio is a percentage, your expenses go up if the value of your fund investment goes up, and vice versa.

Tip A 1% expense ratio might sound like a small amount, but the expense ratios you pay for all the funds in your retirement, college savings, and other investment accounts can really add up. To see what your mutual funds really cost, run them through the SEC cost calculator (*http://tinyurl.com/7qbtg*). The total price tag may convince you to switch to lower-cost options.

Here are the different types of fund fees you might come across and how to handle them:

Fee	Description	Maximum	What to do
Expense ratio	Covers administrative and back-office expenses (bookkeeping, customer service, and processing purchases and sales), management fees (salaries, research costs, and running a trading desk).	0.5% for an index fund; 1% for an actively managed fund.	Keep as low as possible, because this fee comes right out of your returns.
Redemption fees	Usually 1% or 2%, these fees are meant to prevent traders from buying and selling fund shares quickly over a short period.	Less than 1% for 6 months or less.	For funds you buy for the long haul, don't worry. If two funds have similar performance, go for the one without a redemption fee.
Marketing and distribution expenses	Also known as 12b-1 fees, this is money the fund spends on marketing and promotion. Although a fund must disclose 12b-1 fees when they're more than 0.25%, don't pay a fund company to find new investors.	Avoid.	Pass on a fund with 12b-1 fees unless you simply must own it.
Fund brokerage commissions	What a fund company pays to brokerages to buy and sell securities in the fund portfolio.		What a fund pays in brokerage commissions is hard to determine from the prospectus, but you can keep them within reason by investing in low-turnover funds (page 90).
Wrap fee	An extra administrative charge often found with a fund-of-funds or life-cycle fund (a fund that buys other mutual funds).	0.25% or less.	As with expense ratios, the lower the wrap fee, the better.

If you buy funds through a financial advisor, his cut comes in three possible flavors, shown as share classes (the share class usually appears at the end of the fund's name):

- **Front-end loads** are assigned to Class A shares. The front-end load is your financial advisor's commission. It comes right off the top of the money you invest, and it often runs 5.75%. It sounds bad, but it's often the least expensive option if you have to pay a commission.

- **Back-end loads,** assigned to Class B shares, means the fee comes out of the proceeds when you sell your shares. Your financial advisor gets extra commissions every year, and this expense is part of the fund's expense ratio. However, the back-end load usually goes down and eventually disappears if you own the fund long enough (several years, typically). Back-end loads for the first year are usually about 5.75%. If you're sure you'll hold onto your shares forever, Class B shares cost less. But Class A shares are better, just in case you have to sell earlier than you expect.

- Avoid **level loads,** known as Class C shares, like the plague. You pay a commission every year that's buried in the fund's expense ratio, which sends your expense ratio into the stratosphere.

 With load funds, you may get a break on the commission if you invest $25,000 or more.

How to Pick Funds

Now that you know the basics about funds and how they work, you're ready to hunt for the funds that meet your needs. Because index funds (mutual fund or ETF) and actively managed mutual funds don't have the same characteristics, you evaluate them a little differently. Here's a summary of how to choose different types of funds.

Choosing an Index Fund or ETF

The big challenge in picking an index fund or ETF is the number of choices. Depending on the index you're looking at, you may have hundreds of index funds or ETFs to choose from. As with actively managed mutual funds, take a look at the fund's prospectus, which you can find on the fund sponsor's website.

However, picking a fund is as easy as 1-2-3:

1. **Choose the index (or combination of indexes) you want to invest in.**

   The index you want depends on the asset allocation you've chosen (page 162) and your experience as an investor. As a beginner, you may opt for a total market index that invests in stocks and bonds of all kinds. With time, you may decide to go with a mix of stock from large, medium, and small companies, with some foreign stock thrown in for good measure.

   Generally, the more companies an index includes, the better it represents the section of the market it covers. For example, the S&P 500 index tracks 500 companies compared to the MSCI Broad Market index fund, which includes 3,900 companies.

2. **Find funds that track that index or cover that portion of the market.**

   Page 95 tells you how to screen for funds by index or category.

3. **Choose the index fund with the lowest expense ratio.**

   Because an index fund is supposed to mirror a specific index, you shouldn't have to pay a big management fee. Look for expense ratios of 0.5% or less.

4. **Choose the fund with the most experienced manager.**

   Managers don't matter as much with index funds as they do with actively managed funds. But for a tiebreaker, choose the fund with the most experienced manager. (The Quote tab on a Morningstar fund web page shows managers and when they began managing the fund.)

5. **If you're looking for ETFs, choose the ETF with a high trading volume.**

   The trading volume indicates how many shares investors buy and sell during a period. The higher the trading volume, the easier it is to find buyers or sellers for your ETF, which in turn means that the ETF price is usually reasonable. ETFs that have been around for a while and are sponsored by larger companies tend to have higher trading volume. The Quote tab on a Morningstar ETF web page shows the volume and the average volume.

 Note Avoid ETFs or index mutual funds with the words "leveraged," "long," or "short" in their name. These funds use exotic short-term strategies to produce returns, but they're incredibly risky.

Evaluating Actively Managed Mutual Funds

Year after year, investors throw millions of dollars into actively managed mutual funds that are expensive, inefficient, or just plain bad at what they do. Get ahead of those investors by looking for actively managed mutual funds that fit the profile in the table below:

Fund feature	What to look for
Fund manager	A manager with at least 5 years managing the fund.
Minimum investment	If you're just starting out, look for minimums like $250 or $500. When you have more money to invest, look for minimums that let you invest in at least 3 different funds.
Costs	An expense ratio of less than 0.5% is ideal, but absolutely no higher than 1% for stock funds, no more than 0.75% for bond funds.
Performance	3-year, 5-year, and 10-year average annual returns that beat comparable market indexes (page 88). At the least, 10-year returns that beat comparable indexes.
Portfolio turnover	For stock funds, no higher than 50%; 20% or less is ideal.
Investment strategy	A strategy that isn't copying an index fund. Many actively managed funds are index funds in disguise (page 85).

Frequently Asked Question

Follow the Leader

What if the fund manager in charge of my fund leaves?

If you decide to buy an actively managed fund, the fund manager and the returns she delivers are usually a huge factor in your decision. Then, if that manager leaves, you may scratch your head wondering whether to hold onto the fund. The short answer is: It depends.

Some funds have a single manager (assisted by a team of analysts), who selects the fund's investments, manages its investment portfolio, and decides when to buy and sell. Other funds have a primary manager, an assistant manager, and several analysts. Team management means 2 to as many as 10 managers collaborate on managing a fund. (They may manage the entire fund as a team or divide the fund's assets into sections that each manager oversees independently.)

If a long-term assistant manager takes over when a manager leaves, sticking with the fund is OK. The assistant manager helped deliver the fund's past performance.

To the contrary, a totally new manager or management team has no track record with the fund. Before you bail out on the fund, consider researching the funds that the manager handled in the past. If those earlier assignments were successful, you can watch the fund performance for 6 months to a year to see how the new management does. If the new manager is an unknown, you may want to sell your shares—perhaps reinvesting the money in the former manager's new fund. Keep in mind, you'll have to pay taxes on any capital gains if you sell your shares.

Note The *Sharpe ratio* helps you figure out whether a fund manager's returns are due to great investment decisions or to an inordinate fondness for risk. It is a ratio of the return you earn to the risk you take, that is, how much the fund returns for the risk taken. The higher the Sharpe ratio, the better a fund's risk-adjusted returns. To find a fund's Sharpe ratio, click the Ratings & Risks tab on a Morningstar fund web page.

Finding Funds

Funds are investor-friendly investments, but finding the right funds isn't a slam-dunk. Besides a ton of funds to choose from, you've got tons of fund information to wade through. And you may need different types of funds for the asset allocation you've picked for retirement investments, college savings, and other goals. Fortunately, mutual fund and ETF online screening tools help you narrow the field.

Fund screening helps you sift through the thousands of funds to separate the wheat from the chaff of funds that don't meet your investment objectives. You can search for funds in the asset class you're looking for, with low expense ratios, the minimum investment you can afford, or a combination. Lots of financial websites offer fund-screening tools. The best of the bunch come from Morningstar (*http://tinyurl.com/ybrfroq*), Yahoo! Finance (*http://tinyurl.com/5t6xg*), and Index Universe (*http://tinyurl.com/yle637f*). Here are some of the criteria you can use to whittle down your list of fund contenders:

- **Category.** Look for broad asset classes such as stock, bond, and blend funds. The category can also represent fund types like index funds, actively managed mutual funds, and ETFs.

- **Fund families.** If you have an account with a large fund company, like Vanguard or Fidelity, you can search for funds that company offers.

- **Manager tenure.** You can search by how long a manager has led a fund.

- **Performance.** You can search for specific returns, say 10% a year, but it's more helpful to look for returns that beat market indexes during a time period.

- **Expense ratio.** Search for funds with expense ratios below your threshold percentage.

- **Turnover.** If you're concerned about fees or taxes, look for funds with low turnover.

- **Minimum investment.** If you have a limited amount to invest, find funds with minimum investments you can afford.

Index Universe's screening tool (*http://tinyurl.com/yle637f*) is jam-packed with options and criteria for weeding through index funds, ETFs, and actively managed mutual funds, as you can see below.

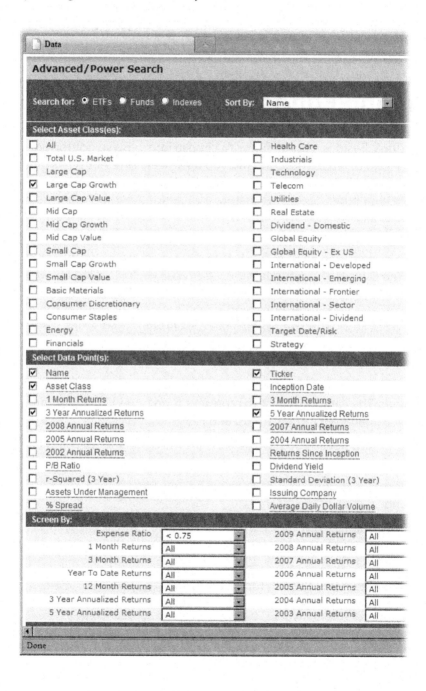

Here's how you use it to find the fund for you:

1. **Select an option for the type of fund you want to find.**

   Select ETFs for exchange-traded funds, Indexes for index funds, and Funds for actively managed mutual funds.

2. **In the Select Asset Class(es) section, turn on the checkboxes for the asset classes you're interested in.**

   Because this tool breaks asset classes down into fine detail, you can turn on as many or as few checkboxes as you want. For example, if you're interested in growth stocks, you can turn on the Large Cap Growth, Mid Cap Growth, and Small Cap Growth, checkboxes.

3. **In the Select Data Point(s) section, turn on the checkboxes for the values you want to see in the results.**

   The basic 411 for funds includes Name, Ticker (the ticker symbol for the fund), 3 Year Annualized Returns, 5 Year Annualized Returns, Expense Ratio, and "Number of holdings". For bond funds, turn on Dividend Yield and "30-day SEC Yield".

4. **In the Screen By section, choose the values you want to use to filter the results.**

   For example, for Expense Ratio, you might pick "< 0.75" to look for funds with expense ratios of less than 0.75%.

Tip Setting up a fund screen doesn't guarantee that a fund exists that meets all your criteria. If you run a fund screen and don't get any results, try loosening up the criterion that's least important to you. For example, look for lower 3-year-average annual total returns.

Deciding When to Sell

If a fund is performing badly, investors are prone to making one of two mistakes. Some sell in a panic, while others hold onto the fund hoping it will turn things around. Most funds give a few warning signs before they crash. If you learn to spot those warnings, you can review a fund that looks like it might be headed for trouble, make an educated decision about selling, and possibly sell *before* the fund hits the skids. Here are fund red flags to watch for:

- **Departing manager.** If you own an actively managed fund, the fund manager delivers the fund performance. If the longtime manager is leaving, but co-managers or the management team is staying in place, don't sell just yet. If brand-new managers are coming in, check out their track record to see if their experience is on par with the old manager's reputation. If it isn't, consider replacing the fund.

- **Proposed fund merger.** Fund companies get rid of their dogs by merging those funds into other funds. If you learn that your fund is merging with another, evaluate the new fund as you would a brand-new fund purchase to make sure it's right for you.

- **Changing investment strategy.** Review your funds' investment objectives and the securities in their portfolios. If you notice that a fund has started to invest differently by, for example, buying large-cap stocks instead of mid-cap stocks, you may want to replace the fund with one that fits your financial plan.

- **Big increase in assets.** Really successful funds rake in oodles of new money. That's not necessarily good for future performance, because the fund managers may have a hard time investing all that cash. Small and mid-cap stock funds are especially vulnerable, because it's hard to find enough suitable investments to deliver the same kinds of returns they've produced in the past. If the fund management closes the fund to new investors, don't sell. They're watching out for your best interests by keeping the fund at a manageable size. If the fund continues to accept new investments, watch the fund's performance closely, and get out if it starts to falter.

- **Bad long-term performance.** Don't sell a fund because of poor performance for a short period like 3, 6, or 12 months. The fund may do better in up markets or down markets, or may have gotten temporarily derailed. But if performance falls behind the comparable market index and the competition year after year, look for a replacement.

- **New or higher fees.** Higher fees take money away from your investment returns, so they're never good. But, if the amount's small (less than 0.1%) and the fund is doing well, it's usually worth staying put. If a fund makes large increases in fees or increases its fees regularly, start looking for a new one.

- **Turmoil.** If a fund family is bought or sold or a star manager leaves (taking staff with him), that chaos can distract fund managers from their jobs and drag returns down.

- **Rising turnover rate.** If the turnover rate increases and stays at higher levels, your expenses and tax bill are likely to climb as well.

Never trade in a fund based on a hot tip you heard around the water cooler at work, at the gym, or from your landscaper. Don't automatically replace funds just because your broker gives you a suggestion. Always do your homework first.

Even if red flags aren't waving, you may decide to sell for other reasons:

- **You need the money.** Selling a fund because you need the money for something is perfectly OK. That's why you invest in the first place.

- **Balance your portfolio.** When you review your portfolio and find that your asset allocation is slightly out of balance, you should sell fund shares in the areas that are over-allocated and buy more in the areas that are under-allocated.

- **Changing goals.** If your life changes, so will your goals. If your child earns a big honking scholarship, you can look at reinvesting the college savings you've amassed into something else.

- **Sleep.** If you're losing sleep over your investments' performance, it's time to make some changes. Ratchet down the risk until you sleep comfortably at night.

- **Taxes.** If you sell a fund that generates capital gains, you may decide to sell a fund with losses to offset the gains.

 You can find out how much you'll pay in taxes and fees when you sell by running your fund numbers through AOL's Wallet Pop "Should I sell my funds now and invest the money elsewhere?" calculator (*http://tinyurl.com/yl8bn7s*).

Managing Your Funds

Chapter 9 explains how to manage your entire portfolio. But mutual funds come with a few special management challenges. This section tells you how to handle each one.

Avoid Overlapping Funds

If you own lots of funds, you may think your portfolio is diversified. But funds with overlapping investment objectives and portfolios could leave your portfolio less diversified than you think. You can review your funds' investment objectives, categories, and portfolios on the Morningstar website.

The trick is to sign up for Morningstar's Premium membership for a free 2-week trial period. At the top-right of the Morningstar website, click Subscribe, and then click "14-Day Free Trial". Don't forget to cancel the trial, unless you like the premium features enough to pay the monthly membership fee.

On the Morningstar horizontal navigation bar, click Tools, and then click the Similar Funds link. This tool helps you find funds with similar portfolios and investment styles when you want to replace a fund, but it can also tell you if your funds overlap. For example, if it shows that you have three large-cap blend funds, you can decide which one you want to keep and sell the other two. Or, you can move some of your money into different areas of the market based on the asset allocation you've picked.

Managing Taxes

You make the most money when you keep your investment dollars working in your portfolio. One way to do that is by paying as little in taxes on your investments as possible.

Tax-advantaged accounts (ones that defer the taxes you pay or eliminate taxes altogether) are the best way to reduce your investment tax bill. (See page 64 to learn what these accounts can do for you. You can also find out which types of investments are best in taxable or tax-advantaged accounts on page 68.) Here are a few guidelines for minimizing the bite taxes take out of your returns:

- Invest money you have in taxable accounts in low-turnover stock funds or ETFs. Those funds distribute fewer capital gains, and capital gains are taxed at the lowest rates.

- Put bond funds, money market funds, and REIT funds in tax-advantaged accounts, so you avoid paying taxes (at higher ordinary income rates) on their interest and dividends. See page 67 to learn more about using tax-advantaged and taxable accounts.

Making the Most of Limited Choices

Most company-sponsored 401(k) and 403(b) plans offer limited investment choices. To make the most of those choices, look at all the options offered by your different accounts—your company's 401(k), your spouse's 401(k), and so on. If one of your accounts offers great choices in a particular area (stock funds, say), use it for that segment of your asset allocation. You can use your IRAs, taxable investment accounts, or other investment accounts with a variety of choices to fill in the gaps in your allocation, such as small companies or foreign investments.

You can see an example of this in the table below. Say your spouse's 401(k) has a great menu of foreign stock funds, so you put your foreign stock allocation there. Your IRA has bond funds galore, so you invest bond money in it. If all your accounts have good U.S. stock fund choices, come up with a division for U.S. stocks based on what you think of the choices in those accounts.

Asset class	Your 401(k)	Spouse's 401(k)	Your IRA
Large-cap U.S. stocks	50%	50%	
Mid-cap U.S. stocks	50%	25%	25%
Small-cap U.S. stocks		50%	50%
U.S. bonds			100%
Foreign stocks		100%	

Investing in Hedge Funds

What are these hedge funds that I've heard about, and should I invest in them?

Hedge funds often say their goal is to return 10% or 20% per year. To pursue that goal, they may buy and sell stocks, bonds, commodities, currencies, and real estate. Managers may bet on where the market's going by selling short or by trading derivatives.

What the heck are "selling short" and "trading derivatives"? That's exactly why hedge funds cater to wealthy investors, who buy them to diversify their extravagantly large portfolios. Hedge funds invest in complicated and risky investments to try to produce incredibly high returns. That's also why hedge funds require investors to meet substantial minimum requirements like hundreds of thousands of dollars in annual income to millions in investable assets.

Hedge funds also restrict withdrawals, so you may not be able to get your money out when you want. Fees are usually sky high, because many hedge fund managers rake in a slice of the fund profits as well as million-dollar salaries.

Even if you can get your foot in a hedge fund door, it's a risky investment. Many hedge fund strategies can backfire in the blink of an eye, leaving you with big losses. Unless you're willing to put a lot of dough on the line, your best bet is to stick with the investments outlined in this chapter and elsewhere in this book.

6 Stocks

Warren Buffett, one of the most famous investors ever, has this to say about owning stocks: "Most investors, both institutional and individual, will find that the best way to own common stocks is through an index fund that charges minimal fees." If the study of individual stocks described in this chapter turns you off and you decide to follow the Oracle of Omaha's advice, simply go back to Chapter 5 to learn all about index funds.

Buffett's advice to investors who choose to own individual stocks is simple, though not necessarily easy to follow: "Your goal as an investor should simply be to purchase, at a rational price, a part interest in an easily under-standable business whose earnings are virtually certain to be materially higher 5, 10, and 20 years from now." Few companies meet these succinct criteria, so when you find one that does, buy a bundle of shares.

Many people try all sorts of strategies to make money in stocks. *Technical analysis* is akin to reading stock price tea leaves: Its practitioners, called technical analysts, study patterns in stock prices and the volume of shares sold each day to try to forecast where the price will go next. Technical analysis has a purpose, though. Long-term investors with lots of money to invest use analysis to help choose good times to buy, because they buy so many shares that each penny counts. This book won't get into technical analysis, because you can invest successfully without it.

Day traders, as they were called in the late 20th century, buy and sell stocks all day long trying to emulate the strategies the brokers and other professional high-frequency traders use. However, this style of investing has a ridiculously high failure rate, so you won't learn about that in this book.

Purchasing stocks based on company fundamentals, called *fundamental analysis* or *fundamental investing,* is a more serene and less time-intensive way to invest. You focus on the fundamental measures of a company's performance—financial statements, revenues, debt, assets, operations, business strategy, competition, and the capabilities of the management team—as if you were buying the business outright. And well you should, because buying a share of stock *is* buying a part of the company. Fundamental investors look for companies whose profile is so strong that they feel confident they can own the shares for the long term. Fundamental analysis boils down to three major criteria: *growth, quality,* and *value,* which you'll learn about throughout this chapter.

You'll also learn how to evaluate the fundamentals of a company. First, you'll dissect company financial statements, which you use to determine a company's financial strength, potential for growth, and value. Then, you'll learn what the different measures in fundamental analysis represent, how you calculate them, the values you want to see, and the values that warn you to stay away. You'll also learn how to compare a company to its competitors and how to compare a company's performance from year to year so you can watch for trends.

Regardless of how good a company's fundamentals are, its stock price still may go up or down, seemingly without reason. Investors are human and their emotions sometimes move stock prices irrationally (page 45), which is why diversification is so important, as you'll learn in Chapter 9.

 You can find most of the numbers you need to evaluate stocks on websites like Yahoo! Finance (*http://finance.yahoo.com*) or MSN Money (*http://money.msn.com*). This chapter tells you where to find values and ratios.

Buying into a Business

If you own your own business, you're already familiar with income statements, balance sheets, and statements of cash flow: the trio of financial statements you must produce for the IRS, your partners, or your own analysis of your company's performance. If you haven't had this joyful experience, here's what all the fuss is about.

The Income Statement

An income statement is like a video of financial performance over a period of time, usually a month, a quarter, or a year. It shows the money the company brings in (income) at the top, as you can see here. Expenses, the money the company spends to run the business, come next. Finally, at the bottom of the statement is the profit or loss that results when you subtract the expenses from income (also called *net income*). Here's how the income statement progresses from revenue to net income:

- **Income or revenue.** The first category in an income statement is income, another name for the revenue the company generates by selling products, services, or both.

Johnson & Johnson - Company Finan...			
Income Statement **Balance Sheet** **Cash Flow** **10 Year Summary**			
⊙ Annual ○ Interim		Financial data in U.	
		Values in Millions (E	
	2009	2008	2007
Period End Date	12/27/2009	12/28/2008	12/30/2007
Period Length	12 Months	12 Months	12 Months
Stmt Source	8-K	10-K	10-K
Stmt Source Date	01/26/2010	02/20/2009	02/26/2008
Stmt Update Type	Updated	Updated	Updated
Revenue	61,897.0	63,747.0	61,095.0
Total Revenue	**61,897.0**	**63,747.0**	**61,095.0**
Cost of Revenue, Total	18,447.0	18,511.0	17,751.0
Gross Profit	**43,450.0**	**45,236.0**	**43,344.0**
Selling/General/Administrative Expenses, Total	19,801.0	21,490.0	20,451.0
Research & Development	6,986.0	7,577.0	7,680.0
Depreciation/Amortization	0.0	0.0	0.0
Interest Expense (Income), Net Operating	361.0	0.0	0.0
Unusual Expense (Income)	1,073.0	181.0	1,552.0
Other Operating Expenses, Total	-526.0	-1,015.0	534.0
Operating Income	**15,755.0**	**16,929.0**	**13,283.0**
Interest Income (Expense), Net Non-Operating	0.0	0.0	0.0
Gain (Loss) on Sale of Assets	0.0	0.0	0.0
Other, Net	0.0	0.0	0.0
Income Before Tax	**15,755.0**	**16,929.0**	**13,283.0**
Income Tax - Total	3,489.0	3,980.0	2,707.0
Income After Tax	**12.266.0**	**12.949.0**	**10.576.0**
Total Extraordinary Items	0.0	0.0	0.0
Net Income	**12,266.0**	**12,949.0**	**10,576.0**

Done

- **Cost of Goods Sold.** The products and services a company sells usually come with some initial costs, for example, the wholesale cost of the products the company resells, shipping costs, or the cost of sales. These costs appear in the second section of an income statement, called "Cost of Goods Sold" or, sometimes, "Cost of Revenue".

- **Gross Profit.** Gross profit is the money the company earns after subtracting the cost of goods sold from income. For example, as you can see above, if the company has revenue of $61.9 billion and paid $18.4 billion in cost of revenue, its gross profit is $43.5 billion.

- **Expenses.** The next section covers all the things the company spends money on to run the business, such as office space rent, research, salaries, and so on.

- **Operating Income.** Operating income is how much money is left after subtracting all the expenses.

- **Other Income/Expense.** Income and expenses that don't relate to the primary business, such as interest paid on loans, fall into the Other Income/Expenses category. Income taxes also appear near the bottom of the income statement.

- **Net Income.** Finally, net income appears at the end of the statement. It's the aptly named bottom line: the money left after the company subtracts all costs and expenses. If net income is positive, the company made a profit (the Wall Street term for a positive net income). If the number is negative, the company had a loss (a synonym for negative net income).

The Balance Sheet

A balance sheet is a snapshot of company finances. This financial statement shows the value of assets the company owns, how much the company has borrowed (its liabilities), and the equity in the company at a given point in time. In a balance sheet, the total assets *always* equal the total of the liabilities and equity, as you can see below. As the company owns more or borrows more, the value of the equity changes to balance the equation. As you'll learn later in this chapter, a healthy balance sheet doesn't have an excessive amount of debt (page 113).

Johnson & Johnson - Company Finan...

Assets			
▶	Cash and Short Term Investments	12,809.0	9,3
▶	Total Receivables, Net	9,719.0	9,4
	Total Inventory	5,052.0	5,1
	Prepaid Expenses	3,367.0	3,4
	Other Current Assets, Total	3,430.0	2,6
	Total Current Assets	**34,377.0**	**29,9**
	Property/Plant/Equipment, Total - Net	14,365.0	14,1
	Goodwill, Net	13,719.0	14,1
	Intangibles, Net	13,976.0	14,6
	Long Term Investments	4.0	
	Note Receivable - Long Term	0.0	
	Other Long Term Assets, Total	8,471.0	8,0
	Other Assets, Total	0.0	
	Total Assets	**84,912.0**	**80,9**

Liabilities and Shareholders' Equity			
Accounts Payable		7,503.0	6,9
Payable/Accrued		0.0	
Accrued Expenses		9,200.0	10,2
Notes Payable/Short Term Debt		3,732.0	2,4
Current Port. of LT Debt/Capital Leases		0.0	
Other Current Liabilities, Total		417.0	2
Total Current Liabilities		**20,852.0**	**19,8**
▶ Total Long Term Debt		8,120.0	7,0
Deferred Income Tax		1,432.0	1,4
Minority Interest		0.0	
Other Liabilities, Total		11,997.0	9,2
Total Liabilities		**42,401.0**	**37,6**
Redeemable Preferred Stock		0.0	
Preferred Stock - Non Redeemable, Net		0.0	
Common Stock		3,120.0	3,1
Retained Earnings (Accumulated Deficit)		63,379.0	55,2
Treasury Stock - Common		-19,033.0	-14,3
Other Equity, Total		-4,955.0	-6
Total Equity		**42,511.0**	**43,3**
Total Liabilities & Shareholders' Equity		**84,912.0**	**80,9**

Here's what each section of a balance sheet represents:

- **Assets.** Assets are what a company owns, like equipment, product inventory, accounts receivable, cash, and even brand names.

- **Liabilities.** Liabilities (debt) include accounts payable (expenses that haven't been paid), loans, and even future expenses, such as pensions. Debt on its own isn't bad, but *too much* debt is a problem, particularly when business slows down, because the company has to make debt payments every month, whether it makes money or not.

- **Equity.** Equity on a balance sheet is like the equity you have in your house. When you buy a house, your down payment is your initial equity. If your house increases in value or you pay off your mortgage, your equity in the house increases. Similarly, equity in a company is its dollar value after you subtract liabilities from assets.

The Statement of Cash Flows

Cash flow tells you whether a company generates enough cash to keep the doors open. A balance sheet may look sweet—$50 million in real estate and only $5 million in debt. But if the company has a $50,000 payment due and only $10,000 in the bank, cash flow is a problem. Cash flow is simply the cold, hard cash that flows in and out of a company—not the noncash transactions, such as depreciation, that appear on an income statement. Companies can generate cash in three ways:

- **Operating activities.** The way you want to see a company generate cash is through operating activities, that is, from ongoing operations like selling products and services.

- **Investing activities.** Buying and selling buildings or making money in the stock market are called investing activities. Although they can generate cash, they typically can't continue forever.

- **Financing activities.** Borrowing money and selling stock are financing activities. New companies often have no other source of cash. However, when an established company uses financing to raise cash, a red flag starts waving. Mature companies should be able to generate cash from their primary business operations.

Investing in Growth

When a company's earnings increase over time, the company becomes more valuable. It owns more assets; it has more money to plow back into the company to produce additional growth; shareholders' equity in the company is higher; and for a dividend-paying company, the dividend usually increases, too. Investors are willing to pay more to own a more valuable company, so the price of the company's stock goes up.

Companies can grow sales and earnings several ways:

- Introduce new or improved products.

- Expand the territory they sell into.

- Increase their market share.

- Build new stores.
- Acquire competitors.
- Increase prices.

If you've ever driven behind someone going one mile per hour faster than the car they're passing, you know it takes forever to make any progress. For the same reason, you want to invest in companies that grow sales and earnings faster than the growth of inflation, or your portfolio won't get ahead. As you'll learn on page 110, you look for companies that grow faster than their industry competitors. You want to own the best companies—and above-average industry performance is one indication of quality. Consistency is good, too. If a company has weathered storms without financial performance suffering unduly, the company is more likely to be stable in the future.

Like children, companies grow at different rates at different times in their lives. On page 156 you learn that small-company stocks have produced an annual average return of 11.7% since 1926, compared to 9.6% for large-company stocks. One reason for small companies' higher returns is they tend to grow faster than large companies—their values increase faster, so their stock prices go up faster. But small companies are risky. Tastes change; products quickly grow obsolete; a large competitor bullies a small company out of the market. On the other hand, growth usually slows as companies get larger. Growing a large company is like trying to make a left-hand turn in an oil tanker. It takes time and a lot of energy. Slower but more consistent growth is fine, too. That's why you want a portfolio that invests in companies of different sizes (page 162).

 Tip Regardless of the size of the company, you must watch for companies that don't keep up their performance. If growth starts to decline or turns into consistent losses, it's time to look for another investment.

Percentages are key to evaluating growth, just as they are for many other financial measures. Comparing absolute values isn't fair, particularly if the contestants are companies of different size. For example, say a small company and a large competitor in the same industry increase their earnings by $1 million. But the small company went from $1 million to $2 million, while the large company increased earnings from $100 million to $101 million. Although the dollar amount is the same, the small company increased its earnings by 100%, while the large company grew by a mere 1%.

There's a bit more to growth rates, though. Time is another factor. How long does it take a company to increase its earnings? An *annualized return* (or *compound annual growth rate*) is a better way to compare growth rates, because it takes into account compounding over time. For example, a 100% increase in dollar value over 5 years represents a compound annual growth rate of 15%. Over 10 years, the same 100% increase is a bit more than 7% per year. See page 16 to learn more about compounding.

To use the MSN Money website (*http://money.msn.com*) to see the growth rate for a stock, type the company ticker symbol into the Get Quote box and click Get Quote. In the left navigation bar, click Financial Results and then choose Key Ratios. Under Key Ratios, choose Growth Rates. As you can see below, MSN Money shows growth rates for sales and earnings for the company, the industry, and the S&P 500 (the comparable market index in this example).

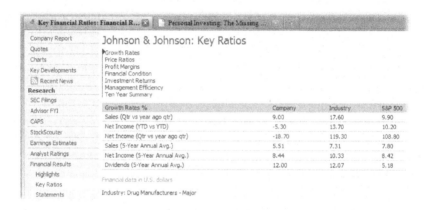

Growth Rates %	Company	Industry	S&P 500
Sales (Qtr vs year ago qtr)	9.00	17.60	9.90
Net Income (YTD vs YTD)	-5.30	13.70	10.20
Net Income (Qtr vs year ago qtr)	-18.70	119.30	108.80
Sales (5-Year Annual Avg.)	5.51	7.31	7.80
Net Income (5-Year Annual Avg.)	8.44	10.33	8.42
Dividends (5-Year Annual Avg.)	12.00	12.07	5.18

Financial data in U.S. dollars

Industry: Drug Manufacturers - Major

Tip Comparing the results for one quarter to the same quarter in the previous year is important, indicated by "(Qtr vs year ago qtr)" above, particularly when business is seasonal. For example, a company in the grocery industry might not see much variation in sales and earnings from quarter to quarter, but for a toy company, the holiday season during the fourth quarter of the year produces more sales than the first quarter. Growth trends are easier to see when you compare numbers for the same quarters each year.

For Yahoo! Finance (*http://finance.yahoo.com*), type the ticker symbol in the Search box. In the left navigation bar, under Company, click Key Statistics. Under Income Statement, look for "Qtrly Earnings Growth (yoy)", which represents the earnings growth from the most recent quarter to the quarter one year ago.

Investing DRIP by DRIP

If you want to regularly invest small amounts of money (as little as $10 in some instances) in a company's stock, a dividend reinvestment plan is a great way to go. Many companies sell shares of their stock directly to investors through their dividend reinvestment plans (DRIPs). Typically, to open a DRIP with a company, you need only one share of that company's stock. Once the DRIP is in place, you pay little or no commission when you buy additional shares of stock or when the company reinvests your dividends in your name. It takes a while to complete a purchase or a sale, so these plans aren't for impatient traders. Use them to invest in a company for the long term.

If a company offers an Optional Cash Purchases (OCP) or direct stock purchase (DSP) option, you can purchase additional shares of stock on a regular schedule—monthly or quarterly, for example. Learn more about these programs by downloading the free online book on the DRIP Central website (*http://www.dripcentral.com*).

Investing in Quality

Sure, you can try to earn money fast by buying a brand-new company with a hot product or one you hope will turn its bad luck around. But those investments can turn into big losses if the story doesn't turn out as you hope. Most successful long-term investors, like Warren Buffett and his mentor Benjamin Graham, build portfolios of long-term investments in strong, quality companies. Here's Benjamin Graham's explanation of why to invest in quality: "For the vast majority of common stocks, the average relationship between price and earnings will reflect the quality and growth of the issue." Investing in quality growth companies provides better returns with less risk. In addition, you don't have to spend as much time watching the stocks you own, because their performance is more consistent.

Quality in companies starts with consistent growth. Any company can turn in one great year of growth. Companies that grow consistently year after year are much harder to find. Quality also means consistent overall financial performance and strength. This section explains the financial characteristics you use to rate a company's quality. Here's a quick synopsis of the factors that investors like Benjamin Graham use to evaluate quality:

- Strong historic growth of sales and earnings per share (EPS) compared to the growth rates of competitors (see page 110 to learn how to compare growth between competitors).

- Consistent historic earnings per share (which is also a sign of management's skill).
- Strong profitability compared to the profitability of competitors.
- Financial strength.
- Consistent dividend payout and growth.
- Competitive strength in its industry.
- Strong management.
- Outlook for the company business and industry.

Tip Quality isn't just about numbers. When you look for quality companies, you should evaluate other factors, too, like the skill of the management team, the company track record in introducing new products, how well it takes advantage of business opportunities, and its way of dealing with problems. For example, quality companies may use their strength to grab market share from weaker competitors during tough times.

Quality often costs more initially, but quality companies often hold or increase their value over time. If you've ever purchased a product for pennies, only to have it fall apart the first time you used it, you know that cheap isn't the same as inexpensive. If you pay a premium for a quality product, it may cost less in the long run. For example, most stock prices fall in a down market, just as all boats lower as the tide goes out. But quality stocks often go down less and come back faster.

Tip Bob Adams, a popular investment instructor, developed a free Excel spreadsheet for analyzing a company's financial status (*http://tinyurl.com/bobadamsstock*). Not only can you use it to evaluate companies, but it's also great for learning about financial analysis, because it explains the importance of the ratios it calculates and highlights red flags in company performance. It can even download the data it needs to calculate ratios.

Dealing with Debt

If you're going to own stock in a company for the long term, financial strength is important. You don't want to own shares in a company that does the business version of maxing out its credit cards or runs out of money at the first whiff of a problem. A few simple ratios can tell you how healthy a company is.

Websites like Yahoo! Finance (*http://finance.yahoo.com*) and MSN Money (*http://money.msn.com*) provide these ratios, so you don't have to calculate them. For example, on MSN Money, type the ticker symbol for a company into the search box. In the left navigation bar, click Financial Results and then choose Key Ratios. Under Key Ratios, choose Financial Condition to see the measures discussed in this section, as shown below.

Debt-to-equity ratio

A public company can raise cash by selling shares of stock, issuing bonds (see Chapter 7), or by borrowing from a bank. With debt (bonds or bank loans), the company has to repay the principal and also pay interest. If a company can borrow at 5% and earn a return of 8% growing the business, the company comes out ahead. However, if the company doesn't earn a higher return on the borrowed money or business drops off, the debt and interest still must be repaid. Then, the company has to take money away from its operations to pay the interest and principal, which decreases growth.

The *debt-to-equity ratio* helps you evaluate whether a company can manage its debt. It's the total debt divided by shareholders' equity (the amount owners have invested in the company plus the total retained earnings).

A lower debt-to-equity ratio means more financial safety. A debt-to-equity ratio greater than 40% (listed as 0.40) or 50% (0.50) is usually a red flag, because a company could struggle to pay off debts if revenues decrease or interest rates go up. (Though some industries, like utilities, often run just fine with high levels of debt, so you need to compare a company to its peers.) For example, in the figure above, Johnson & Johnson has a debt-to-equity ratio of .29 (29%). Notice that the industry average is 1.15 (115%), much higher than the rule-of-thumb 40% to 50%.

However, debt can be good if it helps a company grow. If a company is increasing its debt, see if there's a good reason. For example, building new stores around the country may be a good reason to borrow, because sales will increase with more stores. Decreasing debt year after year often indicates increasing financial strength. For Johnson & Johnson, the debt-to-equity ratio varies over the years, from a low of 7% in 2006 to a current high of 29%. (To see 10 years of ratios, on the MSN Money's Key Ratios page, click Ten Year Summary.) In this example, some research uncovered that JNJ added about $4 billion in debt in 2007 to finance the acquisition of Pfizer's customer health-care business.

Interest coverage

Interest coverage tells you how easily a company can pay the interest it owes over the next 12 months given its current profits. An interest coverage ratio above 4.0 means that a company can easily repay loans and bond payments. An interest coverage ratio below 1.5 is a serious red flag. Interest coverage measures the company's earnings before subtracting interest expenses and taxes divided by the interest expense, both listed on the income statement. JNJ's interest coverage is 44.6. No problem there.

Current ratio

This ratio is the most common test of a company's financial strength. It measures a company's ability to pay off *current liabilities,* debts due in the next 12 months, with *current assets* (or working capital), that is, readily available money like cash, accounts receivable, and inventory. You calculate this ratio by dividing current assets by current liabilities. Although current ratios vary by industry, a current ratio between 2.0 and 7.0 means that the company has two to seven times as much in current assets as it does in current liabilities, which is usually enough to pay the bills if business slows for a short time. If you want to calculate the current ratio, get the values for current assets and current liabilities from the company's balance sheet. JNJ's current ratio is 1.8, right in the ballpark.

When the current ratio drops below 1.5 and unexpected expenses come up, a company may have to borrow money to pay the bills. However, companies that keep low levels of inventory and accounts receivable (McDonald's, Walmart, and Amazon, for example) often have current ratios less than 1.0. Because these companies convert inventory to cash in a flash, they often get paid by customers before they pay their suppliers. For them, a low current ratio means they're running their operations super efficiently.

Quick ratio

A tougher test of working capital is the quick ratio, which omits inventory from current assets, because it can take time to convert inventory into cash. This ratio's calculation is current assets minus inventory divided by current liabilities. For most companies, the quick ratio should be greater than 1.0, and the higher, the better. Like the current ratio, the quick ratio doesn't apply to cash-based businesses. JNJ's quick ratio is 1.6, a reasonable value.

Management Effectiveness

You want company management to use assets and shareholders' equity (page 108) to produce a good return. *Return on equity* (ROE) shows whether management increases the value of the shareholders' equity at an acceptable rate. Another measure of management effectiveness, *return on assets* (ROA), shows the profit the company earns for every dollar it owns in assets.

Return on equity

Return on equity is a company's annual net income divided by the shareholders' equity. Consistently high ROE means management increases the value of the company using the money shareholders invest in it (aka equity). For example, Johnson & Johnson's return on equity is 26.4%, shown on the next page. That means that the company produces $26.40 of income for every $100 in shareholders' equity each year. To see return on equity and return on assets for a company on MSN Money, on the stock page, click Financial Results, then in the navigation bar click Key Ratios, and then click Investment Returns.

A common rule of thumb is to look for ROE higher than 15%. In addition to ROE for the current year, you can learn a lot by comparing ROE from year to year, as well as comparing ROE to other companies in the same industry. Increasing ROE is great, but it can't go on forever. An ROE that holds steady at an above-average rate is still good. For example, in the figure below, you can see that the 5-year average ROE is 27.8%. The 5-year average for the industry (drug manufacturers) is 24.3%, so Johnson & Johnson is not only steady but above the industry average. In addition, its ROE is close to twice the ROE of the S&P 500 index.

ROE can vary widely by industry, which is why you want to compare a company to its competitors. For example, drug manufacturers, like Johnson & Johnson, produce ROE around 25%, while grocery store ROE is closer to 12%.

 Tip To look at trends in company performance for the past 10 years, on the MSN Money stock page, click Financial Results. In the navigation bar, click Key Ratios. Then, above the Key Ratios area, shown above, click Ten Year Summary.

Return on assets

ROE compares net income to shareholders' equity, so a company that borrows heavily may have an attractive ROE without being particularly effective at using shareholders' equity to grow the company. Return on assets (ROA) is the annual net income divided by the company's total assets. Because assets may come with debt (in other words, the company borrowed money to buy the assets), ROA shows how well a company uses the total of debt *and* shareholders' equity to generate value. For example, Johnson & Johnson's ROA is 13.7%, half the rate of the company's ROE. A quick peek at JNJ's balance sheet shows total debt of $42.4 billion, which is why the company's ROA is lower than its ROE.

Like ROE, ROA varies by industry. For example, drug manufacturers have an average ROA of around 11%, while automobile manufacturers require factories and parts to build cars and have an ROA of around 1%.

Turnover ratios

What's the point of owning assets, like buildings, inventory, and cash, if you're not making the most of them. Another way to measure management effectiveness is with turnover ratios: *asset turnover ratio, inventory turnover ratio,* and *receivable turnover ratio.* Turnover ratios vary by industry, so it's important to compare the turnover ratios for a company to the corresponding ratios for competitors and the industry as a whole.

 To see turnover ratios, on the MSN Money stock page, click Financial Results. In the navigation bar, click Key Ratios. Then, above the Key Ratios area, click Management Efficiency.

Asset turnover ratio shows the sales a company generates for each dollar of assets it owns (including office buildings, equipment, inventory, and so on), and the higher the ratio, the better. The asset turnover ratio is revenue for a period divided by assets (typically the average asset value for the time period). Companies with high asset turnover ratios mean the companies sell a high volume of products, usually at a slight increase over cost. These companies can survive and even thrive with these low profit margins (see page 118 for more on profit margins). Johnson & Johnson has an asset turnover ratio of 0.7, which is slightly higher than the industry average (0.6) and just below the average for the S&P 500 (0.8).

Inventory turnover ratio shows how quickly a company moves its inventory into the hands of customers. That's total revenue for a period divided by the average inventory for that period. Basically, this ratio shows how many times the average inventory is sold during a period. Like asset turnover, the higher the inventory turnover ratio, the better. JNJ's inventory turnover is 3.6, which means it sells 3.6 times its inventory each year. The average for the drug manufacturer industry is 2.5, so JNJ is above average.

Grocery stores usually have high rates of inventory turnover, because they sell a lot of low-cost products. On the other hand, companies that sell services instead of products don't have inventory, so this ratio doesn't apply to them. A low inventory turnover ratio may mean that a company's products aren't selling in the marketplace, whether they're obsolete, of poor quality, or for another reason.

Accounts receivable (also called receivables) represent income owed to the company by its customers (unpaid invoices, for example). The third turnover ratio is the *receivables turnover ratio,* which shows how many times a company collects its receivables during a period (revenue divided by average receivables). Higher receivables turnover ratios are better than lower ones. Very high receivable turnover ratios, for example, 73 for the Whole Foods grocery chain, indicate a highly efficient company that collects income quickly, often before it has to pay its own bills. As you would expect, cash-based businesses like restaurants and grocery stores have very high receivables ratios, while heavy industry like auto manufacturers have low ones. Johnson & Johnson's receivables turnover ratio is 6.4, above average for the drug manufacturer industry.

Profitability

Purchase stock in companies whose earnings grow consistently, because that translates into higher stock prices over time. Companies can increase earnings by selling more, but how much profit they earn on those sales is important, too. As with other financial measures, you evaluate profit with a percentage. A *profit margin* is the percentage of profit a company makes on its revenues.

Profit margin can give you early warning that trouble is brewing. For example, if a company's profit margin starts to pull back, earnings are often next, which eventually leads to a lower stock price. Profit margins come in several flavors. In this section, you'll learn about *gross margin, pre-tax profit margin,* and *net profit margin.*

MSN Money shows profit margins for companies, as you can see below. On a company stock page, click Financial Results. In the navigation bar, click Key Ratios. Then, above the Key Ratios area, click Profit Margins.

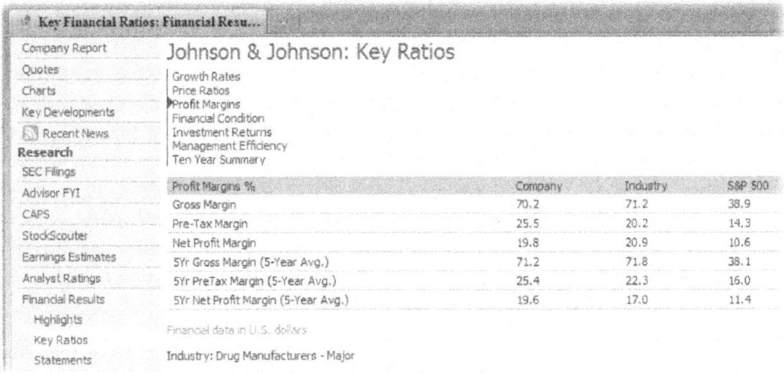
Key Financial Ratios: Financial Resu...
Company Report
Quotes
Charts
Key Developments
Recent News
Research
SEC Filings
Advisor FYI
CAPS
StockScouter
Earnings Estimates
Analyst Ratings
Financial Results
Highlights
Key Ratios
Statements
Johnson & Johnson: Key Ratios
Growth Rates
Price Ratios
Profit Margins
Financial Condition
Investment Returns
Management Efficiency
Ten Year Summary

Profit Margins %	Company	Industry	S&P 500
Gross Margin	70.2	71.2	38.9
Pre-Tax Margin	25.5	20.2	14.3
Net Profit Margin	19.8	20.9	10.6
5Yr Gross Margin (5-Year Avg.)	71.2	71.8	38.1
5Yr PreTax Margin (5-Year Avg.)	25.4	22.3	16.0
5Yr Net Profit Margin (5-Year Avg.)	19.6	17.0	11.4

Financial data in U.S. dollars

Industry: Drug Manufacturers - Major

- ***Gross margin*** is a first cut at the basic profitability of a company, so it has the highest value of the three profit margins in this section. You calculate it using the gross profit (the total revenue minus the cost of goods sold, both described on page 106) divided by the company's revenue. It shows how inexpensively a company can make or buy the products it sells. If a company keeps its raw material and manufacturing costs low, it has more flexibility in pricing its products.
- Company management usually doesn't have much control over the income taxes the company pays. To look at profit margin without the variations due to taxes, you can look at a company's ***pre-tax profit margin.*** Calculating pre-tax profit margin is easy. It's the net income before taxes divided by total revenue. However, as you see in the figure above, pre-tax profit margin is significantly lower than the gross profit margin. That's because net income before taxes is the company's income after you subtract ***all*** the company's expenses (not just the cost of the goods sold).
- ***Net profit margin*** represents how much a company makes after it pays its expenses and taxes. It's no surprise that this margin is net income after taxes divided by total revenue.

As you do with other measures, you compare a company's profit margins to those of its competitors. Grocery stores have very low net profit margins, as do high-volume retail businesses. On the other hand, drug manufacturers have high margins. As you can see in the previous figure, Johnson & Johnson has a net profit margin of 19.8%, close to the average net profit margin of 20.9% for the industry. By comparison, Whole Foods has a net profit margin of 2.1%, slightly lower than the industry margin of 2.9%.

Sometimes, even success can be a problem. Extraordinarily high profit margins are great news for a company for a while. However, high profit margins are bound to attract competition. If other companies figure out how to sell similar products or services for less, the company has to cut its prices, lowering its profit margin, and eventually, its stock price.

Investing in Good Value

Just because a stock price is low doesn't mean you should buy the stock. In fact, a price that looks too good to be true probably is. Poor-quality or slow-growth stocks almost always come with low prices. At the same time, paying too much for the best quality growth stock can produce a low return on your investment. The sweet spot is buying quality growth stocks at reasonable prices—a great way to earn attractive returns with moderate risk.

What if you find a stock you like, but the price is too high? In many cases, you just have to be patient. You may have heard about the *efficient market theory,* which says that the market takes all available information into account so investment prices are always "right." In reality, the market often overreacts, especially to bad news. A problem for one company in an industry can drag the prices of its competitors down with it. If you do your homework and are confident about a company's future, use those short-term price drops as opportunities to buy.

Price Ratios

The most popular measure of the value of a stock is the *price/earnings ratio* (also called the P/E ratio, PE, or multiple). The P/E ratio compares the stock price to how much money the company earned during a year (share price divided by current annual earnings per share). You can think of the P/E ratio as how much investors are willing to pay for each dollar of company earnings. In that light, the P/E ratio is a measure of the confidence investors have in a company's future. The more they're willing to pay for a dollar of earnings, the more confident they are that the company will perform well in the future.

The P/E ratio is a great way to see whether the current price of a share is reasonable compared to a company's share price in the past (see page 122 for more). You can compare the current P/E ratio to the stock's average P/E ratio, average high, and average low P/E ratios for the past few years to gauge whether the stock is a bargain or overpriced. For example, as shown below, JNJ's P/E ratio is halfway between the company's 5-year high and 5-year low. Although it's not a bargain, you wouldn't be paying top dollar either.

Key Financial Ratios: Financial Resu...			
Company Report	**Johnson & Johnson: Key Ratios**		
Quotes	Growth Rates		
Charts	Price Ratios		
Key Developments	Profit Margins		
Recent News	Financial Condition		
Research	Investment Returns		
SEC Filings	Management Efficiency		
	Ten Year Summary		

Price Ratios	Company	Industry	S&P 500
Current P/E Ratio	14.8	14.2	20.9
P/E Ratio 5-Year High	20.5	9.7	67.3
P/E Ratio 5-Year Low	10.5	3.6	9.7
Price/Sales Ratio	2.89	2.98	2.24
Price/Book Value	3.54	5.16	4.14
Price/Cash Flow Ratio	11.90	10.30	15.70

Financial data in U.S. dollars

Industry: Drug Manufacturers - Major

Tip P/E ratios drop when investors pay less for a stock for whatever reason. But they also decrease when company earnings go up faster than the stock price. If the P/E ratio drops because earnings are growing faster than the stock price, the share price represents better value. But decreasing investor confidence is a red flag. If you see a company's P/E ratio decreasing, investigate why.

In addition to seeing whether a stock's price is reasonable, you can use P/E ratios to compare the value of two stocks. Is Johnson & Johnson at $65 a share a better deal than Pfizer at $17? For example, if Johnson & Johnson's P/E ratio is 14.8 and Pfizer's is 12.5, you pay a small premium for Johnson & Johnson.

Tip To see P/E and other price ratios, on the MSN Money stock page, click Financial Results. In the navigation bar, click Key Ratios. Then, above the Key Ratios area, click Price Ratios. You can see 10 years' worth of price ratios by clicking Ten Year Summary. Morningstar (www.morningstar.com/) is another site that offers 10-year comparisons. Type a ticker symbol in the Quote box on the Morningstar home page, and then select the Valuation tab on the stock page. To see 10 years' worth of ratios, select the "10-Yr Valuation" tab above the table.

P/E ratios vary by industry, size of company, and stability. For example, smaller companies may have higher P/E ratios because it's easier for them to grow quickly. On the other hand, well-respected, stable companies may command a higher P/E ratio because of their reputation.

The most common P/E ratio is the price divided by the earnings from the last four reported quarters. These earnings are usually abbreviated as *TTM,* which stands for "trailing twelve months." Some data providers calculate P/E ratios based on earnings per share (EPS) from the *last* two reported quarters plus the estimates for the *next* two quarters. The *projected P/E ratio* is calculated with the estimated EPS for the next four quarters. The projected P/E ratio comes in handy if you're studying companies with very high EPS growth rates, because the current P/E ratios for these fast-growing companies are almost guaranteed to be off the charts.

Power Users' Clinic

Buying and Selling at Rational Values

When stock prices are plummeting, it's hard to remain calm and hold onto good stocks. It's just as tough to be patient and realistic about stock prices when the stock market is on a tear. You can make rational decisions instead of overreacting by assessing a reasonable price for a stock based on long-term P/E ratio performance.

Because the P/E ratio fluctuates constantly as a stock's price changes, the P/E ratio at any given moment isn't all that useful. However, the *average* P/E ratio over 5 to 10 years can give you an idea about a P/E ratio that the company's stock may return to from higher or lower values (the *signature PE*). Say a company's P/E ratio bounces between a high of 32 and a low of 8 over 10 years, like Johnson & Johnson did between 2000 and 2009. You calculate the average P/E ratio for the 10 years and find that it's 21.3.

If the current P/E ratio is higher than the long-term average PE, the current P/E ratio may eventually decline to the average value. If the P/E ratio is lower than the long-term average, the current P/E ratio may increase.

The *rational price* of a stock is the price if the stock sells at its long-term average PE. To calculate the rational price, multiply the long-term average PE by the company's earnings per share. For example, say that the EPS for the example company are $4.40. With a long-term average PE of 21.3, the rational price for a share of the company's stock is $93.72. With Johnson & Johnson selling at $65 in the spring of 2010, the rational price says that the share price may increase. On the other hand, if the stock were selling for $120, the rational price hints that the share price may decrease.

Other price ratios

P/E ratios can sometimes be misleading. For example, companies that grow very quickly often have outrageously high P/E ratios, reflecting what investors expect in the future. On the other hand, companies with problems may have abnormally low P/E ratios, because investors are scared. Other price ratios can help you decide the value a stock's price represents:

- The *P/E to growth ratio* (PEG) is a measure of whether a company's growth rate supports the P/E ratio that the stock price produces. The PEG ratio is the stock's current P/E ratio divided by the estimated future EPS growth rate. The rule of thumb for PEG ratios is that a PEG of 1.0 means the stock price is reasonable—the stock's P/E ratio is equal to the company's EPS growth rate. A PEG of 0.5 may represent a bargain, while a PEG of higher than 1.5 may mean the stock price is high.

 The PEG ratio doesn't work well for industries valued on their assets, such as financial institutions, real estate operations, and airlines. If you're looking at companies like these, use the price/book value ratio instead.

- The *price/book value ratio* (also known as the price/book ratio) was made popular by Benjamin Graham after the 1929 stock market crash. The price/book ratio is the foundation of *value investing,* investing in companies that represent good value. *Book value* is another name for shareholders' equity (page 108). You use book value per share (shareholders' equity divided by the number of shares outstanding) to calculate the price/book value ratio, which helps you determine a stock's value. A price/book ratio of less than 1.0 means the share price is less than the book value for one share, which means you can purchase the company for less than its net worth.

The price/book value ratio can help you find good investment deals, because accounting practices are conservative about depreciating assets on a company's books, like real estate. For example, a company may own buildings that are worth millions, but if those buildings are fully depreciated, they have a value of $0 on the company books. If that's the case, you could purchase the company for less than the company's assets are worth. If you sold the assets, you'd make an immediate profit.

- The *price/sales ratio* (PSR) is another way to measure a stock's value, especially for companies that don't have any earnings (because the P/E ratio is meaningless if a company has no earnings). Remember to be extra careful when evaluating speculative investments. The price/sales ratio is simply the stock price divided by the sales per share.

- Cash flow (page 108) analysis has become much more popular among investors. The *price/cash flow ratio* is a great way to get past any tricky accounting business a company may use to hide unsavory performance. The price/cash flow ratio is helpful for comparing a stock to its industry. Depreciation is a noncash expense that lowers earnings, so the price/cash flow ratio is particularly helpful when you study companies that have ginormous depreciation expenses, such as steel manufacturers and automakers (who have lots of factories and equipment to depreciate). If a stock's price/cash flow ratio is lower than the industry average, the stock may be selling at a discount.

Dividends and Yield

Many companies reinvest profits into their business to finance further growth. At some point, company management can't find ways to use the money the company earns, so they pay a portion of the profits to investors as *dividends.* Dividend payments are crucial for investors who use income from their investments to pay for living expenses.

You use the *dividend yield* to compare the dividends paid by different companies or to compare a dividend to the interest you could earn on a bond or savings account. The dividend yield is the annual dividend divided by the share price.

Keep in mind that dividends also boost your overall return on investment. For example, if the dividend yield is 3% and you also earn a 6% return because the stock increased in price while you owned it, your total return is 9%. Morningstar shows dividend yield along with price ratios, as shown below.

Johnson & Johnson JNJ | ★★★★

Add to Portfolio   Get E-mail Alerts   Print   PDF Report   ? Data Question

Quote   Chart   Stock Analysis   Performance   Key Ratios   Financials   **Valuation**   Insider

Current Valuation | 10-Yr Valuation | Forward Valuation | Yields | Wall St. Estimates

Valuation Ratios				03-19-10
	Stock	Industry	S&P 500	Stock's 5Yr Average*
Price/Earnings	14.8	16.8	19.3	16.2
Price/Book	3.5	3.1	2.2	4.3
Price/Sales	2.9	2.5	1.3	3.2
Price/Cash Flow	11.0	9.0	7.1	20.2
Dividend Yield %	3.0	1.6	1.8	---

* Price/Cash Flow uses 3-year average.

Show Data Definitions | Feedback | Permissions/Reprints | Ticker Lookup

Watching for Trends

One way to get an early warning about problems is by comparing recent financial results to the same period a year ago. If you see numbers getting significantly worse, find out why. Consult the management discussion in a company's annual report; press releases; news reports on the company, its competitors, and the industry itself; or answers from investor relations representatives.

 For quarterly results, you need to compare the same quarter from the current year and the previous year, for example, the fourth quarters for fiscal years 2008 and 2009. Many companies do better during specific times of the year. For example, bookstores and retailers do particularly well in the last calendar quarter because of holiday buying. Home improvement stores often do better during the summer months.

Here's a quick synopsis of evaluating trends:

- **Revenues.** A company can only grow its profits over the long term by growing revenues. Small companies usually grow faster than large companies, so a slowdown in revenue growth is typical as small companies grow larger. In established companies, decreasing revenues can be a sign of trouble. For example, Johnson & Johnson has increased its annual revenues from $50.5 billion in 2005 to almost $62 billion in 2009, a strong upward trend during a poor economy.

- **Earnings Per Share (EPS).** Because investors watch company EPS closely, you can usually find a company's explanation for earnings performance. If EPS are decreasing, you have to decide whether the factors contributing to the decline are likely to affect earnings in the future. At the bottom of JNJ's income statement (see page 109 to learn how to find that on MSN Money), EPS increased from $3.38 in 2005 to $4.40 in 2009.

- **Debt.** If a company has been borrowing money, dig deeper to see if the debt is financing expansion or simply helping to pay the bills. For example, if a company is building new stores, an increase in debt is understandable. (Page 113 gives the background on JNJ's debt.)

- **Assets.** If a company's current assets are growing, the company may be increasing its cash on hand, which is good. On the other hand, if accounts receivable are increasing, the company may be struggling to collect what customers owe. Look at the changes in cash, receivables, and inventory to determine why assets are changing. For example, Johnson & Johnson's assets increased from $58.8 billion in 2005 to $84.9 billion in 2009. However, the company's debt increased from $20.1 billion to $42.4 billion during the same period. So, Johnson & Johnson was borrowing money to purchase assets (other companies, as it turns out). Because JNJ's return on assets is good, the company is making wise investments with the money it borrows.

- **Inventory.** Increasing inventory may mean that customers aren't buying the products that the company sells, or it could represent plans for expansion. If inventory is increasing, read the company's annual reports and press releases to learn why. JNJ's inventory increased slightly from 2005 to 2009, from $3.9 billion to $5 billion.

- **Accounts payable.** If accounts payable are growing, the company may not be able to pay its bills and may be delaying payment to vendors. On the other hand, maybe sales are increasing and accounts payable have increased as the company expands. If accounts payable decrease, the company may have negotiated better terms with its suppliers. However, accounts payable may also decline because sales have dropped off.

- **Cash.** If a company's cash is declining, find out why. Using cash to expand operations is fine, but financing operations with cash because revenues have dropped isn't. For example, JNJ's cash fell from $16 billion in 2005 to $9 billion in 2007, perhaps due to the poor economy. However, in 2008, cash was back up to $12 billion, so the dip is probably temporary.

7 Bonds

Many investors disparage bonds as conservative and boring income investments, and go out and search for more exciting opportunities with higher returns. Some safety-conscious investors give bonds *too much* credit and assume they're risk free. The truth is somewhere in between—bonds *can* be conservative and a little boring, but they do come with risks. And some bonds are riskier than others.

Bonds do several things for your investment portfolio. They provide income, which is helpful if you're retired or simply prefer to gad about carefree. Bonds can increase in value before they mature, delivering capital gains (of course, they can decrease in value, resulting in losses). Finally, bonds can reduce the risk in your overall portfolio. But to gain these advantages, you have to use bonds correctly and purchase them wisely.

This chapter begins by looking at why you'd want to invest in bonds. Then you'll learn what bonds are, how they work, and how you can use them to make money. You'll also find out what's important in bonds, whether you're thinking about buying them for income, capital gains, or both. To help you keep your bond investments in the green as much as possible, this chapter also explains the risks you may face when you invest in bonds, and how you can keep those risks at your comfort level.

Why Invest in Bonds?

As you saw above, bonds can play several roles in your investment port-folio. But don't expect a single bond to do everything all the time. Here's a quick overview of what bonds can do for you (the rest of the chapter explains how they do it in detail):

- **Produce income.** Because most bonds pay regularly scheduled interest, many people invest in them and then live on those interest payments. But bond returns typically aren't high enough to *grow* your nest egg to achieve long-term goals, so you probably can't afford to invest *all* your money in bonds. As you'll learn in Chapter 10, you may end up using bond interest, mutual fund distributions (page 63), and, in some cases, small withdrawals of your portfolio's principal to foot the bill for retirement expenses.

- **Produce capital gains.** Bond prices go up when interest rates go down (get the full scoop on page 136). If you buy bonds when interest rates are high and sell them when rates fall, you actually get more money for the bonds than you paid for them. That happens when you buy bonds that pay a high interest rate (to stay competitive with *market* interest rates). If market interest rates fall, bonds that pay higher-than-market rates are worth more. Keep in mind, however, that investing in bonds for capital gains is a lot riskier than holding bonds until they mature, so most individual bond investors simply hold bonds to maturity. Suppose you buy bonds and interest rates go higher instead of lower, and you get into a situation where you *have* to sell them; your bonds will be worth less than what you paid for them and you'll lose money.

- **Reduce your portfolio risk.** If you hold a bond until it matures, you earn income based on the original interest rate the bond issuer quoted (called the *coupon rate*). With top-quality products like U.S. Treasury bonds or AAA-rated corporate bonds, holding them to maturity is al-most a sure bet that you'll make money. Bond prices may go down, but they usually don't drop percentage-wise as much as stock prices.

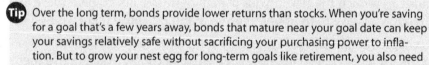

Tip Over the long term, bonds provide lower returns than stocks. When you're saving for a goal that's a few years away, bonds that mature near your goal date can keep your savings relatively safe without sacrificing your purchasing power to infla-tion. But to grow your nest egg for long-term goals like retirement, you also need higher-risk/higher-return investments (see page 156).

How Bonds Work and How You Use Them

If you lend money to friends, you call that an IOU. If you lend your friends money and charge them interest, that's a loan, and you're smart with your money. So what if you lend money to a corporation or a government entity instead? Voilà! You're the proud owner of a bond.

Because bonds are a lot like loans, you already understand a lot about how they work. They borrow money and pay interest on that money for an agreed-upon time, at which point they have repaid the original amount of the loan. Bond investors not only get their original loan back, but they also benefit from the interest on that loan in the interim.

Here's what happens when you buy a bond:

1. **You lend money to a company or government entity.**

   In bond-speak, the company or government entity that borrows your money is called the bond *issuer.* The issuer gives you (the investor) a binding promise—a bond—to pay interest on the borrowed money at a specific rate (the *coupon rate*) for a specific period of time (which ends on the bond's *maturity* date).

2. **The issuer pays you interest on a regular schedule, usually twice a year, until the bond matures (reaches the end of its duration).**

   The borrowed amount is known as the *principal* or the *face amount* of the bond; it's typically $1,000 per bond. For example, if you invest $10,000 in a new bond issue, you buy 10 bonds, each with a face value of $1,000.

3. **When the bond matures, the issuer gives you your principal back.**

Sounds simple, but there's a little more to it. The rest of this section explains what you have to pay attention to and how to choose bonds wisely.

 Note You don't have to hold onto a bond until it matures. However, the price you get when you sell a bond can vary, as you'll learn on page 136.

Many entities issue bonds: the federal government, municipalities, corporations, federal agencies, and foreign governments. You can also buy bonds backed by mortgages or assets (called mortgage-backed or asset-backed securities, because they use the mortgages or assets as collateral). Depending on who issues the bond and the bond's characteristics, you may see bonds referred to as bills, notes, debt securities, or debt obligations.

> **Tip** If you hold bonds in a taxable account, you have to think about the tax implications when you choose which bonds to buy. For example, you don't have to pay state or local income taxes on interest from U.S. Treasury bonds. Municipal bonds from an issuer in your state come completely free of federal, state, or local income tax on the interest they pay. Like everything tax-related, it's complicated. You have to evaluate the federal alternative minimum income tax, your tax bracket, and other taxing minutiae to decide whether bonds with tax advantages make sense for you.

You'll also find funds that invest in bonds, but bonds and bond funds don't work the same way. If you own an individual bond, you can sell it whenever you want to—at maturity, when the bond's market value is higher than its face value, or when you simply need the money. Bond *funds*, on the other hand, *have* to sell bonds when fund investors redeem their shares, regardless of market conditions. By the same token, they *have* to buy bonds when current bonds mature or when investors add to the fund, whether or not the market's favorable. All this means that interest rates affect the returns of bond fund investors more than they affect the returns of individual investors who can pick and choose when to buy and sell their bonds. The table below compares the features of bonds and bond funds and explains why you might choose one over the other.

Bonds	Bond funds
Bond pricing may make it hard for individuals to invest. Bonds have fixed incremental costs of $1,000 (if you buy them when they're issued), and you can't buy just part of a bond.	You can invest small amounts of money and contribute on a regular schedule.
You can buy bonds based on their maturity date, so that they mature when you need your money back.	You can reinvest dividends into the fund.
You can hold a bond to maturity, so you won't lose money.	You can get to your money with less risk than selling a bond before it matures.
You can earn capital gains if interest rates fall, thereby increasing the value of your bond (although most individual investors don't bother with this aspect of bonds).	You can earn capital gains from increasing bond prices if interest rates fall.
Commissions to buy new-issue bonds are lower than mutual fund expenses.	Bond funds diversify your bond investments, which reduces your exposure if you choose to invest in lower-quality but higher-yielding bonds.

Bond Credit Quality

Because bonds pay interest, the first thing you might consider when you buy them is their interest rate. But, in fact, credit quality is your first order of business. As you learned in Chapter 3, owning investments that are riskier than you're comfortable with can cost you plenty. So you want to make sure that the risk level of the bonds you buy gives you a warm and fuzzy feeling.

Credit quality gives you an idea of whether the bond issuer is likely to send your interest payments on time and return your principal when the bond matures. Because most people invest in bonds to reduce their risk, the rule of thumb is "stick with high-quality bonds." This section tells you how to gauge quality.

Avoiding default

If you don't pay your mortgage, your mortgage lender may foreclose on your house. If a bond issuer doesn't make interest payments on time or doesn't return principal to its investors, it's in *default*. When that happens, bondholders like you get in line with a lot of other investors to get their money back. Although you don't want a bond in default, there *is* a bright side: Bondholders have a higher priority than stockholders when a bond issuer cashes in its assets to restructure or liquidate.

Bonds go by different names depending on their claim to company assets. For example, secured bonds are considered the safest, because issuers back them with some type of collateral, that is, assets that the bond issuer pledges toward repayment. The diagram to the right shows the pecking order for investors involved in a default. The lower a security is in the default pecking order, the higher the interest rate it pays because of the higher risk it represents:

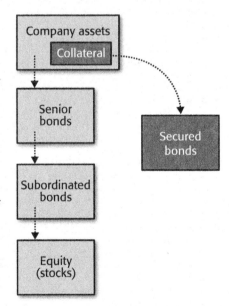

- *Secured bonds* are the safest, because they're backed by collateral. Secured bondholders get first dibs on the collateral.

- *Unsecured bonds* aren't backed by specific collateral. If the issuer defaults, bondholders get in line.

- **Senior bonds** get top priority of all unsecured bonds.
- **Subordinated bonds** get to stake their claim on company assets after senior bonds.
- **Equity** (stock) is last in line after all debt claims.

Much as publicly traded companies have to divulge their finances to shareholders, bond issuers have to spill the beans on their creditworthiness and financial health. (Look for this info in the bond **prospectus**, which describes the bond's terms, features, and risks.) But you don't have to rely solely on the bond issuer for a report on its fiscal health. You can turn to independent rating agencies like Standard & Poor's Corporation (S&P), Moody's Investors Service, or the Fitch Group, which analyze bond issuers' finances and rate the bonds' credit quality.

Just as with school grades, A's go to the top of the bond class. But bond ratings shoot for the moon, because the highest rating from S&P and Fitch is triple-A (listed as **AAA**), and from Moody's it's **Aaa**. Any bond rated BBB/Baa or higher is considered **investment grade**—relatively safe from default. Bonds with lower ratings are called **high-yield** or **speculative** bonds. They pay higher interest rates, but have a much higher risk of default. The table below shows the bond ratings from S&P, Moody's, and Fitch.

What the rating represents	Standard & Poor's	Fitch	Moody's
Top-of-the-line safety	AAA	AAA	Aaa
High quality	AA	AA	Aa
Investment grade good quality	A	A	A
Lowest investment grade (keep your eye on it)	Baa	BBB	BBB
Slightly speculative	Ba	BB	BB
Speculative	B	B	B
On thin ice	Caa	CCC	CCC
Very speculative, possibly in default	Ca	CC	CC
Total junk	C	C	C

 Not all bonds face default risk. Bonds issued by the U.S. government (all Treasury securities and savings bonds, in other words) have the reputation of being risk free of default, because the financial world considers default by the U.S. government impossible.

Unless you're hunting for high returns and are willing to accept the high risk that comes with them, stick with investment-grade bonds. To be on the safe side, start with bonds that have a minimum of an A rating.

Credit ratings can change, especially for longer-term bonds. If you think about it, lots can happen in five years, so it's almost impossible to accurately predict credit quality more than five years into the future. The bottom line: You have to keep an eye on your bonds' ratings. You can ask the broker you used to buy the bond to flag you if the rating changes. Or you can go to one of the rating company websites and look up the rating. For example, on the Standard & Poor's website (*www.standardandpoors.com*), you can type the bond CUSIP number in the "Find a Rating" box to see the current rating.

 The CUSIP numbering system (Committee on Uniform Securities Identification Procedures) provides nine-digit numbers (akin to ticker symbols for stocks) that identify individual bonds. Because each bond has specific characteristics, and because bonds can have confusingly similar names, it's important to find exactly the bond you're buying (or selling); use the CUSIP number to find the right one.

How credit quality affects bond interest rates and prices

Credit ratings aren't just a measure of risk. They affect the interest rate a bond issuer offers, because investors expect higher returns for higher risks. The most creditworthy bond issuers can offer lower interest rates, while risky bonds have to pay higher rates to attract buyers.

Although a bond's coupon rate can't change, the price can (page 136). And it will if the bond's credit rating changes. A bond's price declines if its credit rating drops (and sometimes even before the credit rating drops, if the financial rumor mill is active). While ratings changes affect bond prices, market interest rates have a much stronger effect on prices (page 136).

 Usually, a rating change is minor, one level higher or lower. However, more serious changes include when a bond's rating drops below investment grade, drops more than one level, or drops several times in a brief period. Those are red flags for trouble ahead.

Bond Maturity

For a bond, maturity has nothing to do with acne or voting privileges. Bond maturity is the date in the future when you, the bondholder, get back the money you lent the issuer (the principal). Most bonds mature somewhere between 1 and 30 years from their issue date. You might think that you simply choose bond maturity based on when you want to get back the principal. But bond maturity affects just about every aspect of a bond: the interest rate it pays (see below), how risky it is (page 131), how much its price fluctuates (page 136), and so on.

Bond maturity comes in three categories:

- **Short-term** is any duration up to five years. Short-term bonds usually offer lower returns because they're less risky. (You get your principal back sooner, and they're less sensitive to market interest rates, as you'll learn on page 138.) Those in the know refer to bonds with a duration of less than 1 year as "paper" and use "note" for bonds with a duration between 1 and 10 years.

- **Medium-term** represents durations of from 5 to 12 years.

- **Long-term** is for maturities longer than 12 years. Long-term bonds usually pay the highest returns in exchange for the highest risk and greater price fluctuations.

> **Tip** Bond maturity tells you when you'll get your principal back. However, some bonds (referred to as "callable" bonds) have *call provisions,* which let the issuer redeem the bond before maturity (usually on a specific date and for a specific price). For example, if interest rates drop dramatically, the bond issuer may *call* the bond (pay back the outstanding debt) and then issue new bonds to borrow money at a lower rate. Before you buy a bond, ask your broker if the bond has a call provision, or read the bond offering document that the bond issuer provides. Because this feature protects the bond issuer, you should get a higher annual return than you do for bonds without a call provision.
>
> If you buy a bond at face value and the issuer calls it, you get your money back, but you'll have to invest it in another bond, more than likely at the current lower interest rate.
>
> On the other hand, if you pay a premium for a bond and it's called in early, you could lose a lot of the premium you paid. For example, if you paid $1,100 for a $1,000 face-value bond, you get back the face value only, losing $100 per bond.

Bond Interest Rates

If you're investing for income, the interest rate a bond promises to pay (the coupon rate) is pretty important. But the original interest rate can also determine whether you make or lose money (page 136) when you invest in bonds for capital gains.

Most bonds pay a fixed interest rate (a percentage of the bond's face amount) from the time they're issued until they mature. For example, a bond with a face amount of $1,000 and a 6% interest rate pays $60 in interest each year. (Most bonds pay interest twice a year, so each payment is half the annual amount, $30 in this example.)

 Interest payments are called *coupon payments,* which is why bondholders in the old paper-based days talked about "clipping coupons." They would clip the paper coupons attached to their bonds and send them in to collect their interest payments.

Zero coupon bonds work a little differently. First, instead of making regular interest payments, this type of bond pays one lump sum at maturity that combines interest and principal payments. In addition, you buy a zero coupon bond at a discount from its face value. When the bond matures, you receive the face value, which is the purchase price and all the interest you earned, compounded at the bond's interest rate (coupon rate). For example, a bond with a $1,000 face value that matures in 20 years and has a 6% interest rate may sell initially for $307. At the end of 20 years, you get $1,000, which is your purchase price plus the interest at 6% (compounded twice a year).

One characteristic of zero coupon bonds is their variability in price. For complex financial reasons that would try the patience of Ben Bernanke, zero coupon bond prices fluctuate more than those of regular bonds, so you may notice that variation if you compare the two types of bonds.

 Zero coupon bonds are great when you're saving for a goal in the future. You can invest a smaller amount today in zero coupon bonds that mature when you need the money. In between, you don't have to worry about reinvesting the bond interest.

Convertible bonds are corporate bonds with an option to convert the bond into shares of the company's common stock. They offer the lower risk and more stable returns of a bond along with the potential upside of a stock. For that reason, the interest rates they pay are lower than for regular bonds.

Understanding Bond Prices

As you learned on page 129, when you buy a bond, you get regular interest payments based on the interest rate set when the bond was issued. That original rate doesn't change, whether it's higher or lower than current market interest rates. One of the benefits of a bond is the comfort of knowing your rate of return so long as you hold onto it. Bond *prices* are birds of another feather entirely. They zig when interest rates zag—going up when interest rates go down, going down when interest rates go up.

After a bond is issued, its market price varies, based on its interest rate (coupon rate), market interest rates, the date it matures, the issuer's credit quality, market supply and demand, and more. If you intend to hold onto a bond until it matures, you can skip this section, because face value is the only price you need to know. But plans change, so it's a good idea to understand how bond prices can change, just in case.

When a bond's price is higher than its face value, the bond is selling at a *premium.* When the bond's price is below face value, it's selling at a *discount.* Face value is also known as trading at *par.*

 Note Most of the time, the price quotes you see for bonds aren't based on face value, the way stock quotes are. Instead, bond quotes are a *percentage* of face value, which moves the decimal left one digit. For example, if the face value of a bond is $1,000 and the bond price is now $1,011.26, that's 101.126% of the face value, and the bond's price quote shows up as 101.126. You get the bond's price simply by multiplying the price quote by 10 (101.126 x 10 = $1,011.26). One website where you can see bond quotes is *www.bondsonline.com*, or check the bond section of the Financial Industry Regulatory Authority website (*http://tinyurl.com/finrabonds*).

How market interest rates affect bond prices

When market interest rates go down, prices for issued bonds go up. When market interest rates go up, issued bond prices go down (also known as interest rate risk). Why this contrary behavior? The short answer: to compete with new bonds issued at a higher or lower interest rate.

Here's how this competition works:

- The original interest rate (the coupon rate) is the rate promised when a bond is issued, say 5%.

- After the bond is issued, it has to compete on the open market, with new bonds being issued. Say a new bond pays 6% interest, compared to your bond's 5% coupon rate. Then say you need some cash, and you decide to sell your bond. Your bond's annual interest payments are still

$50, so how can you get someone to buy your bond when new issues pay $60 in interest a year? Somehow, you have to sell your bond so that the buyer gets a 6% interest rate. The way you do that is by dropping the price of your bond.

When someone buys your bond, the *current yield* is the annual interest it generates ($50 in this example) divided by the price they pay—just like the interest rate you get for the bond is the annual interest ($50) divided by the face value ($1,000; $50/$1000 = 5%). To figure out what you can charge for your 5% bond in a market of 6% bonds, you need to remember your algebra. The price you can charge a buyer so that he ends up with 6% interest is your bond's annual interest ($50) divided by the current yield (6%): $50/0.06 or $833.

On the other hand, if a new bond pays 4%, your bond's price would increase to $1,250, because $50 annual interest represents a 4% yield on $1,250.

 Note Financial types love their numbers, and they resort to all sorts of terms of endearment. Bond yield is usually shown in *basis points,* instead of as a percentage. And there's a good reason for that. Say interest rates increase from 5% to 6%. That isn't a 1% increase; it's a 20% increase. Whoa! That's one too many percentages in the translation. So, instead of talking about percentages of percentages, bond traders and investors use basis points to talk about changes in percentages. One hundred basis points is equivalent to 1%, so an increase from 5% to 6% or from 8% to 9% is still 100 basis points.

- Current yield isn't the final earnings on your bond, though. *Yield to maturity* takes into account the interest that the bond pays plus any gain or loss of principal, that is, the total return you get if you hold the bond until it matures. That comes in handy when you want to compare bonds with different maturities and interest rates. Say someone buys your bond for $833. Not only does the new owner earn a 6% yield, but by holding the bond until it matures, she gets back the bond's $1,000 face value, not the $833 purchase price.

Tip Some bond prices, like those backed by mortgages, are based on the *average life* of the bond instead of its maturity. Because homeowners typically prepay mortgages when interest rates go down, the average life of a mortgage-backed security decreases when interest rates drop. If mortgage rates go up, the average life of the security increases.

Interest Rate Risk

You've heard it before: The higher the risk, the higher the return. The flip side is that safer investments offer lower returns. *Interest rate risk* is the risk of losing money on a bond if interest rates go up, and it's a big consideration if you think you might sell your bond before it matures. The simplest way to avoid interest rate risk is to hold a bond until it matures. That way, you don't have to worry about price changes.

But if you plan to sell before maturity, you need to know how much is at risk from interest rate changes. The longer the bond's duration, the more its price jumps around when interest rates change. That's because longer-term bonds have a longer stream of interest payments that don't jibe with current rates.

 If interest rates go down, you make *more* money on long-term bonds than on shorter-term ones.

You can use bond duration as a rough gauge of how much a bond price may change each time the market interest rate goes up or down by 1% (100 basis points). For example, the face value of a bond with a 5-year duration drops about 5% when the market interest rate increases by 100 basis points. The bond's price increases by 5% if market interest rates fall by 100 basis points. So the price of a bond with a 12-year duration would fall 12% for each 1% increase in market interest rate.

 You can take a cue from professional bond managers and adjust your average bond portfolio's duration based on where you think interest rates are headed. If you think interest rates are headed down, increase the duration of your portfolio to turbo-charge how much your bonds increase in price. If you think interest rates will go up, decrease the duration of your bonds so their prices don't drop as much.

Buying Bonds

Buying individual bonds isn't like buying shares of stock. First of all, buying bonds when they're issued is a lot like buying stock in an initial public offering. To get in on the ground floor, you usually need to know someone—like a banker handling the new issue or a financial advisor with an "in."

Even buying individual bonds on the secondary market (that is, from an investor) can be challenging. If you're looking for bonds with specific characteristics (for example, a 10-year AAA-rated corporate bond), you may have to shop around with several dealers to find it. Your best bet is to go to large broker-dealers (well-known brokerages such as Charles Schwab, Merrill Lynch, Scottrade, and so on).

When you buy or sell a bond (or shares in a bond fund), the price quote includes a bid price and an ask price. The difference between the two is called the *spread,* and it's the commission the broker/dealer gets. For example, if a bond quote is 102 bid/104 ask, someone buying the bond pays 104 (actually, $1,040, as you learned on page 136), and the person selling the bond gets 102 ($1,020). The broker gets the remaining 2 ($20).

Spreads can vary from 0.5% to as high as 4%. Low-risk actively traded bonds have the lowest spreads. The more difficult a bond is to sell, the higher the spread. A spread at the high end (4%) could mean the bond is tough to resell, or it could be on shaky ground.

 Say you buy a bond and you see that the price is higher than the quote you received. Don't worry, the broker didn't get greedy. The difference between the price and the quote is from *accrued interest.* Here's what happens: Bonds pay interest twice a year, but the bonds actually accrue interest every day. When you buy a bond, you're entitled to the interest for every day that you own it.

If you buy someone's bond that's in between payment dates (say 2 months after the last payment date), the previous owner is entitled to 2 months' of accrued interest. When you buy the bond, the accrued interest is added to your purchase price and goes to the previous owner. Then, on the next payment date, you receive the interest for the entire period and you're even.

If you want to buy U.S. Treasury bonds, you can get them directly from the government at auction (meaning you pay no sales commission) using the Treasury Direct program (*http://www.treasurydirect.gov/about.htm*). To do so, you open an account with Treasury Direct (so your account is with the Federal Reserve Bank). You can purchase Treasury securities with as little as $1,000 and in additional increments of $1,000. Your account can hold all your Treasury securities, and you can designate another account to receive your interest payments and principal.

Building a Bond Portfolio

As with the rest of your investment portfolio, diversification is the key to success. In other words, don't put all your eggs in one bond. Buy bonds with different maturities to reduce your interest rate risk (page 138). If you want relatively safe bond investments, go for medium-term investment-grade bonds with maturities of 5 to 10 years. Buy bonds from different issuers to spread out the credit risk.

8 REITs

Although the real estate market was really ugly in 2007 and 2008, investing in real estate is still a good way to diversify your investment portfolio. But if you scratched and clawed your way to save for the down payment on your house, you may wonder how you can afford to *diversify* in real estate. Who has the money to buy one rental property, much less several? The good news is, you don't have to have that kind of money: You can diversify in real estate with a small amount of cash by investing in real estate investment trusts (REITs), companies set up specifically to invest in real estate. Some REITs specialize, for example, in shopping centers or office buildings, while others focus on real estate in certain geographic regions.

REITs trade on U.S. stock exchanges, so you buy shares just like you do in any other stock. For even more real estate diversification, you can buy into a REIT mutual fund or REIT exchange-traded fund (page 62).

Like the economy and other parts of the stock market, real estate is *cyclical*, which means that prices cycle up and down over time. With the United States just beginning to emerge from a horrendous real estate market crash, you might blanch at the idea of investing in real estate, but it's probably a good time to buy (see page 143 for reasons why).

This chapter begins with the pros and cons of investing in REITs. If you're interested in branching out into REITs, you'll learn about the different types. Then, the chapter dives into what to look for in REIT investments. Finally, you'll learn how to find individual REITs, REIT mutual funds, and REIT ETFs.

Is REIT Investing Right for Me?

For most folks, buying individual investment properties is out of the question. Coming up with a down payment to buy real estate and then making ends meet is tough. Then, as a landlord, you have to deal with finding tenants, running credit checks, collecting rents, keeping up with maintenance, and evicting deadbeat renters. Even if you *can* afford to buy a building or two or three, REITs are a no-muss no-fuss alternative to the hassle of owning individual properties. By owning shares in a REIT, you turn over all those icky property-management tasks to a professional building manager.

The Pros

By law, REITs have to invest primarily in real estate and pay out 90% of their income to shareholders. So when a REIT makes money, shareholders get dividends—and usually attractive ones. In addition, a REIT's share price goes up if its earnings and the market's perception of the value of its holdings and management skills increase. So with the right REIT, you can earn good income *and* capital gains. (Of course, shares can go down, as many have during the recent real estate market crisis.)

Most REITs own hundreds of properties, something you could never afford to do, unless you're Donald Trump. Because many REITs specialize in property types or geographic regions, you can use REITs to diversify your portfolio *and* the types of real estate investments you make.

The Cons

As with other pooled investments like mutual funds, you count on REIT investment managers to make advantageous decisions. If they don't, REIT share price and yield are both at risk.

Although REITs usually pay high dividends (5% or 6% isn't uncommon, as you can see on page 143), the government taxes them at ordinary income rates, not at capital gains and dividend tax rates, which are lower. You can get around that by holding REITs in a tax-advantaged account, like an IRA or Roth IRA.

A Lesson in REIT Returns

Like other types of investments, REIT returns vary, as their share prices go up or down. The good news is that REIT *dividends* are a great source of income and don't vary the way the REIT share price does. Most REITs set their dividend payout and leave it there. They avoid reducing their dividends, because that's the investment's main attraction. The table below shows REIT returns and dividends from 2003 to 2009 (from the US Real Estate Index, published by the National Association of Real Estate Investment Trusts, a REIT trade association). Oversupply and over-borrowing contributed to the dramatic plunge in REIT prices in 2007 and 2008. But better-managed REITs are taking advantage of the opportunity to pick up foreclosed properties in 2009 and into 2010 and stand to gain when the market and the U.S. economy recover.

Year	Total return	Dividend yield
2003	38.97%	5.75%
2004	30.41%	4.97%
2005	8.29%	5.06%
2006	34.35%	4.06%
2007	−17.83%	5.29%
2008	−37.34	8.37%
2009	27.45%	4.63%

Types of REITs

Like other types of investments, REITs come in a variety of shapes and sizes. If you opt to buy individual REITs, you can fine-tune the portion of the real estate market you invest in.

How REITs Make Money

REITs can invest in physical real estate, or in mortgages that other parties take out to buy physical real estate. So REITs come in three types:

- **Equity REIT.** A REIT that makes a profit by buying, selling, building, renovating, and managing real estate.

- **Mortgage REIT.** One that invests in real estate mortgages and earns money by lending to Equity REITs.

- **Hybrid REIT.** A REIT that invests in both real estate and mortgages.

REITs that buy property sometimes specialize in segments of the real estate market. If you think health-care real estate is going to explode as baby boomers retire, you may decide to stick to a REIT in that area. However, specialized REITs are riskier if a downturn hits their target investments. Here are some of the industries and types of property that equity REITs specialize in:

- **Retail.** Invests in retail-oriented real estate, such as shopping malls, strip malls, and convenience stores.

- **Residential.** Includes residential condos and apartment buildings.

- **Industrial/office.** Invests in warehouses, industrial parks, and office buildings.

- **Health care.** Represents medical offices, surgery centers, assisted living, and nursing homes.

- **Lodging/resort.** Invests in hotels, motels, and resort properties.

- **Self-storage.** As you may have guessed, focuses on self-storage properties.

- **Entertainment.** Includes movie theaters, theme parks, and other entertainment-related properties.

- **Specialty.** This a mish-mash of specialty properties, such as timberland and gas stations.

Picking Individual REITs

Choosing individual REITs to invest in is a lot like choosing any individual company. First, look at a REIT's strategy to see how it tries to make money, and then dig into the bottom line to see whether it's succeeding. Check out the REIT's track record for things like increasing earnings, sales, and dividends. Then compare its performance to other REITs.

Looking at Strategy

Identifying a REIT's strategy (the types of property it invests in) is similar to checking out a fund's investment objectives. REITs spell out their strategies in their annual reports and on their websites (look for the About Us or Press section).

Because REITs invest in real estate, the characteristics you evaluate are a bit different from those of other investments. Here's what to look for:

- **Property type.** The types of properties the REIT invests in. If you simply want to diversify into real estate, you can look for REITs that aren't specialized. However, you can invest in specialized REITs to take advantage of economic trends. For instance, residential REITs may catch your eye if you think that a big increase in house foreclosures means higher occupancy in apartment buildings.

- **Property location.** Where those properties are located. If you're considering a regional REIT, look for an area that's growing—or at least, not in a real estate crisis. (In early 2010, California, Florida, Nevada, Arizona, and Michigan were still the poster children for real estate problems.)

- **Total square footage.** Total square footage in millions. The more square footage a REIT owns, the more diversified it is. Even if one building runs into trouble, others in the REIT portfolio can keep performance from deteriorating too much.

- **Occupancy rate.** The percentage of total square footage leased to tenants is particularly important because it tells you how much owned space earns rent from tenants and how much is vacant. An occupancy rate of 85% is the minimum you want to see; 90% or more is great. A high vacancy rate almost always means the REIT is losing money.

- **Percentage of total annualized base rent.** This measures how much of the REIT's total rental income comes from a particular tenant each year. A REIT that's overly dependent on a single tenant or type of tenant could end up with lots of vacant space and lots less revenue if a major tenant leaves or goes out of business. The top 10 tenants should account for no more than 3% to 5% of total annualized base rent.

- **Tenants.** A list of the top 10 tenants. If the top 10 tenants do represent a big chunk of the REIT's square footage, you can use this list to see whether those tenants are on solid financial footing.

Looking at the Bottom Line

A well-managed REIT pays dividends and often increases in share price. Of course, shares can go down, too. In that case, you may want to hold on to or buy more shares while the price is low. To make good decisions, you have to do your homework. Here's the bottom-line performance you want:

- **Steadily increasing dividends over several years.** Because REITs pay dividends out of profits, a REIT that isn't consistently profitable can't afford to increase dividends. Steady dividend increases mean that the REIT has been profitable in the past and that management is confident revenues and earnings will increase in the future.

- **Reinvesting cash into new opportunities, buying buildings, or developing new projects.** REITs have to pay out the bulk of their income in dividends, so they either borrow money or issue stock to finance the purchase of buildings or to develop new projects. To find out what a

REIT is working on, check out the projects under development in its annual report. You can also see whether the REIT has borrowed money or issued stock recently from the shareholder annual report, the 10-K (the annual report that the SEC requires), and the 10-Q (the SEC-mandated quarterly report).

- **Increasing profits.** REITs increase profits on the properties they own by raising rent and lease prices in favorable markets. When times are bad, however, as they are now, that's hard to do. REITs often have to cut rents and lease rates or offer special deals to lure tenants. At the same time, they can't neglect property maintenance and improvements. In times like these, you have to adjust your expectations of performance: Some REITs may increase their profits, but for many, flat sales and earnings or losing less money than other REITs is about the best you can hope for.

To sort out the good REITs from the bad ones, focus on the quality of management. Smart REIT managers avoid problems like chronic construction delays and cost overruns. To see the status of a REIT's projects, check out the company's annual reports, its 10-K, and its 10-Q. In the "Management Discussion and Analysis" section of the 10-K and 10-Q, watch out for signs of development projects dragging on from year to year. Some construction delays are unforeseen—for example, the bank providing financing being seized by regulators. But if projects are continually delayed due to funding, permits, or resources issues, it's a sign of poor management.

 Location, location, location is just as true for commercial real estate markets as it is for residential properties. While many commercial real estate markets are reeling (California and Florida come to mind), other markets are holding up. For Washington, DC, and suburban Maryland and Virginia, 2009 was a good year. The federal government expanded, and businesses working with the federal government did, too.

Depreciation and Real Estate

Because REITs' major assets are real estate, they account for depreciation differently from most other companies. You need to look at a few specialized financial measures to gauge a REIT's performance.

Assets like equipment lose value over time. Using regular accounting rules, depreciation and amortization reduce a company's revenues and earnings per share. But real estate usually increases in value. For that reason, funds from operations, adjusted funds from operations, and operating net income per share are a better gauge of performance than earnings per share:

- **Funds from operations** (FFO), also known as *income from continuing operations,* doesn't include depreciation, gains, or losses from sales of property, so it shows how much money the REIT makes from rents and leases.
- **Adjusted funds from operations** (AFFO) is a version of FFO that includes special depreciation calculations designed to better measure a REIT's operating cash flow.
- **Operating net income per share** focuses on a REIT's net income after operating expenses but excludes income taxes and interest.

As with revenue and earnings per share for other companies, with REITs you want to look for steady increases in the money generated by operations, adjusted funds from operations, and operating net income per share, which are better than flip-flops of big increases to losses from year to year.

A REIT reports income and expenses much like other types of companies, as you can see below. To see REIT income and expenses using Morningstar.com, do the following:

1. **At *www.morningstar.com*, in the Quote box, type the REIT's name or ticker symbol.**

   As you type letters in the box, a drop-down list shows the investments that match what you've typed so far.

2. **On the horizontal navigation bar, click Financials. Then, click the 10-Yr Income tab.**

   The 10-Yr Income tab shows you values from the previous 10 years, perfect for seeing how consistent a REIT's performance is.

3. **To calculate operating income per share, first find the operating income and the number of shares (shown in millions at the very bottom of the page). Then, divide operating income by the number of shares.**

Most REITs include FFO and AFFO information in their quarterly reports and SEC filings, which you can access from their corporate websites.

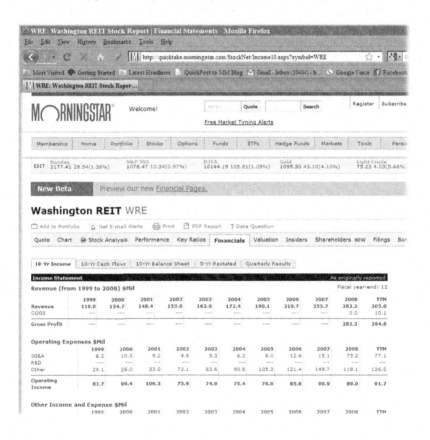

Finding the Right REITs and REIT Funds

Just as with other types of investments, the best way to find a REIT or REIT fund is with a screening tool, as you can see below.

Screening REITs

For individual REITs, MSN Money's stock screener is a great place to start (*http://tinyurl.com/qqh9*). Here's what you do:

1. **To find REITs that don't specialize by industry, select REIT - Diversified.**

   If you want to invest in a specific part of the real estate market, scroll to REIT in the drop-down list, and then pick one of the specialized REIT entries, like REIT-Healthcare Facilities.

2. **If you want a REIT to fit into the large-cap, mid-cap, or small-cap portion of your portfolio, in the Market Cap box, choose the size you want.**

   If you don't care, select Any.

3. **In the Dividend Yield box, select Any.**

   You want income, but if you start your screen with "As high as possible", you may not get any results. All REITs pay dividends, so choosing Any starts you off with several candidates.

4. **In the Revenue Growth box, select "As high as possible".**

   Although you filter by revenue growth, don't put too much weight on year-over-year growth. Long-term growth trends are more important. Still, this filter delivers decent REITs you can inspect for long-term sales and earnings growth.

5. **With a short-list of candidates, put them under the microscope as described on page 144.**

Screening REIT Funds

If you really want to diversify in real estate, REIT *funds* cover more ground than individual REITs and often offer low costs and low minimum investments. By investing in a REIT fund, you spread your risk among all the REITs it owns. Just like other types of funds, REIT funds come in actively managed, index, ETF, and closed-end flavors, and have the same pros and cons as they do (see page 72 in Chapter 5 for what they are).

Screening is the key to wading through hundreds of REIT funds and ETFs. Morningstar's basic screening tool is the best way to whittle down the hordes of REIT funds (see the image below). Here's how:

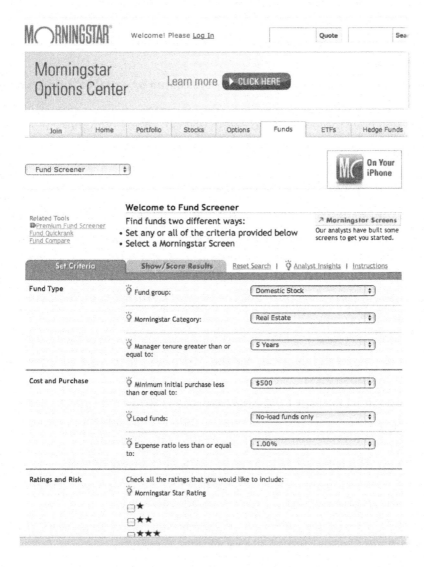

1. **On Morningstar.com's home page, in the horizontal navigation bar, click Tools. Under Screening Tools, find the Basic Screener section, and click the "mutual fund" link.**

   The mutual fund screener page appears.

2. **In the "Fund group" box, choose Domestic Stock. In the Morningstar Category box, choose Real Estate.**

   These two choices ensure that the results you see are REIT mutual funds.

3. **In the "Manager tenure greater than or equal to" box, choose "5 Years".**

   That way, you find funds whose managers have a track record you can evaluate.

4. **In the "Minimum initial purchase less than or equal to" box, choose $500.**

   If you have more money to invest, you can choose a higher value.

5. **In the "Load funds" box, choose "No-load funds only".**

   As you learned on page 89, paying a load takes away from the money you invest and the returns you earn.

6. **In the "Expense ratio is less than or equal to" box, choose 1.00%.**

   If you don't find any funds that meet your criteria, you may consider increasing this to 1.5%. Expenses reduce the returns you earn every year, so keep them low.

7. **In the Returns section, set the 10-year return boxes to "Category average".**

   There's no reason to look at REIT funds with below-average returns.

8. **In the Portfolio section, for the "Turnover less than or equal to" box, choose 75%.**

   If you don't find any funds that meet the 75% test, you may try increasing turnover to 150%. If you buy the fund in a tax-advantaged account, higher turnover isn't as harmful, as you learn on page 90.

9. **To see the funds that pass your tests, click Show Results.**

   If the filter doesn't have any funds that pass your tests, you can change some of your tests to "Category average" or "Any".

For REIT ETFs, use the Index Universe screen described on page 95. Under Select Asset Classes, turn on the Real Estate checkbox.

9 Manage Your Portfolio

Y ou invest because you want your money to work hard to help you reach your financial goals. Low-return, low-risk investments won't grow your nest egg to where it needs to be. But high returns come with the risk of large losses. So, crafting a successful investment portfolio is a balancing act between return and risk.

"Don't put all your eggs in one basket" is sage advice, whether you invest in stocks, bonds, real estate, or (especially) Fabergé eggs. If you dump all your dough into one investment, you could win big or you could lose it all. Sadly, regardless of how carefully you choose investments, you won't pick a winner every time. The simple solution to earning a decent investment return without risking everything you've got is *asset allocation,* that is, investing in different types of investments (stocks, bonds, funds, and real estate, for example) in your portfolio at the same time. You can diversify your portfolio further by diversifying each type of investment within your portfolio. For example, in the stock portion of your portfolio, you might invest in firms of different sizes, industries, sectors, or geographic regions.

Of course, you have to *build* an investment portfolio before you can *manage* one, but the two tasks are similar. This chapter starts by giving you an overview of returns and risks for different types of investments. Then you'll learn about asset allocation, investing portions of your portfolio in different investments to obtain the combination of return and risk you want. Because diversifying is more challenging when you're just beginning and have only a small amount of money, this chapter gives you some hints on how to get started.

Once you have your portfolio plan in place, you have three main tasks. Every so often, you tweak your portfolio to keep your asset allocation on target (page 170). At the same time, you play defense, that is, you keep an eye on your portfolio so it doesn't get hurt. For example, if an investment starts to nosedive, you want to get out before it hits the ground. Finally, you look for ways to improve your portfolio by, for example, looking for funds with lower expenses, higher returns, or less volatile performance.

What's Investment Portfolio Management?

Portfolio management starts with planning. The financial goals you identified in Chapter 2 kick-start the process, because that's where you determine how much money you need and when. After that, you figure out how you're going to invest and keep an eye on your portfolio to make sure it stays on track.

Here are the basic steps:

1. **Identify your tolerance for risk, and understand the investment risks you face.**

   As you learned on page 156, you have to build an investment portfolio whose risk is in line with what you can tolerate. Your tolerance for risk is probably different from that of other investors. And it can change based on life events like retirement. Although investment risks are explained in detail in other chapters, page 158 provides a quick review.

2. **Choose the percentage of your portfolio you want to allocate to different types of investments.**

   On page 160, you learn about *asset allocation,* dividing your money between different investments to reduce your overall risk and to provide a smoother ride of investment returns.

3. **Document your investment plan and the guidelines to follow.**

   Memories have a way of fading or playing tricks. As page 45 explains, investors' best intentions can get tripped up by psychological pitfalls. To help you stay on course, put your portfolio plan in writing: Record the risks you're willing to take, your target asset allocation, the guidelines you'll use in evaluating your investments, and the triggers for when you buy or sell.

4. **If you haven't opened any investment accounts yet, now's the time to do so. Start contributing to your accounts and buying investments according to your plan.**

   Chapters 10, 11, and 12 describe the different types of accounts you can use to invest for retirement, a college education, and health care. While you're at it, set up automatic deposits so your financial institution regularly withdraws the amounts you want to contribute from your checking or savings account. (You usually don't miss what you don't see in your checking account.)

5. **Review *individual* investments regularly, for example, with individual stocks at least quarterly to make sure they're performing up to your expectations (see Chapters 5 through 8 for more detail).**

   The best way to make sure you do quarterly reviews is to have your investment statements delivered automatically. Depending on the brokerage you use, you may be able to set up reminders that notify you when quarterly reports or earnings are released. You may also be able to set up alerts to notify you of important events like prices at which you may consider buying or selling.

   Tip Don't overreact. Analyze investment performance and the reasons behind it before you decide whether you really want to buy or sell.

6. Review your overall investment portfolio regularly, too, although you can do it annually or semiannually, and make changes if necessary.

   For example, you usually adjust your asset allocation to reduce risk as you approach retirement. Page 168 tells you how often to review your overall portfolio.

Return vs. Risk

Stocks are risky in the short term, because they can drop like a rock in any single year (sometimes in any single week). Over the long term, though, they produce the kind of returns you need to grow your portfolio. Fixed-income investment returns aren't nearly as volatile (especially when you hold bonds until they mature), but they don't deliver enough growth hormones to your nest egg. So what kinds of returns can you expect from different types of investments and at what risk? Can you earn attractive returns without too much risk? It turns out you *can* have it both ways, as you'll learn on page 160.

The table below compares returns for intermediate- and long-term fixed-income investments, large stocks, and small stocks, from 1926 through the end of 2008. As you can see, the long-term average annual returns and real returns (that is, the return adjusted for inflation) for stocks are almost twice those for fixed-income investments. For example, the real return for government bonds beats inflation by only a few percentage points. (Treasury bills [not listed below], which are short-term government bonds, delivered a real return of only 0.7% during the same period.)

The single best years for stocks are likely to make you salivate. However, if you had everything riding on small-company stocks and retired just before the Depression, you would have lost almost 90% of your retirement fund between 1929 and 1932, which is why the Great Depression was so grim and why you want a diversified portfolio that delivers more consistent returns from year to year.

Investment type	Annualized return	Real return	Single best year	Single worst year	Return from 1929 to 1932
Intermediate-term bonds	5.4%	2.3%	14.7%	0.0%	20.3%
Long-term government bonds	5.7%	2.6%	40.4%	−9.2%	19.7%
Large-company stocks	9.6%	6.4%	54.0%	−43.4%	−64.2%
Small-company stocks	11.7%	8.5%	142.9%	−58.0%	−88.0%

You probably noticed in the table above that stock returns for 1-year periods are all over the map (the largest 1-year loss for large stocks was 43.4%; in 1931, small stocks fell 58%), but the risk of losing money in stocks literally melts away with time. The combination of higher long-term returns and lower long-term risk is why stocks are essential to long-term investment plans.

The graph below shows the real returns that stocks and bonds provide over different holding periods. Over 20-year periods, stocks not only haven't lost money, they've delivered positive real returns (page 156) of between 1% and 12.6%. Fixed-income investments (bonds), though, had one 20-year period where the real return was –3%. During that period, a bond portfolio would have lost almost half its purchasing power! Even over 30 years, bonds still had one period where the real return was –2.0%.

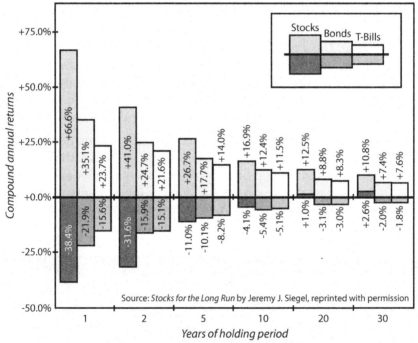

Source: *Stocks for the Long Run* by Jeremy J. Siegel, reprinted with permission

Years of holding period

Maximum and minimum real holding period returns, 1802-1997

Tip If your company has an employee stock purchase plan, don't overindulge at the company stock buffet. If your company starts to struggle, you could end up out of work and losing money in your retirement plan as well.

Face Your Fears: Understanding Investment Risks

You can't avoid risk no matter how you invest your money. You worry that your nest egg will spoil from stock price gyrations or mayhem in the markets. At the same time, you know inflation is picking away at your boiled nest egg every moment. Some risks decrease over time, while others get worse. Here's a quick review of the different types of investment risk and how you can manage them:

- **Inflation risk.** Chapter 1 showed just how dangerous inflation (the steady increase in prices) can be. It's the one investment risk that gets worse with time. The higher returns of owning stocks long-term are the sure antidote to inflation risk (page 14).

- **Economic risk.** This is the risk of losing money in investments because the economy tanks. The economy tends to cycle up and down every 5 years or so. The down cycle, known as a recession, can last from a few months to, occasionally, a few years. As with inflation, owning stocks for longer than the typical economic cycle helps overcome economic risk. You can also avoid economic risk by keeping near-term spending money in safer investments like short-term bonds or a savings account.

- **Market risk.** Sometimes, perfectly good investments go down in value just because the market as a whole goes down. And sometimes, mediocre investments go up because the overall market goes up. The key to managing market risk is researching the investments you buy and sticking to your plan as long as those investments are still fundamentally sound.

Up to Speed

Don't Forget Dividends

Although the dividends investments pay may seem small, they're a big part of the long-term returns you receive. The key to success is reinvesting those dividends into additional shares of stocks or bonds. That way, you put compounding (page 16) to work for you again. Every time you get a dividend, you reinvest it into buying more shares. Therefore, your next dividend will be even larger, which means you can reinvest into even *more* shares. And of course, you *own* more shares, so your portfolio value increases more when the stock price goes up.

Say you invested $100 in the Standard & Poor's 500-stock average in 1926. If you spent all the dividends you received, your portfolio would have reached approximately $7,079 by the end of 2008. That's a 708% increase! It sounds good until you see that reinvesting your dividends would have grown your $100 to $204,945, a 2,049% increase!

- **Equity risk.** Many investors are afraid of losing money on a bad investment, which is called equity risk. True, companies can go under, taking your investment with them. But equity risk is easy to manage by diversifying your portfolio, that is, by buying several different investments to dilute the effect of one underachiever.

- **Holding period risk.** This is the risk that you have to sell an investment when its price has fallen. It's a good idea to keep some money in short-term investments so you don't have to sell long-term investments when their values are down.

- **Reinvestment risk.** When you invest in bonds, bills, or even certificates of deposit and hold them until they mature, you face reinvestment risk, the risk that interest rates are lower when your fixed-income investment matures and that you have to reinvest your money in a new investment with a lower interest rate. Unfortunately, reinvestment risk is a fact of life with any kind of fixed-income investment you hold to maturity.

- **Interest rate risk.** If you buy a bond and sell it before it matures, you face interest rate risk, the risk that the bond price drops because interest rates rise (see page 136).

- **Currency risk.** If you invest in foreign stocks or bonds, currency risk comes into play. If the dollar falls compared to your investment's currency, your investment loses value. Currency exchange rates work in your favor when the dollar is strong compared to other currencies.

 Tip When your portfolio grows large enough or you're well ahead of your plan, you may yearn to gamble on higher-risk investments, such as *micro-company stocks* or *high-yield bonds*. As a rule of thumb, the average investor shouldn't invest more than 10% in high-risk investments.

Asset Allocation

Smart investors don't pursue the current investment rage (because they know it's already old news). Nor do they try to trounce market averages. Instead, they use a simple approach that delivers the goods: asset allocation. This strategy involves divvying up your investment portfolio among different types of investments (called asset classes) based on the level of risk you want. In short, you invest in stocks for long-term higher returns, bonds to reduce your overall risk and to earn income, and cash for near-term expenses. The allocation you choose for your risk level, in turn, determines the average return your portfolio is likely to achieve. Once you know the level of risk you want (as you learned on page 156), you choose an asset allocation appropriate for that risk level, invest according to your allocation, and stick with it.

Different types of investments present different types of risks (page 158 describes the most common ones). Using asset allocation to diversify your portfolio helps reduce your risk and improve your returns in several ways:

- **Playing to each asset class's strength.** Instead of worrying about each type of investment risk you face, you can play them off each other. For example, long-term average annual returns for stocks are three times that of inflation or the return on Treasury bills, so they're a perfect investment for long-term goals. A one-two punch of stock investments and time defeats inflation risk and equity risk.

What's Your Risk Tolerance?

Balancing return and risk is essential, because greed and fear can mess up the best financial plans. (See page 45 to learn about psychological mistakes many people make when investing.) By matching your portfolio risk to your personal risk tolerance, you can sleep soundly while your investments are hard at work.

Figuring out your true risk tolerance is more complicated than the approaches taken by most online tools. But you can get a sense of your tolerance with any of the following tests:

- MSN Money offers a risk tolerance quiz (*http://tinyurl.com/msnmoney-risk*) that tells you two things: how comfortable you are taking risks and whether your personal circumstances are such that you can afford to take risks.
- The Rutgers University website offers a risk tolerance quiz (*http://tinyurl.com/rutgers-risk*) that identifies how comfortable you are with risk.
- CalcXML.com (*http://www.calcxml.com/do/inv08*) determines your tolerance for risk by asking 10 questions about you, your financial situation, and how you would respond to several situations.

Your brokerage may also offer a tool for determining risk tolerance. For example, the Charles Schwab website has a risk profile questionnaire (*http://tiny.cc/k4xp7*) that analyzes your risk tolerance and investment timeframe to determine what type of investor you are.

But because your stocks need time to recover from the bottom of a business cycle or bad news about a company, you also need other types of investments. Enter fixed-income investments, which deliver more dependable returns. Although bond returns sometimes don't beat inflation, you use bonds and other fixed-income investments for overall portfolio stability. In effect, you take on small risks, like interest rate risk and reinvestment risk, to counteract the risks from stocks. REITs offer both attractive dividends and potential capital appreciation, so they help reduce overall risk further.

 Tip As you'll learn on page 190, you also keep money you'll need in the near future in very safe investments like short-term bonds, money market accounts, certificates of deposit, or savings accounts. By keeping an emergency fund, you counteract economic risk, holding period risk, and interest rate risk.

- **Building a broad base.** Commuting in a car with four wheels is easier and more stable than riding a bicycle, which is more dependable than a unicycle, which is preferable by far to using a pogo stick. By owning different types of investments, you ensure that your overall portfolio doesn't zigzag wildly. Some types of investment do well in environments that put other types of investments into a tailspin. For example, high market interest rates mean more income for investors who buy and hold bonds, but high rates drag stock prices down. (That's because investors would rather buy bonds, which are less risky than stocks, when bonds deliver a return that's close to that of stocks.) With a mixture of asset classes, your portfolio returns from year to year are more consistent.

If you buy individual stocks or bonds, diversification means no one investment can seriously harm your portfolio. Regardless of how thoroughly you research investments, some do better than you expect, some do worse, and most perform about on target. If you own one stock and it drops 50%, you lose 50%. If you divide your investment equally among 10 stocks and one drops 50% while the others remain at their original prices, your portfolio loses only 5%. If another one of those 10 stocks does spectacularly well, you may still come out ahead.

 Tip If you want to learn more about asset allocation, check out the SEC (Securities and Exchange Commission) article "Beginner's Guide to Asset Allocation" at *http://tinyurl.com/SEC-assets.*

Other Ways to Diversify

If you're just starting out in personal investing, you can keep diversification plain and simple, as you learn on page 166. With time and a larger portfolio, you may decide to diversify your investments in several ways: by different-sized companies, by market sectors and industries, or by geographic regions. The following table explains how these types of diversification can help your portfolio.

Diversification by	Effect
Asset class	A mixture of stocks, bonds, REITs, and cash offers better overall returns with more dependable year-to-year performance.
Company size	Large companies often grow more slowly but more consistently than small companies. Small companies may grow quickly, but they're riskier.
Sector and industry	Take advantage of sectors and industries that can benefit from circumstances, such as pharmaceuticals as the baby boomer generation ages and needs more medications. Protect your portfolio from sectors and industries that fall out of favor or that get hurt by unfavorable government regulations.
Geography	U.S. and foreign companies sometimes cycle through peaks and valleys at different times.

 Tip If you invest in individual securities or in funds because you want to outperform the market, don't diversify *too* much. If you diversify among industries, sectors, regions, and individual securities, your portfolio starts to echo the market. Although you spend time managing your investments and paying commissions and fees, your portfolio may deliver the same return you could have gotten more easily from an index fund. Page 85 tells you how to compare your portfolio to an index.

Choosing an Asset Allocation Plan

Your tolerance for risk is unique, as is each of your financial goals, so you have to choose an asset allocation that fits both your risk profile and the goal for which you're investing. For example, the asset allocation you use for retirement is different from the one for your kid's college education. The key to success is sticking to your plan, so you have to buy and sell investments from time to time to keep your allocation on target (page 170).

At the same time, change is inevitable, so your asset allocation isn't cast in concrete. When major life events such as marriage, children, divorce, or retirement occur, it's time to reevaluate and reset your asset allocation plan (page 188).

The table below shows how different types of asset allocation work for people in different phases of their life.

Asset allocation return and risk	Retirement	College	Financial situation
5% to 6.5% return. Low risk.	Elderly retired couple who live on portfolio income and capital and can't afford losses.	Family paying expenses for children in college.	Family with little disposable income.
6.5% to 8.5% return. Medium risk.	Younger retired couple with many years of retirement ahead and enough assets to tolerate occasional losses.	Family saving for college 3 to 5 years in the future.	Family that can save some money.
8.5% to 10.5% return. High risk.	Young couple saving for retirement 30 to 40 years in the future.	Young couple starting a college fund before child is born.	Dual-income couple with no children.

You're probably wondering about the asset class allocations that deliver those pairings of return and risk. Suppose you start with a basic allocation of stocks, bonds, REITs, and cash. For a major goal like college education or retirement, figuring out the percentage for each of these asset classes is as easy as 1-2-3:

1. **Put the money you need within the next 5 years into safe short-term investments.**

   Create a cash reserve of low-risk low-return investments to cover your goal expenses for the next 3 to 5 years; that's the time it typically takes stocks to recover from recessions and other temporary setbacks. For example, when you're 5 years away from retirement or already retired, keep 5 years' worth of living expenses in safe choices like savings accounts, money market accounts, certificates of deposit, and short-term bonds.

2. **With your cash reserve set aside, choose the percentage of stocks based on your return-risk profile.**

Once you have your cash reserve in place, you can put 10% of the remaining portfolio money in stocks, even if you want a low-risk portfolio. The typical low-risk asset allocation contains between 10% and 30% in stocks. A medium-risk allocation has between 30% and 60% in stocks. A long-term high-risk portfolio invests from 50% to 100% in stocks.

As you gain more experience, you may decide to split your asset allocation into finer slivers by allocating, for example, a percentage of your funds to foreign stocks or small company stocks. You'll see some examples of different types of allocations on page 167.

If you have very little money and your financial goal is near at hand, you may not have much money to put in stocks or bonds. In that case, set up your cash reserve first. Then, apply your stock percentage to the money that's left. For example, if you have $10,000 saved, but need $5,000 for upcoming expenses, allocate the remaining $5,000 to stocks and bonds.

3. **Choosing the percentage for bonds and REITs is easy. It's what's left after you complete steps 1 and 2.**

As you can see, both the money and time you have at your disposal affect your asset allocation. When retirement is decades away, you don't need a cash reserve. But if retirement is at hand, you must be more conservative with your asset allocation.

 Some financial professionals recommend a rough rule of thumb for retirement asset allocation: Use your age as the percentage of bonds in your portfolio. For example, when you're 20 years old, you invest 20% in bonds and 80% in stocks. At age 90, you would have 90% in bonds and only 10% in stocks. However handy, this guideline doesn't consider your marital status, health, lifestyle, and so on.

Be Reasonable

The asset allocation you choose takes the lead in delivering the average annual return you earn. As the table on page 163 shows, 7% is a middle-of-the-road goal. That return beats inflation by a respectable amount. You can achieve this return without spending every weekend studying investments or taking high risks trying to beat the market.

You may be tempted by high returns that some funds or investments have delivered in the past. Keep in mind that no actively managed fund has consistently beaten the market over long periods of time (10 years or more). Investments that appear to beat the market often come with sky-high expenses, which bring their returns back to the market average (see page 90).

Using an Online Asset Allocation Tool

Online asset allocation tools help you choose your asset allocation plan based on your financial situation and risk tolerance. You tell the tool things like your age, how much money you have already, how much you can contribute each year, how much you'll spend in the future, and so on. The tools show you percentage allocations in different asset classes based on your choices. Major brokerages often have online asset allocation tools to help clients decide how to invest. Here are a couple of examples:

- **SmartMoney's One Asset Allocation System.** This free tool (*http://tinyurl.com/smartmoneyallocator*) helps you choose your asset allocation by dragging sliders to the left or right, as you can see below. You set your age, your current portfolio value, your yearly savings, how much you'll spend in the next 10 years (for example, for retirement living expenses), the percentage income you require from your portfolio, your tax bracket, your risk tolerance, and your perception of the strength of the economy. The web page explains asset allocation and how to use the tool.

- **Charles Schwab Portfolio Solutions.** Charles Schwab offers a simple tool (*http://tinyurl.com/schwab-portfoliosolution*) that helps you choose an asset allocation based on your risk profile. It has five risk profiles, from conservative to aggressive. When you point to a profile, a pie chart shows the suggested asset allocation and provides some details about it, such as the time horizon and the average annual return. To see mutual funds that Schwab suggests for each asset class, click "See sample portfolio" below the pie chart.

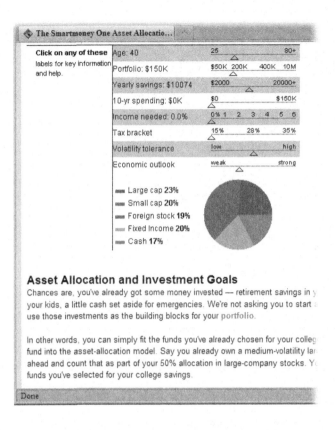

Asset Allocation Made Ridiculously Easy

In Chapter 5, you learned how index funds are a low-cost way to diversify your portfolio among all sorts of investments. They provide instant diversification, because they own many individual investments within categories like large and small companies, industries and sectors, bonds, and geographical regions. Because they follow indexes, their expenses and turnover are low. In this chapter, you've learned how allocating your money to different types of investments is the biggest factor in balancing the return and risk of your portfolio. Put those two ideas together, and you get the no-muss no-fuss method for successful investing: the *lazy portfolio.* You choose your asset allocation plan and then set up automatic purchases of index funds (mutual funds or ETFs) for each asset class. That's it! No need to peruse every inch of the *Wall Street Journal* or to hide in a cave when the markets turn ugly. Sit back and relax while your asset allocation, investments, and time do their jobs.

As you learn on page 168, you revisit your portfolio and asset allocation every so often to make sure they still meet your needs.

Building a Lazy Portfolio

If you contribute to your employer's 401(k) or 403(b) plan, you're already on your way to a lazy portfolio. All you have to do is set up your contributions according to the asset allocation percentages you chose (assuming that your employer's plan offers funds for the asset classes you want). Then, with each paycheck, your company's plan administrator takes care of investing your money per your instructions. You can do the same with college savings plans that offer different investment options.

Even outside of employer retirement plans or college savings plans, building a lazy portfolio is easy. It wouldn't be a lazy portfolio otherwise!

1. **Open an account with a brokerage firm or index fund company.**

    ETFs that track the indexes you want are a great way to build a lazy portfolio. Because ETFs trade on exchanges like stocks, you can buy them in smaller dollar amounts than many mutual funds. However, be sure to buy them through a discount brokerage so the brokerage commissions don't eat up your regular contributions.

    Vanguard (*http://www.vanguard.com*) is the top dog when it comes to low-cost index mutual funds (their index fund expense ratios are about 0.2%). They're great if you have enough money to meet the minimum initial purchases, which can be $1,000 to $3,000 or more. You don't pay commissions on purchases, just the expense ratio.

2. **Set up an automatic deposit for the first asset class.**

    Take the amount you contribute toward your goal each month, and multiply it by the percentage for the first asset class. Set up an automatic deposit for that amount for the index fund that represents the asset class, such as the Vanguard 500 Index Fund for large company stocks.

    Automatic deposits are the ultimate in laziness, because you set them up and let them rip. (You can adjust them later on, if necessary.) Automatic deposits also help you succeed by regularly contributing to your plan through thick and thin, good times and bad, high prices and low (read about dollar-cost averaging on page 4).

3. **Repeat step 2 for each additional asset class.**

    That's it! Easy, huh?

John Bogle, the founder of the Vanguard Group, Inc., is a pioneer of low-cost mutual funds and has written several great books (*http://tinyurl.com/boglebooks*) about the benefits of index funds.

Stealing a Lazy Portfolio from an Expert

If you don't want to design a lazy portfolio of your own, you can use one that financial experts have put together. Keep in mind that these lazy portfolios use fixed percentages for each asset class so the portfolios come with a fixed return/risk level. You have to decide if the lazy portfolio's allocation makes sense for your financial situation. Here are some of the best-known and laziest portfolios around:

- **The Couch Potato Portfolio.** Scott Burns, a financial writer for the *Dallas Morning News*, espouses a two-fund portfolio, split 50-50 between stocks and bonds, using the Vanguard 500 Index (VFINX) and the Vanguard Total Bond Market Index (VBMFX). Learn more about this moderately conservative lazy portfolio at *http://tinyurl.com/LP-potato*. Burns has a three-fund portfolio that's split equally among Vanguard Total Stock Market Index, Vanguard Total International Stock Index, and Vanguard Inflation-Protected Securities (VIPSX). Go to *http://tinyurl.com/LP-cookbook* to read about other lazy portfolios Burns has cooked up.

- **William Bernstein's No-Brainer Portfolio.** A retired neurologist, William Bernstein is a big fan of asset allocation and has written books including *The Intelligent Asset Allocator* (McGraw-Hill, 2000) and *The Four Pillars of Investing* (McGraw-Hill, 2002). His no-brainer portfolio is a simple four-index portfolio with moderately high risk: 25% Vanguard 500 Index (VFINX), 25% Vanguard Small-Cap Index (NAESX), 25% Vanguard Total International Stock Index (VGTSX), and 25% Vanguard Total Bond Market Index (VBMFX). Learn more at *http://tinyurl.com/LP-nobrain*.

- **The Second-Grader Portfolio.** This three-fund portfolio is another moderately high-risk portfolio, suitable for longer-term goals. That makes sense, because Allan Roth, a certified financial planner and certified public accountant, developed it to explain investing to his young son. The portfolio includes 40% Vanguard Total Bond Market Index (VBMFX), 40% Vanguard Total Stock Market Index (VTSMX), and 20% Vanguard Total International Stock Index (VGTSX).

- **Yale University Lazy Portfolio.** David Swensen, author of *Unconventional Success* (Free Press, 2005), offers this five-fund portfolio as a simplistic replacement for the portfolio management strategy he uses for Yale University's endowment fund. The portfolio includes 15% Vanguard Inflation-Protected Securities (VPISX), 20% Vanguard REIT Index, 15% Vanguard Short-Term Treasury Index (VFISX), 30% Vanguard Total Stock Market Index (VTSMX), and 20% Vanguard Total International Stock Index (VGTSX).

Reviewing Your Portfolio

How often you review your portfolio depends on how you invest. If you use asset allocation to divvy up your portfolio by asset classes, a yearly checkup may be all you need—just like seeing your doctor for your annual physical. On the other hand, if you own individual stocks, you may want to see how they're doing every time quarterly reports come out. Significant life events, like marriage, divorce, the birth of a child, or retirement, are signals to revisit your objectives and risk tolerance, and possibly to revise your target asset allocation.

> **Tip** As the timeframe for withdrawing money grows near, don't forget to adjust your portfolio to a lower-risk allocation (page 163). In addition, move money you plan to spend in the next 5 years to very safe investments, like short-term bonds, certificates of deposit, money market accounts, or savings accounts (page 190).

Checking Your Asset Allocation

Sticking to your target asset allocation requires occasional portfolio maintenance. Asset classes and individual investments perform differently (page 156), which can unbalance your asset allocation. An off-kilter asset allocation can mean unacceptable returns or unpalatable risk.

> **Tip** Checking up on your portfolio daily or weekly is a bad idea. Watching the values of your investments bounce around like crickets in a hot frying pan could tempt you to make portfolio changes you don't need. You fret; spend money on commissions, taxes, and other fees; and may end up hindering your portfolio's performance.

Say you have $100,000 in your portfolio and have chosen an asset allocation of 60% in stocks and 40% in bonds. After 1 year, your stocks increase 11% to $66,600, while bonds increase 4% to $41,600. Your new allocation is 61.5% stocks and 38.5% bonds—still close to your target. However, after several years of returns like that, stocks could grow to 70% of your portfolio, while bonds drop to 30%, which may be a riskier allocation than you had in mind.

When you review your portfolio, don't drive yourself crazy reallocating if your asset classes are a few percentage points off target. Maintaining a meticulously accurate allocation leads to turnover, which increases your fees, commissions, and taxes. Instead, keep your allocations within, say, 5% of your target. For example, if your target stock allocation is 60% and your actual allocation is 61%, leave it alone. If the actual stock allocation grows to 66%, it's time to rebalance.

Checking Up on Funds, Stocks, and Bonds

In addition to your asset allocation, you need to keep an eye on the investments you own:

- **Index mutual funds.** Make sure that fund expenses remain low.

- **Actively managed mutual funds.** Review the fund's returns, expenses, turnover, portfolio, and management, as described on page 94.

- **Stocks.** If you buy individual stocks, check up on their performance and financial measures, as described on page 108.

- **Bonds.** For individual bonds, look for rating changes (page 133). If you own bond funds, see page 129.

 Note If you buy individual stocks, you can use the same approach to keep one stock from growing to an inordinately large percentage of your portfolio.

Rebalancing Your Portfolio

Bringing your portfolio back into balance means taking money out of the investments that grew faster and buying more of the investments that didn't keep pace. Remember, some investments simply don't grow as fast as others; for example, the average bond return is lower than the average stock return. So, when stocks have been on a roll, you have to move money from stocks to bonds to keep your asset allocation percentages on target.

Likewise, if small company stocks have fallen more than large company stocks, you rebalance your allocation to put more in small company stocks, because eventually their returns are likely to catch up and pass those of large stocks. You can rebalance your portfolio several ways:

- **When you have taxable and tax-advantaged accounts.** Reallocate in your tax-advantaged accounts first. That way, you don't have to pay taxes on your capital gains. In taxable accounts, sell funds *before* they make their annual distributions, and buy funds *after* their distributions, so you don't have to pay taxes on gains and dividends.

- **When you no longer contribute to your portfolio.** You have two ways to reallocate a portfolio you no longer contribute to. One option is to sell some of the over-allocated investments and to use the proceeds to buy more of the under-allocated ones. For example, the worksheet below shows that long-term bonds are 2% ($2,000) above their target and that small stocks are 8% ($8,000) above their target. The negative numbers in the +Buy/–Sell column tell you how much you would have to sell to bring them back on track. At the same time, large stocks are 10% ($10,000) below target. You could sell $2,000 worth of long-term bonds and $8,000 of small stocks to purchase the $10,000 of large stocks you need. You can download the Portfolio_Rebalancing.xls spreadsheet from *www.missingmanuals.com/cds*.

If you're withdrawing money from your portfolio, the other way to rebalance is to sell portions of your better performers for your withdrawals.

	A	B	C	D	E	F
	Portfolio_Rebalancing					
1	Monthly contribution ($)	1000				
2						
3	Portfolio	Actual $	Target %	Actual %		+Buy/-Sell
4						
5	Cash	5,000	5%	5%		0
6	Short-term/Intermediate-term bonds	10,000	10%	10%		0
7	Long-term bonds	12,000	10%	12%		-2,000
8	Small stocks	18,000	10%	18%		-8,000
9	Large stocks	30,000	40%	30%		10,000
10	International stocks	15,000	15%	15%		0
11	REITs	10,000	10%	10%		0
12						
13	Total	100,000	100%	100%		

- **When you still contribute to your portfolio.** If you continue to add money to your portfolio, you can use dollar-cost averaging (page 4) to rebalance your portfolio. Invest your new contributions in the investments or asset classes that have fallen below their target allocations. That way, you simply add more money to the investments that fell behind instead of selling your better performers. For example, in the portfolio above, you could invest your $1,000 monthly contributions in large stocks until they reach their target allocation.

Getting Back On Track

Your finances never stay exactly on track, but sometimes, they get horribly derailed. Whether the economy falls into a protracted tailspin, you lose your job, or your spouse gets sick and medical bills pile up, you have to figure out how to get back on track. Just because your plan is broken, all is not lost. However, you do have to re-evaluate your objectives (page 22) and make choices about what to do to correct your course:

- **Work.** If you haven't built up a safety cushion of stable assets (page 190) and your nest egg cracks as you're about to retire, delaying your retirement date offers several advantages. First, you give your portfolio time to recover. You also give it an extra boost by continuing to make 401(k) or 403(b) contributions. In addition, you can increase your monthly Social Security benefits by postponing their distribution (page 192). If you're already retired, a part-time job or going back to work full time may be the answer. The longer you leave your retirement nest egg alone, the more likely it will get back on track.

 If you need more money to reach your goals and you're already working, you might consider a part-time job and contribute the extra income to your investment accounts.

- **Contribute more.** If you're still contributing to your portfolio, one way to get back on track is to spend less and to contribute those savings to your investment accounts. If you're over 50, the federal government offers additional tax-advantaged make-up contributions (pages 178 and 181) to help you get your retirement portfolio where it needs to be.

- **Withdraw less.** If working or higher contributions are out of the question, your other option is to ratchet your plan down to a more modest level (page 22). Plan to withdraw less money each year during retirement, provide your children with less money toward their college expenses, or set your sights lower on other goals.

 You may be tempted to take on more risk in your portfolio to make up for what you lost. Remember, more risk means more chance of larger losses, so that approach could put you in even deeper doo-doo.

Part 3
Manage Your Investments

10 Investing for Retirement

Some folks shrug off saving for retirement with a casual "I'm going to work until the day I die." The problem with that approach is that it's not very realistic—working until you drop isn't much fun, and most people want some down time after a lifetime of toil. So how do you plan for the day you cash your last paycheck and need to live on other sources of income?

Chapter 2 showed you how to build a retirement investment plan, and Chapter 9 explained how to set up and manage your retirement portfolio. But if you've ever had days when nothing went the way you expected, you can imagine how much can change when you try to forecast your retirement needs 40 years in the future. In addition, retirement accounts and Social Security come with so many options and rules that you could devote most of retirement to mastering them all.

This chapter focuses on fine-tuning your retirement plan. You start by learning how to change key retirement-plan decisions to make your strategy work—or how to bring a derailed plan back on track.

You'll also learn how to make the most of the retirement accounts you learned about in Chapter 4: employer-sponsored 401(k) and 403(b) accounts, traditional IRAs, and Roth IRAs, all of which offer tax advantages that help you invest for retirement. Even taxable investment accounts can play a part in retirement investing. This chapter helps you choose the right types of retirement accounts and use them wisely.

This chapter also shows you how to adjust your asset allocation as you approach and then enter retirement. With Social Security a significant part of most retirees' income, you'll learn ways to squeeze more from your Social Security benefits.

Finally, you'll learn how to withdraw money from your retirement plan. When you start spending your nest egg, reducing risk becomes more important than higher returns, so you need to adjust your portfolio to hold more conservative investments. This chapter shows you smart ways to withdraw from your accounts to make your money last as long as you do.

The Key Retirement Decisions

Whether you want to fine-tune your retirement plan or get it back on track, your strategy stems from two important decisions: when you're going to retire and the retirement lifestyle you desire. Once you adjust your key decisions in this chapter, you can jump back to Chapter 2 and see whether your new and improved retirement plan works.

When You're Going to Retire

The trend for longevity shows no sign of stopping, so chances are good you'll spend decades in retirement. You may already know when you want to retire, and that's a good start. But you can change your retirement date to solve retirement plan problems. Here's a quick review of how your retirement date affects your plan:

- **How long you have to save.** The more time you have to save and invest for retirement, the easier it is to finance a comfortable retirement. Whether you contribute smaller amounts regularly for 40 years or invest a $50,000 inheritance when you're 20, compounding investment returns (page 16) strengthens your portfolio the more years it has to work. A longer timeframe also means you can choose to start your plan with a more aggressive asset allocation (page 163) to aim for higher returns with less overall risk.

- **The number of retirement years you have to pay for.** If you postpone retirement, your retirement war chest doesn't have to pay for as many years of living expenses. Because inflation increases the cost of living each year, a year of retirement expenses isn't small potatoes. Removing a few years from your plan could drop your retirement price tag by several hundred thousand dollars (page 16).

- **Your Social Security benefits.** Postponing when you start taking your Social Security benefits can boost your monthly income in several ways (as you'll see on page 192).

What Retirement Will Cost

How much you want to spend each year in retirement is the other big question. Many of your expenses—food, utilities, clothing—don't change (except, of course, for increases due to inflation). You may choose to spend more extravagantly on travel, hobbies, and other fun, or plan for higher health-care bills. If you're like many people, you can leave several types of expenses you pay now out of your retirement budget: mortgage payments, college tuition, and those pesky contributions to retirement savings. In addition, you're likely to have less taxable income during retirement, so your income tax rate may drop. Either way, Chapter 2 shows you how to estimate annual retirement spending based on your living expenses today.

If you need to repair a retirement plan and don't want to postpone retirement, you can lower what you plan to spend each year in retirement. Be realistic. Don't set an impossibly low target to make your plan work, or you'll suffer through that decision for years.

If you're having trouble saving enough money for retirement, remember that your retirement is more important than your kids' college fund or helping your parents pay their bills. Your children can find other ways to pay for college (page 198). Find ways to help your parents other than handing over cash (page 34). In fact, if you work with them on their finances now, they may not need your financial help later on.

Making the Most of Retirement Accounts

In Chapter 4, you learned about the tax advantages that employer-sponsored 401(k) and 403(b) accounts, traditional IRAs, and Roth IRAs offer. Some accounts let you contribute pre-tax dollars. Some defer tax payments on dividends and capital gains. And some let you skip paying taxes altogether when you withdraw. Even investment accounts that you pay taxes on can help you save for retirement. Because you usually can't save enough for retirement with any one type of account, you'll probably use a mix of several types. This section helps you choose which ones.

 Tip As you learned in Chapter 4, contribute as much as you can to tax-advantaged accounts before you contribute to taxable accounts. After that, keep investments with the highest tax bills in your tax-advantaged accounts, and keep more tax-efficient investments in taxable accounts. Page 68 shows you which types of investments are best suited to tax-advantaged and taxable accounts.

Making the Most of Your 401(k)

401(k) and 403(b) accounts are employer-sponsored retirement savings plans. Although they aren't as sweet as traditional pension plans, where your employer makes the contributions (page 29), they're still a great way to save for retirement.

Why you should contribute to your 401(k)

401(k)s and 403(b)s are tax-deferred retirement accounts. You contribute a percentage of your paycheck, and you don't pay taxes on that money. In 2010, the maximum annual contribution is $16,500. (If you're over 50, you can add a catch-up contribution of up to $5,500.) Here are the big benefits of using a 401(k) or 403(b) plan:

- **Your savings grow faster because you don't pay taxes.** With tax deferral, you can reinvest the full amount of the dividends and capital gains your investments produce, so your money grows as fast as your asset allocation (page 160) allows. Page 63 spells out how much you'd pay in taxes on different types of investments.

- **You may pay less tax when you withdraw.** When you retire, you do have to pay tax on the money you take out of these accounts. But because your taxable retirement income is often significantly lower than your taxable income while you work, you may be in a lower tax bracket in retirement and therefore pay less in taxes than you would today.

- **You aren't likely to miss the money you contribute.** The money comes out before you get your paycheck, so you usually learn to live on the check's net amount. Meanwhile, your 401(k) contributions and retirement account investments quietly grow in the background.

- **You contribute to your plan regularly.** Because your payroll deduction occurs automatically, you aren't as likely to skip a contribution. In addition, because you contribute to your 401(k) or 403(b) every paycheck, that regular investment schedule means that your contributions automatically buy more shares of investments when prices are lower and buy fewer shares when prices are higher.

- **The tax deduction helps you contribute more.** The pre-tax contribution means you can afford to contribute more to your retirement plan. For example, if you're in the 25% tax bracket and contribute $10,000 to your 401(k) or 403(b), you save $2,500 in taxes, so your net out of pocket is only $7,500.

- **Earn a matching contribution from your employer.** Many employers match a portion of what you contribute. A typical match is half of your contribution up to 6% of your salary. (Employers match contributions to coax lower-paid employees to participate in the plan, which is an IRS requirement for these types of plans.) For example, if you earn $50,000 per year and contribute 6% to your 401(k), that's an annual contribution of $3,000. Your employer would contribute another $1,500 to your account. An employer match is like an instant 100% return on that part of your contribution. For that reason, strive to contribute enough to your plan to get the full company match.

The downsides to 401(k)s and 403(b)s

In addition to the contribution limit on these accounts, which may not be enough to get your retirement plan where it needs to go, 401(k) and 403(b) plans have other disadvantages:

- **Many plans offer limited investment choices.** If your plan has a meager selection of investments, they may not play well with your ideal asset allocation (page 160). See page 100 to learn how to work around a limited menu of investment choices.

- **Plans with high fees can eat away advantages.** Sometimes the expense ratios you pay on funds in a 401(k) can run as high as 2% above the expense ratio for the same fund outside of the plan. For example, a fund that has an expense ratio of 0.5% in a regular investment account may charge 1.5% in a 401(k) plan. In addition, your 401(k) may also charge its own management expenses and hidden fees. As you learned on page 90, keeping fees low means a lot more money in your investment account.

Tip If your 401(k) has high fees, you have a few choices. One is to contribute up to your company's matching limit and then contribute additional funds to an IRA—or even a taxable investment account where you put money into low-turnover investments (see page 90). Because many people don't stay at the same job forever, you may choose to put up with the high fees. Then, when you change jobs, you can roll over your 401(k) into a rollover IRA (page 180) with lower fees.

- **You must start withdrawing from your account when you're 70 ½.** The IRS has rules about the minimum amounts you must withdraw each year after you reach age 70 ½. The purpose of required minimum distributions (RMDs), as they're called, is to make sure you use your money to pay for retirement expenses and, in doing so, give the government its cut in income tax on your distributions, instead of passing it on to your heirs (potentially tax-free depending on the size of your estate and on inheritance tax rules). The IRS calculates your annual RMD as the market value of your account divided by your life expectancy in years. Even if the cash value of your account remains the same over time, you have to withdraw a little more each year as your life expectancy decreases. For example, if your account balance is $100,000 and your life expectancy is 20 years, you must withdraw $5,000 that year.

> **Tip** Some employers have begun offering Roth 401(k)s. These plans are employer sponsored, like traditional 401(k)s, except that they have the tax-advantaged features of a Roth IRA. The same decisions you must make in choosing between a traditional and a Roth IRA (page 182) apply to traditional and Roth 401(k)s: in short, whether you can afford to pay taxes on your contributions now and whether you think your income tax rate will be higher or lower during retirement.

Rolling over a 401(k)

If you switch jobs, you can choose whether to keep your retirement funds in your employer-sponsored retirement plan or to move them into a *rollover IRA*. A rollover may be a good idea, particularly if your employer's plan doesn't offer a wide range of investment choices. By rolling your plan into an IRA with a brokerage or a large mutual fund company, you can pick from all the index funds, ETFs, and other investments that financial institution offers.

Another reason to roll over your 401(k) when you switch jobs is fees. As you learned on page 179, many 401(k) plans charge high fees, which eat away at your returns. If you open a rollover IRA at a financial institution with low fees, you may increase your return by 1% or more (for example, from 6% to 7%).

Tip Financial institutions want your business, so they bend over backward to help you roll over your retirement accounts into the IRAs they offer.

Choosing an IRA: Traditional or Roth?

If you don't have an employer-sponsored retirement plan, or you want to contribute more toward retirement outside of your employer's plan, an IRA is another tax-advantaged retirement savings option. In any type of IRA, your money *grows* tax-deferred. That means you don't pay taxes on dividends or capital gains, so the full amount of your contributions, capital gains, and dividends work at full steam to increase your retirement kitty.

As of 2010, the IRS limits your contribution to a maximum of $5,000 each year ($6,000 if you're age 50 or older). That usually isn't enough to reach your retirement goal, which is why you're likely to have an IRA as well as other types of retirement accounts.

Beyond tax-deferred and contribution limits, the similarity ends between traditional and Roth IRAs. This section helps you decide whether a traditional IRA, Roth IRA, or both are the right solution for you.

Traditional IRA

Anyone with earned income (salary, wages, tips, bonuses, and so on—you can get this quickly from line 7 of your 1040 tax form) who is younger than 70 ½ can contribute to a traditional IRA. A traditional IRA is a good choice if you expect your retirement income tax rate to be lower than your current tax rate, because you do pay taxes on the money you withdraw. Similarly to 401(k) plans, you must start withdrawing when you reach age 70 ½ with the required minimum distributions calculated based on the value of your account and your life expectancy (page 180).

The table below shows whether your IRA contribution is deductible.

Filing status	Covered by employer retirement plan	Modified gross income	IRA deduction status of your contribution
Single, head of household	No	Any amount	Full deduction
Married, filing jointly or separately	No	Any amount	Full deduction
Single	Yes	Less than $55,000	Full deduction
Single	Yes	$55,000 to $65,000	Partial deduction

Filing status	Covered by employer retirement plan	Modified gross income	IRA deduction status of your contribution
Single	Yes	More than $65,000	No deduction
Married, filing jointly	Yes	Less than $89,000	Full deduction
Married, filing jointly	Yes	$89,000 to $109,000	Partial deduction
Married, filing jointly	Yes	More than $109,000	No deduction
Married, filing jointly	Spouse covered	Less than $166,000	Full deduction
Married, filing jointly	Spouse covered	$166,000 to $176,000	Partial deduction
Married, filing jointly	Spouse covered	More than $176,000	No deduction
Married, filing separately	Spouse covered	Less than $10,000	Partial deduction
Married, filing separately	Spouse covered	$10,000 or more	No deduction

Roth IRA

Roth IRAs have the same contribution limits as traditional IRAs, and they also offer tax-deferred growth of your investments. Before you go any further, you can't contribute to a Roth IRA if you're single and earn more than $120,000 a year ($176,000 if you're married and filing jointly). Beyond that hard cutoff on contributions, Roth IRAs differ from traditional IRAs in several big ways that make them an obvious choice for anyone who's planning for retirement at least 5 to 10 years in the future. Here's how they differ and why you should care:

- **Roth IRA contributions are not tax-deductible.** That's right: You have to pay taxes on the money you contribute to your Roth IRA. For example, if you're in the 25% tax bracket and contribute $5,000 to your Roth, you still have to pay $1,250 in taxes, so your out-of-pocket cost is $6,250. Ask yourself whether you can afford to make a non-tax-deductible contribution to a Roth. If the answer is no, a traditional IRA is the better choice.

- **You can withdraw from a Roth account tax-free after the age of 59½.** Tax-free withdrawals in retirement are attractive, especially if you expect tax rates to be higher then than they are now. Because you contribute to a Roth after-tax, you can withdraw your *contributions* without paying taxes or penalties. To withdraw your *earnings* tax-free, you must be 59½ and have converted or contributed to the Roth at least 5 years earlier.

- **You can contribute after you reach 70½ if you have earned income (salary, wages, tips, bonuses, and so on).** No contribution age limit means you can keep adding money to your retirement plan into your 70s and beyond. If you plan to keep working after your official retirement, a Roth IRA is one way to continue funding your retirement plan. Remember, because retirement can last 35 to 40 years or more, contributions you make at 75 years of age may still have 20 years or more to grow.

- **You don't have required annual distributions.** Unlike 401(k)s and traditional IRAs, you can leave money in a Roth IRA as long as you want, which makes it a great option for funding the latter years of your retirement: If you have other funds to live on early in retirement, you can let your Roth account grow tax-deferred.

 If you're the beneficiary of an IRA, you can transfer the money into an inherited IRA to keep the tax-deferral going. However, similar to other IRAs, the IRS has rules (*http://tinyurl.com/inheritedIRA*) about when you must start withdrawing money from these accounts.

Should I Convert a Traditional IRA to a Roth IRA?

In 2010, the IRS lifted the income restriction for converting traditional IRAs to Roth IRAs, which triggered an avalanche of talk about whether people should make the switch.

Bean-counter types devote hours to analyzing the effect of time periods, pre- and post-retirement tax rates, required minimum distributions, beneficiaries, and so on. If you answer yes to one or more of the following questions, converting to a Roth may make sense for you:

- **Do you have enough money to pay the taxes on the converted funds without taking money from your current IRA?** When you convert a traditional IRA to a Roth, you have to pay taxes on the tax-free contributions you made to the original account and any capital gains and dividends you've earned. For sizable conversions, those taxes can add up to serious money, because you pay your ordinary income tax rate on the entire taxable amount. (That's right, you don't even get to apply the lower capital gains rate to any capital gains your investments earned.) For example, if you convert an IRA worth $100,000, and your tax rate is 25%, you have to pay $25,000 in taxes. You work hard to save money for retirement, so you don't want to take money out of your current IRA to pay the tax bill.

- **Do you have enough time before withdrawing to recover from paying the taxes now?** The longer you have before you start withdrawing from your Roth, the bigger the conversion advantage is. You want the money in the Roth to have enough time to grow and compound to recoup the taxes you paid when you converted. If you're decades from retirement, chances are good a Roth conversion makes sense: Your IRA balance is probably small, and you have lots of years for your investments to grow.

- **Do you expect your income tax rate to be higher during retirement than it is now?** If you think about it, you pay taxes on money in an IRA at one point or another. With a traditional IRA, you pay taxes on the money when you withdraw it in retirement. If you convert from a traditional IRA to a Roth IRA, you pay taxes on the converted funds now, and then pay no taxes when you withdraw. If your current tax rate is high and you expect your retirement tax rate to be lower, keeping your traditional IRA may make sense. However, if you foresee higher taxes in the future (for example, because of the government deficit or other reasons), paying taxes now and withdrawing tax-free may be the better choice.

Tip If you like the idea of converting to a Roth IRA, 2010 is a good year to do it. Your IRA value may still be off its peak due to the market downturn in 2008, so you'll pay less taxes than you would have a few years ago. In addition, the government introduced special conversion rules for 2010, so you can split the income from the conversion equally between your 2011 and 2012 tax returns. Dividing the conversion income into two smaller amounts may keep the total from pushing you into a higher tax bracket. In addition, you have until April 15, 2012, and April 15, 2013, to save up the money to pay the conversion tax bill.

Using a Roth conversion calculator

You don't have to hurt your brain trying to decide whether a conversion makes sense. Online calculators can help you decide. Here's an example using the calculator offered by The Vanguard Group (*http://tinyurl.com/VanguardRothTool*):

1. **In the "Personal & tax information" section shown below, fill in your birth date (1/31/1950 in this example), marital status (single), the year you plan to convert (2010), your taxable income in the year you plan to convert ($50,000), the average annual rate of return you expect your portfolio to deliver (7%), and whether you want to postpone the conversion tax that's due (No).**

   In 2010 only, individuals who convert to a Roth can spread the taxable income equally between the 2011 and 2012 tax years, so the tax bill doesn't come due as quickly, and each bill isn't as large.

2. **In the "Your total IRA balance" section, fill in the balance of all your IRAs and the amount of any nondeductible contributions you made.**

   Later in the calculator, you can tell it what percentage of your IRA total you want to convert. Also, you don't have to pay tax on nondeductible contributions you made.

3. **Click Next.**

   As you can see on the next page, the Results page shows whether converting to a Roth makes sense. It assumes that you retire at 65; you withdraw $1,000 per month from your IRAs during retirement; and you pay a 28% tax rate during retirement. On the left side of the page, you see how much you would have to pay in taxes ($6,688 in this example). The graph on the right shows the additional money you'd have from a conversion or the number of years less your IRA will last if you convert. In this example, the 60-year-old should not convert to a Roth.

   You can also change the percentage of your IRA total that you want to convert. The tool sets the percentage to 50% initially, but you can reduce or increase that amount.

4. **Drag the first slider to set the year you plan to start withdrawing from your accounts.**

   For example, drag the slider to 2025 to have the 60-year-old start withdrawing at 75 years of age.

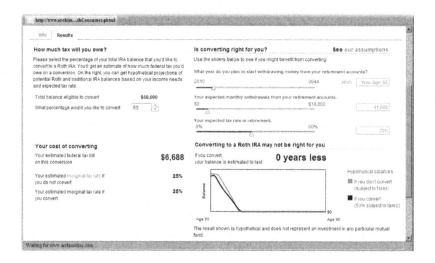

5. **If you plan to withdraw more or less money each month, drag the second slider.**

   You can drag the slider between $0 and $10,000 per month.

6. **If you expect your tax rate to change, drag the last slider to the rate you expect.**

   For example, drag the slider to reduce the tax rate to 25%.

   The graph changes to show the results, as shown below. The gray line on the graph is the value of your retirement accounts if you don't convert and must pay taxes on your withdrawal. The green line is the value of your accounts if you do convert and withdraw tax-free.

   Tip Roth conversions aren't all-or-nothing choices. You can convert a small percentage of a traditional IRA each year. One tactic some people use is to convert only the amount of money that keeps them in the same tax bracket. (If you convert a large amount at one time, the amount you convert increases your taxable income for the year and may bump you into a higher tax bracket.) For example, say your 2009 taxable income is $30,000. The 15% tax bracket tops out at $33,950. If you convert only $3,950, you remain in the 15% tax bracket. However, if you convert $5,000, you'll pay a 25% tax rate on the additional $1,050.

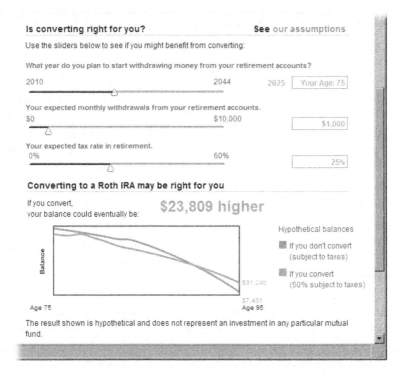

Is converting right for you?   See our assumptions

Use the sliders below to see if you might benefit from converting:

What year do you plan to start withdrawing money from your retirement accounts?

2010   2044   2025 | Your Age: 75 |

Your expected monthly withdrawals from your retirement accounts.
$0 $10,000 | $1,000 |

Your expected tax rate in retirement.
0%   60% | 25% |

Converting to a Roth IRA may be right for you

If you convert,
your balance could eventually be: **$23,809 higher**

Balance

Hypothetical balances
■ If you don't convert
  (subject to taxes)

$31,240

■ If you convert
  (50% subject to taxes)

$7,431
Age 75   Age 95

The result shown is hypothetical and does not represent an investment in any particular mutual fund.

Retirement Plans for Small Businesses

Small businesses have several choices for retirement plans, from employee-contribution plans to employer-contribution plans and several in between:

- **Payroll Deduction IRA.** Some employers don't set up retirement plans, but do let employees contribute to IRAs through payroll deductions.

- **SEP-IRA.** For small businesses and self-employed individuals, the simplified employee pension IRA (SEP-IRA) is the easiest pension plan option. Employer contributions are limited to no more than 25% of your income each year (to a maximum $49,000 in 2010). You can set up a SEP-IRA for a side business even if you already have a 401(k) at your day job. Employers must contribute the same percentage of pay for each employee and can opt to skip payments for a year, if business isn't good, for example.

- **SIMPLE IRA.** Employers with 100 or fewer employees can set up SIMPLE plans. Employees choose how much to contribute, up to a maximum of $11,500 in 2010 ($14,000 for employees age 50 and older). Employers match portions of the employees' contributions.

- **Keogh or 401(k).** Qualified plans like Keogh and 401(k) retirement plans allow high levels of contributions by employees. Paperwork requirements for employers are higher than for other plans, so these may not be the best bet if you own a business of one.

Managing a Retirement Portfolio

In Chapter 9, you learned how to use asset allocation to balance investment return and risk, and how to coordinate investments between multiple retirement accounts. One key ingredient to choosing the right asset allocation is how soon you need the money. Retirement poses a challenge, because the level of safety you need in your retirement investments changes continuously as you grow older. This section shows you how to adjust your retirement portfolio as time passes. You'll also learn how to withdraw money from your portfolio during retirement. To keep the examples simple, this section assumes you allocate your portfolio among stocks, bonds, REITs, and cash.

To plan for retirement, you can choose from a few rules of thumb. Some financial professionals calculate the percentage of stocks in your portfolio by subtracting your age from 100. For example, when you're 20 years old, you invest 80% in stocks and 20% in bonds and REITs. At age 100, you would have 100% in bonds and REITs, and 0% in stocks. More risk-tolerant folks or those who expect to live long past their century birthday may calculate the percentage of stocks by subtracting their age from 120, so even at age 100, you could still have 20% in stocks. This section uses a moderately risk-tolerant investor who uses the 100-age guideline to calculate her stock allocation percentage.

 For couples, life insurance is another tool for your retirement planning bag. Each spouse can get a life insurance policy with the other spouse as the beneficiary to provide additional funds should one spouse pass away. Or, if money is tight, you can take out a life insurance policy on whichever spouse has a shorter life expectancy (women typically live longer than men).

When Retirement Is Way in the Future

When your retirement is decades away, you don't have to worry about setting aside cash to withdraw in the next few years. You can allocate your portfolio solely to stocks, bonds, and REITs. The table below shows the initial asset allocation for a 20-year-old's retirement plan.

 If you want to set some cash aside to purchase great investment deals, you can do that. However, because cash pays such a low return, you're usually better off selling the least attractive investment in your portfolio to buy something you find more attractive.

Asset	Allocation percentage
Stocks	80%
Bonds	10%
REITs	10%
Cash	0%

This 20-year-old has decades until retirement, but that doesn't mean she can let her retirement portfolio languish unattended. She still has to rebalance her portfolio as some investments grow faster or slower than others (see page 170 for the nuts and bolts of rebalancing). And she has to gradually move her money to more conservative investments as she approaches retirement, until she gets to a few years before retirement.

On the one hand, if you're going to rebalance your portfolio every year, you may as well incorporate the gradual move to more conservative investments. However, just as many investors don't keep their asset allocations to within 99.9% of their targets, young investors don't have to notch their stock percentages down every year. For example, if you're 45 years old or younger, you may choose to notch your stock percentage down every 2 to 5 years instead of each year. The table below shows how the woman in the previous example, who is now 25 years old, rebalances her portfolio to move it to a slightly more conservative asset allocation now that she's older.

Asset	Actual allocation at 25	Target allocation at 25	Rebalance percentage required
Stocks	90%	75%	−15%
Bonds	8%	12.5%	+4.5%
REITs	2%	12.5%	+10%
Cash	0%	0%	0%

The Red Zone

Personal finance types call the 5 years before and after retirement the red zone, because drops in the value of your retirement portfolio during this period can really hurt. It's big trouble if retirement is close at hand or has just started and your portfolio sinks along with a down market. The best way to protect yourself from this kind of meltdown is easy: Keep 5 years' worth of cash and short-term bonds in your portfolio.

Selling investments that have lost value to pay for living expenses can chew years off your retirement plan. Say you retired in 2007 at 65 with a $500,000 retirement portfolio. Estimating an average annual return of 7% (with a 3% inflation rate), you figured your nest egg would provide $23,300 of annual retirement income until you reach age 95. In 2008, the S&P 500 index fell 37%. If your portfolio dropped the same amount, it would have decreased to $315,000. If you kept withdrawing $23,300 a year anyway, you'd run out of money when you reached age 80. (To keep the money going for 30 years, you'd have to decrease your annual withdrawal to $14,700.) However, in 2009, the S&P 500 went up 26.5%. That would put your portfolio at $398,475. Your plan wouldn't be completely back on track, but it would be a lot closer.

To avoid those planning problems, create a cash reserve of low-risk, low-return investments like savings accounts, money market accounts, certificates of deposit, and short-term bonds. How much cash insulation you need depends on your other sources of retirement income. If you have a pension plan and Social Security benefits that pay for most of your annual retirement living expenses, you can keep a modest cash reserve, one that covers any other expenses for a couple of years. But if your portfolio is your only source of income, having a robust 5 year's worth of expenses in a cash reserve means you probably won't have to sell investments at a significant loss.

The table below shows an asset allocation for someone 60 years old who intends to retire at 65 on $25,000 per year. Keep in mind that the percentage of cash you hold depends on your annual living expenses and the size of your portfolio. In the table below, 5 years of living expenses is $125,000, which represents 10% of the $1,250,000 portfolio. However, if your portfolio has only $625,000, you would have 20% of your money in cash.

Asset	Allocation percentage	Dollar value
Stocks	40%	$500,000
Bonds	25%	$250,000
REITs	25%	$250,000
Cash	10%	$125,000

 You can gradually increase the percentage of cash in your portfolio, just like you gradually change your asset allocation as you get older.

With your cash reserve in place, you can allocate *the rest* of your portfolio as you would normally, depending on the risk you can tolerate:

- **Low-risk.** Invest 10% to 25% of your remaining portfolio in stocks, 75% to 90% in bonds depending on your age.

- **Medium-risk.** Allocate between 25% and 40% in stocks, 60% to 75% in bonds.

- **High-risk.** Invest between 40% to 55% in stocks, 45% to 60% in stocks.

Troubleshooting Moment

Getting Back on Track

If the market goes south just before you retire, postponing retirement has loads of advantages:

- **Work.** Delaying your retirement not only gives your portfolio time to recover, but you also can continue to make contributions to 401(k) or 403(b) plans and IRAs. In addition, you can increase your monthly Social Security benefits by postponing the date you start taking those benefits (page 192). If you're already retired, you may consider a part-time job or going back to work full time for a while. For example, if you earn $50,000 a year and contribute 15% to a 401(k) account, you'd add another $22,500 to your account if you wait 3 more years to retire. (Your retirement income gets a boost because you also shorten your years in retirement.)

- **Contribute more.** If you're still contributing to your retirement portfolio, beef up your contributions. If you're over 50 years old, the federal government offers additional tax-advantaged make-up contributions (pages 178 and 181) to help you get your retirement portfolio where it needs to be. If you have a Roth IRA, you can contribute to it as long as you have earned income, regardless of your age (page 183).

- **Withdraw less.** Your other option is to adjust your plan to withdraw less money each year for living expenses (page 194).

Making the Most of Social Security

Social Security benefits make up about 40% of the income for people 65 and older, according to a 2006 study by the Employee Benefit Research Institute (EBRI). While that statistic may be due to earlier generations not planning for retirement as well as you do, it still makes sense to get as much out of your Social Security benefits as you can. In most cases, the best way to maximize your Social Security benefits is to hold off when you start to receive them, because the longer you wait, the more you'll get each year, as you'll see shortly. Of course, if you need your Social Security benefits to live on, you don't have much choice but to start them.

In most cases, you're eligible for Social Security if you've worked for at least 10 years. If you're married or were married for 10 years and haven't remarried, you're eligible for half of your spouse's Social Security payment.

The Benefit of Delaying Benefits

The monthly Social Security payment you get when you first start receiving your benefits is the starting point for your payments for the rest of your life. Because Social Security benefits have a delayed retirement credit (8% for each year you delay up to age 70 if you were born in 1943 or later), you can boost your benefits by postponing when you start to receive them.

Social Security delayed retirement credit

Say you were born in 1950, so full retirement age is 66 (the sliding scale increase it to 67 if you were born after 1959), and your current annual earnings are $60,000. Here are the benefits you'd receive the first year of retirement, depending on your retirement age as calculated by the Social Security calculator (*http://tinyurl.com/SSA-Benefits*):

- **At the age of 62.** $14,340 ($1,195 per month).
- **At full retirement age of 66 (for someone born in 1950).** $18,504 ($1,542 per month).
- **At age 70.** $27,792 ($2,316 per month).

As you can see, starting your benefits at 62 years of age reduces your monthly payment by about 22%. (If you were born in 1960 or later and retire at 62, your payment drops by 30%.) On the other hand, if you wait until age 70, your monthly payment increases by 50%! That increase comes in part from delaying the start of benefits (8% per year) and in part from the Social Security Administration's cost-of-living adjustments (on average, an increase of about 2.7% per year).

 The results shown here come from the Social Security quick calculator. You can also download a calculator from the site that asks more questions and produces a more accurate result. However, the printed statements that you receive every January are the most accurate, because they base their estimates on the earnings you reported on your tax returns.

Increased earnings

Higher earnings during the additional years you work are another way your benefits may increase. The Social Security Administration (SSA) calculates your benefits based on the highest 35 years of your earnings. If you postpone retirement and earn a higher salary during those additional years, your Social Security benefits increase accordingly. The formula the SSA uses to calculate your benefits applies different percentages to different "bands" of your annual earnings: 90% for the first $9,000, 32% from $9,000 to $54,000, and 15% for $54,000 to the maximum salary of $106,800.

 In 2010, the maximum annual Social Security benefit is $27,876 a year ($41,814 for a married couple), but you'd have to pay the maximum amount in Social Security taxes almost your entire career to get that much.

Life expectancy

If your health is poor, taking your benefits sooner rather than later may make sense. However, anyone who's planning on a long life can get more from Social Security by waiting. For example, the retiree used as an example on page 192 would receive the same total Social Security benefits by age 82, whether she retired at 65 or 70. However, if she lives to be 95 year old, she would receive about $146,000 more in benefits if she waited until she was 70 to start her Social Security benefits.

Working and Receiving Benefits

Once you hit age 62, you can work and receive Social Security benefits at the same time, but you pay a price. Before you reach full retirement age, your Social Security benefits drop by $1 for every $2 you earn above a certain income level ($14,160 in 2010). In the year you reach full retirement, you lose $1 for every $3 earned beyond $37,680. The good news is that after you reach the month of your full retirement age, you can work and earn money to your heart's content without losing any Social Security benefits.

For example, say you turn 62 in 2010 and your annual Social Security benefits are estimated at $15,000. You continue to work and earn $25,000. Your earnings are $10,840 more than the earned income threshold, so your Social Security benefits drop by $5,420 in this example. You'd receive only $9,580 in benefits instead of $15,000. In fact, if you earned $44,160 or more, you'd wipe out your benefits entirely.

Withdrawing Money During Retirement

After you spend decades living off a paycheck and saving money for retirement, selling investments so you have spending money can be downright unsettling—it's the exact opposite of what you've done your entire life. In addition, you worry about having to sell investments during a down market and hurting your portfolio (page 190). Meanwhile, you have enough on your mind wondering whether you'll get to the local diner in time for the early bird special. You can balance withdrawing cash from your portfolio and making sure your money lasts. This section tells you how.

Figuring Out What You Can Spend Each Year

The whole point of a retirement plan is to save enough money so you can live the way you want during retirement. However, when you retire, you have to be realistic. If you want your money to last, you can spend only a certain amount each year. That amount depends on the sources of income you have:

- Social Security benefits.
- Pension benefits, if you qualify for a pension.
- Part-time work.
- Income from your portfolio.
- Withdrawing principal from your portfolio.

If you're lucky and frugal, you may receive enough money from the first four sources to pay your living expenses. However, most people have to withdraw principal from their portfolios to make ends meet. If you fall into this category, here's how to figure out how much you can withdraw from your portfolio in income and principal each year without worrying about running out of money:

1. **Figure out the real return you expect from your portfolio between now and when you die.**

   The real return is the investment return you expect, reduced due to the effects of inflation. For example, if you expect to earn 7% and inflation is 3%, your real return is 3.9%. (To calculate the real return for yourself, use this formula: (1 + investment return)/(1+inflation rate) − 1, and then multiply by 100 for a percentage.) For simplicity, this example assumes the real return is 4%.

2. **Use the real return you calculated to figure out how much you can withdraw during your first year of retirement.**

Say your portfolio is $500,000. Multiplying your portfolio balance by the real return ($500,000 x 4%), you see that you can withdraw $20,000 the first year.

3. **Calculate the withdrawal for each subsequent year by multiplying the previous year's amount by the inflation rate.**

In this example, you'd increase your second-year withdrawal by 3%, making it $20,600. You'd withdraw $21,218 in the third year of retirement.

 If you opt to withdraw only the income from your portfolio, you may be tempted to weight your portfolio heavily on the bond and REIT side of things. Although you'll be able to withdraw more each year, your portfolio won't grow fast enough during retirement, and you'll run out of money sooner.

Creating a Retirement Paycheck

The withdrawal strategy in the previous section assumes that the annual return is the same each year. But you know that the market has good years and bad years. That's why you set up a cash reserve to cover several years of living expenses (page 190). That way, you won't have to sell investments at a loss to pay your bills. As long as you have a cash reserve, you can set up automatic withdrawals to act as a replacement for the paycheck you grew accustomed to.

Using the $20,000 first-year withdrawal from the previous example, here's how you use your cash reserve to set up a retirement paycheck:

1. **Set aside a cash flow resesrve for 5 years of living expenses.**

To keep things simple, multiply your first year's withdrawal by 5 (totaling $100,000 in this example).

2. **Put 1 year's worth of expenses ($20,000) in an ultra-low-risk savings account, like a money market account.**

You don't earn much interest, but you don't lose any money either.

3. **Invest the second year's living expenses (another $20,000) in a low-expense, short-term bond fund.**

Invest in high-quality bonds to keep your risk low (see page 132). You'll earn a better return than you do in the money market account without much additional risk. If you invest in municipal bonds, your taxes on the income will be low, too.

4. **Invest the remaining 3 years of living expenses in short- and inter-mediate-term bond funds.**

   These investments are still relatively low risk, but provide slightly high-er returns than the rest of your cash reserve, which helps protect your money against inflation.

5. **Set up a monthly transfer from your money market account or savings account (the one in step 2) to your checking account so it acts as your retirement "paycheck."**

   You can live on this money just like you did with your paycheck while you were working. In this example, the monthly amount starts at $1,667. Each year, you increase your monthly withdrawal for inflation, so the monthly amount in the second year is $1,717.

6. **Every year, replenish your cash reserve.**

   Remember, your cash reserve has to increase for inflation. So, if you started with $100,000, the next year's reserve would have to be $103,000.

   Because you have to sell investments to refill your cash reserve, choose what to sell wisely. If you can sell some investments without taking a loss, sell the investments that also keep your overall asset allocation on target (page 162). You can also use these sales to get rid of invest-ments that aren't meeting your expectations. If stocks and bonds are both in the toilet, sell short-term bonds first (they drop the least of any duration bond, as explained on page 138). That way, you give the rest of your portfolio time to recover.

   Because you have 5 years of expenses in your cash reserve, you have time to wait out a bear market. If all your investments have lost money, you can wait before replenishing your cash reserve. For example, you may choose to delay adding to your cash reserve for a year. Then, when the market recovers, you can sell investments to top off your reserve.

Tip If you have money in traditional IRAs or 401(k)s, you have to take required mini-mum distributions (page 180). When you refill your cash reserve, be sure to with-draw your RMDs first. After that, it usually makes sense to withdraw the additional money from your traditional IRAs and 401(k)s, so money in Roth IRAs can grow for as long as possible. (Roth IRAs don't have RMDs, so you can leave the money in as long as you like.)

11 Investing for College

Allin as a parent, you probably dream about your child graduating from college and hope it's from a topnotch school. A college degree means your kid is out on her own and, you hope, out of your hair. That degree opens doors to better jobs, higher salaries, and more personal satisfaction.

Whether your offspring ends up at the University of California at Berkeley, Penn State, or Muriel's Institute of Musicology, going to college isn't cheap. To make matters worse, the price goes up at a frightening pace. As with retirement, sending a kid to college is one of the biggest expenses you're likely to face.

Fortunately, whether you start saving for college before your child is born or when he or she is already into the terrible teens, you've got plenty of savings options. Section 529 savings plans, Section 529 prepaid plans, Coverdell savings accounts, Uniform Gifts to Minors Act accounts, and even taxable investment accounts can help you amass the small fortune you need for college expenses.

This chapter begins with a look at why saving for college is so challenging. Then you'll learn about the tax-advantaged savings plans available and how to choose the one that's right for you. And if you have more than one kid headed for higher ed, you'll learn strategies for contributing to more than one college savings account at a time. Finally, this chapter explains how to spend those college savings once your little darlings start school.

College Costs How Much?

When you see how much it costs to put a kid through college, you may wonder if it's worth it. You betcha. Over their lifetime, college graduates earn about 60% more than folks with just high school diplomas. Although college graduates aren't immune to hard economic times, those with less education do even worse. In November 2009, the U.S. Department of Labor reported an unemployment rate of 4.9% for people with at least a bachelor's degree. During the same period, the unemployment rate for high school graduates was 10.4%.

 Fortunately, most students don't have to foot the entire bill for higher education. Need-based financial aid, merit awards, sports scholarships, and other financial assistance usually cover some of the cost.

But higher ed costs are mind-numbingly high, and tuition increases makes them more daunting every year. From 1999 to 2009, public college tuition and fees rose 4.9% *more than* the general inflation rate, while the private college increase was 2.6% higher than inflation. As the table below shows, 1 year at a private college averages more than $35,000. Whoa! With annual increases, that's almost $150,000 for all 4 years—if you're lucky enough to have a kid who graduates in only 4 years.

Type of school	Average tuition and fees, 2009–10 school year	Room and board	Total
Community College	$2,544	$0	$2,544
Four-Year Public	$7,020	$8,193	$15,213
Four-Year Private	$26,273	$9,363	$35,636

Data courtesy of the College Board

Where does all that money go? Tuition is only the beginning. Here's what college expenses typically include:

- **Tuition.** Schools can charge tuition per credit, per class, or as a flat fee.

- **Room.** This is the cost for on-campus housing. Unless your kid lives at home while attending college, you have to pay for housing on campus or off.

- **Fees.** Expect anything from lab fees to student activities fees in this category.

- **Board.** Many schools require freshmen to buy some type of on-campus meal plan, though upperclassmen can often opt out. Either way, kids still need to eat.

- **Books and supplies.** This expense includes hard copy or eBooks, study guides, and lab workbooks, and averages $1,114 per year, according to the College Board (*http://tinyurl.com/ykvn6x4*).

- **Transportation and travel.** This cost includes trips home and commuting costs for students who live off campus.

- **Medical expenses.** School-provided medical insurance can cost up to $1,000 a year. To opt out, you usually have to provide proof of insurance.

- **Personal expenses.** Late-night pizza runs, laundry, and cell phone bills all add up.

Tax-Savvy Ways to Save for Education

The good news is that you can save for your child's college education several ways, and cut your tax bill at the same time. The following sections spill all the details, but the table below gives you an intro to your options.

Type of plan	Description	Controlled by	Financial aid impact	Contribution limit
529 Savings	Tax-advantaged plans available from all 50 states and Washington, DC. You save money in investment plans set up by the state.	Parent	Low; parents' asset	Varies by state
529 Prepaid	Tax-advantaged plans where you purchase future tuition at today's prices. These plans are available from in-state schools in some states and through a consortium of private colleges.	Parent	Low; parents' asset	Varies by state
Coverdell	Tax-advantaged accounts you set up through a bank, brokerage, or mutual fund company to save for kindergarten through grade 12 private school expenses or for college.	Parent	Low; parents' asset	$2,000 per year until 2011; then $500 per year
Uniform Gifts to Minors Act	Custodial accounts that parents or grandparents set up to pay for any kind of expenses incurred by minor children, not just for education.	Parent until child reaches 18 or 21	High; child's asset	None

Section 529 Savings Plans

Section 529 savings plans are the odds-on favorite for college savings—people squirreled away $89 billion in 529 plans as of the end of 2008, according to the Investment Company Institute. They come with great tax advantages. They're flexible. And they don't put too big a dent in your kid's shot at financial aid. What's not to like? If you decide to go with one of these plans, page 204 tells you how to choose the best one.

Section 529 savings plans let you salt away a boatload of money for college. Many plans have contribution limits higher than $300,000 and that's a lot of moola. Contributions to these plans grow tax-free, and you don't pay capital gains or any other taxes when you withdraw the funds—as long as you use the money for your child's qualified college or graduate school education expenses. What qualifies? Tuition, room, board, fees, and other expenses at any college, university, or trade school (nonprofit or for profit) where you can also take out a federal student loan. (If you spend 529 savings plan money on nonqualified expenses, you have to pay IRS taxes and penalties.)

Every state and Washington, DC, has at least one plan, and most have two or more. You can invest in any plan in any state, but you may get tax incentives and deductions if you go with a plan offered by the state you live in. Pennsylvania, Arizona, Maine, Kansas, and Missouri give tax deductions for investments in any state's 529 savings plan, for example. Tax incentives and deductions often come with income limits and other restrictions, so get the full scoop by checking the state plan's website or reading Savingforcollege.com's description of the plan you're considering (*http://tinyurl.com/ydq39dk*).

 Tip If your state doesn't have a minimum holding period for 529 savings plan funds and gives you a tax deduction or credit for your contributions, you can deposit money into the plan one day, withdraw it immediately to pay expenses, and still get a tax benefit. Sweet!

Most 529 savings plans let you choose from a wide range of investment options, like age-based plans, where the investments get more conservative as your child gets older; single mutual funds, where you choose the investment objectives you want; or a package of funds that invests your money conservatively, moderately, or aggressively. Page 207 explains how these options work.

 Note You can change your investment options only once a year. If you choose an age-based plan, that's not a problem; age-based plans automatically adjust your investments as time passes. But if you pick a packaged option or invest in single funds, you need to switch from more aggressive to more conservative investments as your child gets closer to college age. That way, you aren't as likely to lose principal when you're close to needing the money. When you change your investment options as time passes, you have to choose carefully—or you're stuck with them until the next year.

Section 529 savings plans are also easygoing when it comes to beneficiaries. Say son number one decides to join the Peace Corps, and you don't need his 529 for his college education. You can switch some or all of his funds to your other children. You can even change the beneficiary to yourself or another relative with eyes on a higher education prize, or hang onto the money until you have grandchildren.

As with any other type of asset, 529 savings plans affect how much financial aid your child may receive. Because the plan is held in your name (or a grandparent's name), not your child's, the financial aid eligibility impact is low. Colleges expect you to spend a maximum of 5.64% of Section 529 assets held in your name each year. For example, if you have $20,000 in college savings in your name, you'd have to spend $1,128 on tuition and expenses in a year. The colleges deduct that amount from the financial aid Scooter receives. On the other hand, colleges expect you to spend 20% of any assets in your child's name; in this example, if the 529 plan were in your child's name, that would amount to $4,000!

 Note Another benefit to you controlling a college savings account is that you also control how and when the money is spent.

Section 529 Prepaid Plans

Prepaid plans lock in future tuition costs at today's rates. That's usually a great deal, because tuition increases faster than inflation.

By 2009, only 18 states offered prepaid plans, and a consortium of private colleges offers just one prepaid plan. So why are the prepaid pickings so slim? Section 529 prepaid plans aren't easy to roll over into 529 savings plans or to transfer to other beneficiaries. Moreover, many plans have minimum holding periods before you can use the money toward tuition.

Prepaid plans are great if your child attends an in-state public college. Tuition at public colleges is growing faster than that at private colleges, so you save more money by locking in today's rates. If your ungrateful kid decides to go to school elsewhere, you can convert the funds and use them elsewhere. Most state prepaid plans let you put your money toward tuition somewhere else based on the average public school tuition rates for that year, in that state. Check your 529 prepaid plan documentation or call your state's prepaid plan administrator to find out exactly how much you'd get from a conversion.

 Tip Some states guarantee your investment in 529 prepaid plans, some don't. If you live in a state that doesn't guarantee your investment, be careful. You could lose some or all of your investment if the state runs into financial problems.

Prepaid plans come in two varieties:

- **Contracts.** You agree to buy a specific number of years of college tuition. The purchase price depends on your child's age at the time of purchase and whether you pay a lump sum or pay over time.

- **Prepaid Units.** You purchase a specific number of units, each one representing a percentage of 1 year's tuition. Prepaid units are more flexible than contracts because you can buy as many units as you want in a year. The unit price is the same regardless of how old your children are. The unit price typically rises each year as the cost of tuition increases.

The states that offer prepaid plans usually allow only in-state residents to contribute. Many of the existing plans aren't even accepting new contributions. To get the latest scoop on prepaid plans, check out Savingforcollege.com's plan details (*http://tinyurl.com/ybk4u2h*).

Prepaid plans have the same tax advantages as 529 savings plans. Funds grow tax-free and you don't have to pay any capital gains or other taxes when you withdraw money to pay qualified educational expenses.

 If you're sure your child is destined for Harvard or your private-college alma mater, you may want to check out the independent 529 plan, *www.independent529plan.org*. A consortium of more than 100 private schools offers a no-fee prepaid plan for any of the consortium's member colleges. If your child decides not to go to a member college or isn't accepted by one, you can roll over the balance (your contributions plus a small amount of interest) into a 529 savings plan.

Coverdell Education Savings Accounts

Before Section 529 savings and prepaid plans came around, Coverdell savings accounts were the primary tax-advantaged way to save for college. Their big drawback is a limit of $2,000 for annual contributions. Regardless how early you start, you can't save much in these accounts. But Coverdell accounts do one thing that 529 plans don't: They cover kindergarten through grade 12 expenses.

Qualified expenses for Coverdell accounts are broader than those of 529 savings plans. For students in elementary or secondary schools, you can spend Coverdell funds on private and religious school tuition, fees, and expenses. Qualified college expenses include tuition, fees, books, supplies, room, and board. Or you can buy a computer for students in your family who are in elementary school, secondary school, or college.

Because you can open a Coverdell account at a bank, brokerage firm, or mutual fund company, you can invest your contributions in just about anything you want.

 In 2001, Congress increased the Coverdell annual contribution to $2,000 and expanded qualified expenses to elementary and secondary schools. Those extra perks end on December 31, 2010, unless Congress takes action. Otherwise, the accounts will revert to their $500 annual contribution limits and limit qualified expenses to college costs only. In addition, you won't be able to withdraw from a Coverdell account in conjunction with some federal educational tax credits.

Uniform Gifts to Minors Accounts

The Uniform Gifts to Minors Act (UGMA) account started out as a way for parents and grandparents to gift financial assets to children who weren't old enough to legally own them. These accounts were the original way to save for college. Today, their claim to fame is that you can sock away money for your child for anything, not just college.

Assets in these accounts are irrevocable gifts to a child, but a trustee (usually a parent or grandparent) controls them until the child legally becomes an adult (age 18 or 21 depending on where you live). After that, the trustee has no say over how the child spends the money. College tuition, a Corvette, or a 50-inch HDTV are all fair game.

UGMA accounts are assets in a child's name, which means they reduce your child's potential financial aid more than other types of college savings accounts do, as page 209 explains. UGMA accounts also come with tax issues. Investment earnings up to $1,900 in 2009 are taxed at a child's lower rate (the "kiddie tax"). But investment income above $1,900 is taxed at the parent's higher rate for children ages 14 to 24.

How to Pick a 529 Savings Plan

If you opt for a 529 savings plan, you have to choose from 119 plans in 50 states and Washington, DC. Add in all the features and advantages of each plan, and you end up with some serious homework to pick one that's right for you. This section tells you how to streamline the process.

As you learned on page 201, your state's 529 plan deserves the first look, because most states offer tax deductions or credits to their residents. If your income is low enough, your state may even match your contributions.

But if you're scrimping to save for college, you want as much of your money to go to college as possible. Section 529 savings plans come in two flavors:

- A **direct plan** that the state of your choice runs is almost always cheaper than privately sold plans, because you pay lower fees and no brokerage commissions.

- You purchase a **broker-sold plan** through a financial advisor. If you need help choosing a plan, hiring a financial advisor might be worth the extra cost. Some advisors provide advice for a flat fee, which may cost less than paying a 5% or higher commission for broker-sold plans.

 Tip If you decide to hire a financial advisor to help you pick a 529 savings plan, look for someone with college savings expertise. Find out how they're compensated, and ask why the plan they recommend is better than other options.

Low fees are another reason to consider your state's plans. Some states charge account maintenance fees and enrollment fees only to out-of-state investors.

Most plans calculate their fees by multiplying how much you have in the plan by a percentage, known as an *asset-based expense ratio.* Look for asset-based expense ratios of less than 0.35%, or at the most, 0.75%. Avoid plans that charge fees for anything other than account maintenance.

In addition to tax incentives and fees, you have other options to consider: different investment managers, investment choices, minimum initial contributions, and minimum holding times before you can spend the money in an account. Use this table to see how to evaluate other features of 529 savings plans:

Plan feature	What to look for
Investment manager	An investment manager with low costs, like Vanguard, Fidelity, T. Rowe Price, American Century, or TIAA-CREF.
Management contract	A plan where the state hires an investment manager to run the plan; look for plans where the manager has at least 2 or 3 more years to go on her contract. Otherwise, you may have to choose new investment options if the state fires the current manager.
Minimum contributions	Initial investment minimums that you can afford: $1,000, $250, or even less. For ongoing contributions, $25 or $50 minimums give you the most flexibility.
Investment options	Several choices each of age-based, packaged funds, and single-fund options.

Account access	Online information, enrollment, and management is ideal. At the very least, download plan information and an enrollment form, and mail in the packet with a check. For ongoing access, see if you can check your account balance and make changes to your investments online. For withdrawals, look for transfers directly from your 529 savings plan into your bank account.
Minimum holding period	No minimum holding period or one that's less than a week.

You don't have to sort through all these options on your own. Saving-forcollege.com has a comparison tool (*http://tinyurl.com/ygky9sa*) to help you select the best Section 529 savings plan for you (as shown below). You start by narrowing your search by type of plan, and then you compare up to six features at a time. For 529 savings plans, screen for minimum contributions, age-based or static investment options, account maintenance fees, total asset-based expense ratio, state tax deduction or credit for contributions, and participant/owner change policies. For 529 prepaid plans, include as many contractual features options as you can.

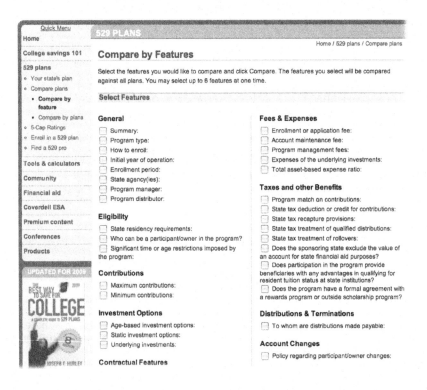

Choosing investment options

Once you pick a plan, the next challenge is choosing how the plan invests your money. You can change your investment option only once a year, so you need to pick carefully. Here are the three major investment options and the advantages of each:

- An **age-based plan** is the easiest option, because the plan automatically changes your investments based on your child's age. When your child is younger, the plan invests your funds more aggressively because time is on your side. You can take more risk in hopes of earning higher returns. As your child gets older, the plan automatically moves your money into more conservative investments so you're less likely to lose money just when you need it.

  Age-based plans vary enormously. Look for a plan that starts out with an 80%/20% stock-to-bond allocation. When your child is in middle school, a 50/50 split between stocks and bonds is good. By the time your child is halfway through high school, the allocation should be 20% stock and 80% bonds. When your child starts senior year and then goes off to college, look for a money market or FDIC savings account option.

- **Packaged funds** offer a basket of mutual funds to suit different levels of risk tolerance: aggressive, moderate, and conservative. Aggressive packages contain mostly stock funds with some bond or money market funds. The allocation is usually 100% stock or 90% stock/10% bonds. Moderate packages are approximately 60% stock/30% bonds/10% money market funds. Conservative packages give the lead to bond funds with small amounts of stock and money market funds, usually 60% bonds/40% stock. The packaged fund option you choose remains in place unless you change it.

- With **single funds,** you choose several funds from a menu of individual mutual funds with different investment objectives. You can allocate your money to several funds by percentages or dollar amounts, or put all your eggs in one basket. If you're a hands-on, knowledgeable investor, the single-funds option gives you the most flexibility. Your choices remain in effect until you change them.

 If you want safe and conservative, most 529 savings plans offer FDIC-insured options, which typically include the CollegeSure CD, a certificate of deposit whose rate is linked to a college-tuition index; CDs of varying maturities; or an FDIC-insured money market or savings account.

Revisit your investment choices each year to make sure they still make sense for you. If you choose a packaged or single-fund option, be sure to adjust your investment options to more conservative choices as your child gets closer to college age.

What to Do with Excess College Savings

Unless you're a multimillionaire, it's hard to save too much for college expenses. If you *do* end up with more money than you need in college savings accounts, you have several options:

- Transfer the money to your other children.
- Transfer the money to yourself, if you're planning to go back to school.
- Hang onto it. You can roll funds over to your grandchildren later on.
- If your child qualifies for a tax-free scholarship or GI Bill educational benefits, withdraw money from a 529 plan without having to pay a 10% IRS penalty. You still have to pay taxes on any gains, though.

Saving for More Than One Child

If you have more than one child, the challenges multiply. If more than one of your kids is in college at the same time, each child will probably get more financial aid. But you'll still be paying the lion's share of multiple college educations. Here are some guidelines to help you survive:

1. **Figure out how much you have to budget for college each month in dollars or as a percentage of your income. The College Board's College Cost Calculator (*http://tinyurl.com/cwfj8n*) helps you figure that out. The amount will change with your circumstances, but it's good to start with a firm number. Don't worry if the College Savings Calculator (*http://tinyurl.com/yf2juam*) says you need more. Page 210 tells you how to make up the difference.**

    Say your kids are 3 and 5 years old and the College Cost Calculator says you need to save $510 a month for the 3-year-old and $554 a month for the 5-year-old to pay for an in-state, 4-year college. If you can save $350 a month total, start with that number.

2. **Divide up whatever you earmark for college among your children.**

    Save the most for your older child, particularly if you didn't start saving when she was born, because you have the least amount of time to save for her. For example, set aside $200 a month for your elder child and $150 for the younger one.

3. **Commit to increasing your monthly savings by a set amount each year, say $50 a month, and allocate half of that increase to each child.**

That way, you add more money without breaking your household budget.

4. **If necessary, shift money from your oldest child's accounts to your younger children to make up any shortfall.**

If your oldest earns a massive sports scholarship or a National Merit Scholarship, you might move some money from her 529 plan account into an account for one of your other children. Fortunately, you can transfer money between accounts at any time, so you can wait to see how much an older child needs, and then transfer any extra funds to younger siblings.

 Tip Whatever you do, don't short your retirement savings to save for your kids' college. Your kids can borrow to pay college costs, but you can't do that for retirement. And you probably don't want your kids to have to support you in your old age. The key to saving for retirement and college is to start early, stick to your plan, and contribute to your retirement plan to earn the maximum amount your employer matches.

The Best Way to Spend College Savings

As you learned at the beginning of this chapter, a college education provides plenty of opportunities for spending money. The trick is spending the money you save in a way that stretches your savings *and* increases your child's financial aid. Here are several steps that help you do just that:

1. **Start by spending assets held in your child's name, because these assets reduce your child's financial aid eligibility.**

These assets include Uniform Gifts to Minors Act accounts and other savings accounts in the child's name. For example, you can use these assets for college-related costs that occur *before* you fill out financial aid forms, such as application and testing fees and college visits.

2. **Divide your college savings by 4 (the number of years you hope your child will take to complete college), and spend a quarter of the savings each year.**

This approach ignores the unfortunate tendency of college costs to rise faster than inflation. For "extra credit," you can use the average rate of college inflation (about 6%) to calculate how much to spend each year.

To calculate the first two years of spending, multiply the one-fourth by the college inflation rate. For example, if you have $5,000 to spend each year, the first year's spending is $4,450, and the second year's is $4,717. To calculate the third and fourth years' spending, increase the one-fourth by the college inflation rate, $5,300 and $5,618, in this example.

If what you've saved isn't even close to what you have to pay, you're not alone. Most parents have to dip into income, take out loans, or do both to make up the difference between savings and actual costs. Here are some steps to take to fill in the gap:

 Tip If you use current income to pay some expenses during your child's first two years of college, you can postpone tapping into your college savings. That delay leaves more money to cover the last two years and also gives your savings more time to grow.

1. **Get your child to sign up for what he qualifies for in federal Stafford loans, a government-funded loan program that he doesn't have to repay until he graduates.**

   The federal government increased loan limits in 2008. See *http://tinyurl.com/yd5hedm* to find out more.

2. **Ask your child to help foot the bill.**

   He can pitch in savings from a summer job, work-study programs, or a part-time job during the school year.

3. **Make an emergency appeal to the college's financial aid office.**

   You may get more financial aid, especially if you or your spouse has lost a job or had any other major financial setback. Call the financial aid office, explain your situation to a financial aid counselor, and ask whom you should talk to. Then write a letter to that person explaining your situation.

4. **Decide whether to take on debt.**

Additional debt should be your last resort. PLUS loans are federal loans parents can take out to help pay for a dependent child's undergraduate and graduate tuition and expenses. If you qualify, a PLUS loan isn't cheap. In 2009, fixed interest rates were 7.9% to 8.5% with up to a 4% origination fee. And you start repaying the loan right away. Find out more at *http://tinyurl.com/q4pr7j*.

Banks, savings and loans, and credit unions offer private student loans, which come as loans or lines of credit. Most come with high up-front origination fees, variable interest rates, and require that you start repaying right away.

12 Investing for Health Care

Face it, health insurance is expensive and getting more so every day. In 2009, the average family of four with employer-provided coverage spent $16,771 on health care costs, including premiums, according to health care consulting firm Milliman. If you can't get an affordable employer-based plan, costs are even higher. In addition, more and more employers are offering high-deductible health insurance plans paired with health savings accounts, which are less expensive for them, and usually more expensive for you.

If you have your own business, your employer doesn't offer health insurance, or he offers coverage that's too expensive, you're on your own—literally. Finding a policy can be complicated, because each one offers different coverage, deductibles, co-pays, and so on. And if you and your family members aren't in good health or have preexisting medical conditions, you may not be able to get health insurance at all.

This chapter describes the ins and outs of health insurance and identifies ways you can save and invest for your health care expenses. First, you'll learn about the different types of health insurance plans and how to choose one.

Because high-deductible health insurance plans are growing more prevalent, you'll find out whether one of these plans is right for you and how to set one up. These plans come with health savings accounts that help you save and invest toward your health care expenses.

Finally, this chapter offers some tips on how you can lower your health care costs and plan for long-term care.

Types of Health Insurance

Health insurance comes in several varieties, which you'll learn about shortly. Choosing the right plan is all about trade-offs. In general, the lower your premiums, the more you pay out of pocket for your medical care. For example, with a traditional indemnity plan (where you pay a deductible before plan benefits kick in), you're free to choose your doctors, but you pay dearly for that freedom. An HMO or PPO (where you have to patronize plan-approved professionals) may mean you have to switch doctors when you join, but you pay less out of pocket. With a high-deductible plan, your premiums are lower, but you pay a high deductible before the plan starts to pay. Here are the basics of the different types of plans:

- **Traditional indemnity plan.** Also known as a fee-for-service plan, an indemnity plan typically covers 80% of your costs after you reach your deductible, which can run up to $1,000 or more per person. You can choose any doctor who accepts your insurance plan.

- **Health Maintenance Organization (HMO).** A managed-care plan that provides benefits only when you see doctors and health providers affiliated with the HMO. To see a specialist, you must get a referral from your primary care doctor. Out-of-pocket expenses are usually low, typically for co-payments (a small cash amount, usually $10 or $20) for doctor visits and prescriptions.

- **Preferred Provider Organization.** A type of managed-care plan, where you choose from an approved list of doctors and other health care providers (what insurance companies call "in-network" providers). You can see doctors outside of your network, but you bear more of the cost for that. Out-of-pocket costs for PPOs are similar to those of an HMO.

- **Point-of-Service.** Like a PPO and HMO combined, a Point-of-Service plan requires a referral from your primary care physician for a visit to a specialist. As with a PPO, you can see an out-of-network specialist, but you pay more of the cost.

- **High-Deductible Plan.** A high-deductible health insurance plan has, unsurprisingly, a high deductible. It starts at $1,200 for individuals and $2,400 for a family and can run as high as $5,950 for an individual and $11,900 for a family. You pay for any expenses up to that amount each year before the plan benefits kick in. These plans usually come paired with a health savings account (HSA), a tax-free savings account you set up to pay for health care expenses the high-deductible plan doesn't cover (page 218).

Choosing an Employer-Sponsored Plan

Whether you get a new job or sign up for another year of health insurance when *open enrollment* (a period once each year when your employer lets you switch plans) rolls around, you need to choose a health insurance plan from the options your employer offers. If you have more than one option, choose carefully, because a mistake could cost you a bundle in either high premiums or high out-of-pocket expenses.

Here's a quick guide to choosing an employer plan:

1. **Read the information your employer provides about the health plan options.**

   Attend the benefits seminar that human resources departments usually sponsor. Many employers have tools on their intranets to help you evaluate your options and pick the best plan for you.

2. **See whether your current health care providers are in the plan you're considering.**

   Ask your doctors, therapists, and other health care providers if they accept the plan. Ask this question even if you stay with the same plan, because health care providers sometimes drop out of plans.

3. **Calculate how much your out-of-pocket costs could be and whether you can afford them.**

   Add up the plan's annual deductibles, *co-pays* (a fixed amount you pay for doctor's visits and prescription drugs), *co-insurance* (a percentage of the total cost that you're responsible for), and any other fees you may have to pay. (Many health insurance plans are switching from co-pays to co-insurance, because, you guessed it, you pay more of the bill that way.) Use your history of medical-care costs to estimate your current costs. Blue Cross/Blue Shield of Minnesota offers a calculator (*http://tinyurl.com/yehrded*) to help you estimate your out-of-pocket costs.

4. **If your spouse also has coverage, compare the costs between the two employer plans.**

   The cost of employer-based family coverage is rising faster than that for individuals. See if you can save money on premiums if you each enroll in your employer-sponsored plan, with one spouse signing up as an individual and the other covering the kids.

5. **Don't be shy about asking questions.**

   Health care benefits can be tough to figure out. Write questions down and ask someone in HR or at the health insurance plan. Don't back off until you understand the answer.

6. **Pick a plan.**

   If you're single and healthy, the cheapest plan option is probably fine. On the other hand, for a family, a PPO, HMO, or Point-of-Service plan is usually better, because your family probably requires more care, so you want reasonable premiums and manageable out-of-pocket expenses. But if you expect lots more medical expenses during the plan year, the deductible for a high-deductible plan could provide your lowest out-of-pocket total.

> **Tip** To help pay for health care, daycare, and other expenses, many employers offer Flexible Spending Accounts (FSAs). You fund an FSA through pretax payroll deductions, and your employer may also contribute. You have to figure out how much to contribute, because you have to spend all your FSA money by the end of the year (or the following March 15 if your employer takes advantage of an IRS rule that extends the deadline). If you don't spend your yearly contribution, you lose the remaining money.

Choosing an Individual Health Insurance Plan

If you aren't eligible for employer insurance, you have to go out on your own. Talk to a local insurance agent, or use online tools to get quotes. For example, eHealthInsurance.com (*http://tinyurl.com/yz7v8h3*) helps you get quotes from health insurance companies in your state, as you can see below.

> **Tip** Group policies are usually less expensive than policies for individuals. If you're self-employed, see whether any groups you belong to offer group health insurance coverage as a benefit.

Here's how to get a quote using eHealthInsurance:

1. **In the Insurance Type drop-down list, choose the type of health insurance you want. In the Zip Code box, type your Zip code. Click Go.**

   You can choose Individual & Family, Small Business, or Short-term. (Short-term policies work for gap insurance coverage for less than a year—for example, when you're in between jobs or waiting for a new group plan to start—and are generally cheaper than individual or family policies.)

2. **Under "Get Quotes for Individual & Family Health Insurance Plans", answer the questions on gender, date of birth, smoking status, and student status for you and anyone else the plan will cover. If you have more than two children, click Add More Children. Click Go.**

   The results show the number of health plans found and the lowest premium available. You can sort plans by best seller, price, deductible, ratings, and company. Each health plan shows the plan type, deductible, co-insurance, cost for an office visit, and the monthly cost.

3. **Click Apply for any plan you're interested in.**

   You usually hear whether you're approved within 24 hours.

4. **If you're overwhelmed, click Help Me Choose below the results.**

   You answer several questions and the site provides recommendations based on your answers.

If you have preexisting conditions, many insurers exclude them from coverage for the first 6 to 12 months, which means you pay for all expenses for those conditions during that period.

High-Deductible Health Insurance Plans

High-deductible health insurance plans are exactly that: insurance plans where the yearly *deductible,* that is, the amount you pay out of pocket for your health care before your plan pays, is high. The higher the deductible you're willing to pay, the lower your premium. If you're healthy as a horse and don't spend much on health care, you can save some big bucks with a plan like this. The amount you pay for covered health care expenses is capped by the IRS at $5,950 if you're single ($11,900 for a family). That's a lot of moola, which is one reason you'll usually see these plans paired with health savings accounts (HSAs), which you'll learn about shortly.

 Some high-deductible health plans offer preventive care with a lower or no deductible. Preventive care includes physicals, prenatal and well-baby visits, immunizations, and health screenings for cancer, vision, hearing loss, and other conditions.

Although anyone can sign up for a high-deductible plan, employers are flocking to them. The Employee Benefit Research Institute estimates that, in 2009, between 15 and 19 million Americans were covered by high-deductible health insurance plans. Employers like them because they cost the employer less. And, in theory, you spend more carefully on health care because it comes out of your own pocket.

Health Saving Accounts

Health savings accounts (HSAs) can help you with those out-of-pocket expenses. They're accounts in which you deposit pretax contributions to cover those expenses, and they're designed to work in conjunction with high-deductible insurance plans. In fact, you can open an HSA only if you have a high-deductible health insurance plan *and* it qualifies under federal rules. To figure out if you qualify, use the Principal Financial Group's Eligibility and Contributions tool (*http://tinyurl.com/yja83ft*), shown below.

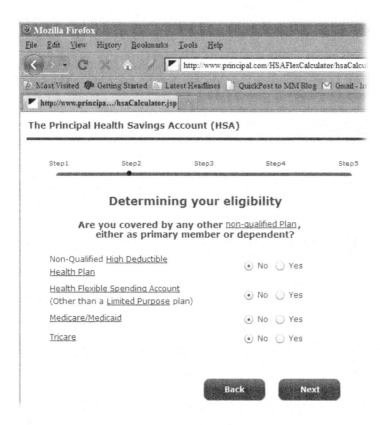

The tool has five steps, with a progress bar at the top:

1. **Give the tool some basic info about you and your health plan.**

   Enter the date you go live with your qualified high-deductible plan, your deductible, and whether you have a single or family plan.

2. **See if you're eligible based on other coverage you have.**

   Some health insurance plans, such as Medicare, Medicaid, or a health flexible spending account, disqualify you from opening an HSA. As soon as you choose an option that disqualifies you, a page appears telling you that you are ineligible.

3. **See if other issues disqualify you.**

   For example, you aren't eligible if someone else claims you as a dependent on their tax return or if you get VA medical benefits.

4. **Think about whether your status will change in a way that may disqualify you from participating in an HSA.**

   For example, if you'll turn 65 later in the year and qualify for Medicare, or if your spouse has a new job and you plan to enroll in a traditional health care plan through that employer.

5. **Click Next to find out if you qualify.**

   If you qualify, the final page says, "Congratulations".

 Tip If you're covered by Medicare, you can't contribute to an HSA. But, if you already have an HSA, you can withdraw funds from the HSA to cover other costs without penalty once you turn 65. You'll have to pay tax on those withdrawals, however. But if you use HSA funds for qualified medical costs, withdrawals are tax free.

Setting up an HSA

You can open an HSA as soon as your qualified high-deductible coverage becomes effective. If you get an employer-based plan, you can make contributions through payroll deductions. Many employers also contribute to your HSA (as much as $500 to $1,000 each year), because it's cheaper than paying for traditional health insurance.

 Note Don't be too optimistic about how much deductible you can afford to pay. Sure, your contribution to a health savings account is tax deductible, and you can use that money to pay out-of-pocket HSA costs. However, you may lose the tax savings if you have to borrow money to cover your out-of-pocket expenses.

The IRS limits how much you can contribute each year, although the limits increase every year for inflation. In 2010, you can sock away $3,050 if you're single and as much as $6,150 for a family. If you're over 55, you can put away an extra $1,000 in both single and family accounts. The deadline for making contributions for a 2009 HSA is April 15, 2010. For 2010 HSA accounts, it's April 15, 2011.

 Tip You can deduct your HSA contributions on your tax return. Employer contributions aren't taxable. But be sure to save your health-care expense receipts in case you're audited.

Choosing an HSA provider

Hundreds of banks, credit unions, insurance companies, and other financial services providers offer HSA services. Here are features to consider when you choose an HSA provider:

- **Fees.** When choosing among HSA providers, get a written list of fees, compare them, and choose the one with the lowest fees. Banks may charge a bewildering variety of fees, from setup charges to maintenance fees to charges for specific transactions such as writing checks. Many charge a fee to close your account.

- **Investment options.** Your HSA investment options depend on what's offered by your bank, brokerage firm, insurance company, or credit union. The IRS permits lots of options for HSA investments including stocks, bonds, mutual funds, exchange-traded funds, REITs, certificates of deposit, and savings accounts. You're usually using an HSA to pay for current medical expenses, so it makes sense to stick with very conservative investments. Go with a low-fee provider that offers savings accounts, money market accounts, and perhaps low-fee stock, bond, and balanced mutual funds.

- **Ease of use.** Look for a plan that lets you pay for your out-of-pocket expenses using a debit card or check directly drawn on your HSA. Submitting receipts, filling out forms, and waiting for reimbursement is too much hassle.

Up to Speed

Choosing HSA Investments

Conservative is the watchword with money in an HSA. You want money to pay for medical expenses, so you don't want to risk losing a lot in the stock market. Here are some guidelines for different levels of HSA investments:

- **Less than $5,000.** Keep the money in a money market account or a savings account linked to a debit card or checking account.
- **Between $5,000 and $10,000.** Keep a minimum of $5,000 in a money market account or checking account, more if you anticipate higher medical bills in the near future. For the rest, consider a balanced mutual fund that invests in both stocks and bonds (see page 78).
- **More than $10,000.** Keep $5,000 or more in a money market account or checking account. Invest the next $5,000 in a balanced fund. Anything above that can go into a stock or bond fund, depending on the risk you're willing to take (page 156).

What are qualified medical expenses?

Before you spend money from your HSA, make sure your expenses qualify, because some don't. The IRS publishes a list of qualified expenses every year, which you can find in IRS publication 969 on the IRS website (*http://tinyurl.com/yopnep*) and in IRS Publication 502 (*http://tinyurl.com/34pgy*).

Qualified medical expenses run the gamut and include prescription drugs (including birth control pills), glasses, contact lenses, dental expenses, dentures, psychological therapy, crutches, wheelchairs, health insurance premiums, massages, and more. However, hair removal, diaper services, illegal drugs, health club dues, vitamins, over-the-counter drugs, maternity clothes, teeth whitening, and funeral expenses do *not* qualify. If you spend funds from your HSA on nonmedical expenses, you have to pay taxes on those withdrawals plus a 10% penalty.

 You can use HSA funds to install special equipment in your house or to renovate it to accommodate a medical condition or disability, such as a wheelchair ramp or railings in a bathroom. If improvements or renovations result in an increase in the value of your house, you have to subtract that increase from the overall cost of the improvements to determine the net expense of the improvements. You can pay for the net expenses with HSA funds.

If you have an individual HSA, you can use HSA funds only for your qualified expenses. With a family HSA, you and your spouse can each set up individual HSAs and use those funds for your expenses and those of your dependents. For tax purposes, dependents include your children, stepchildren, nieces, nephews, and grandchildren who live with you and whom you claim on your tax return as dependents.

 If you leave your high-deductible health insurance plan with money still in your HSA, don't fret. You can't contribute any more money, but you can keep your HSA open and pay for qualified medical expenses. If you go back to a high-deductible health insurance plan later, you can resume contributing to your HSA.

Why Go High-Deductible/HSA?

High-deductible health plans aren't for everyone. For example, you may be more comfortable knowing that your insurance plan will cover most of your health care expenses and be willing to pay a higher premium for that comfort. However, if you're healthy, don't have any kids, or want lower premiums, a high-deductible plan may make sense.

To compare a high-deductible plan to a traditional plan, use the HSACenter tool (*http://tinyurl.com/hsacentertool*), as shown below.

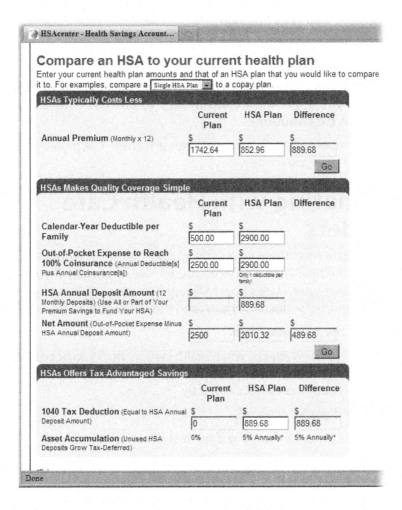

Here's how to see whether a high-deductible plan makes sense:

1. **In the drop-down list, select Single HSA Plan or Family HSA Plan. For Annual Premium, fill in the annual premium for your current plan and the HSA you're considering.**

   The Difference box shows the difference between the annual premiums.

2. **Under "HSAs Makes Quality Coverage Simple", fill in your annual deductible, out-of-pocket expense to fulfill the 100% co-insurance limit, and the HSA annual deposit amount (how much you plan to deposit in your HSA this year).**

   The calculator calculates the cost difference between your current plan and the HSA.

3. **Under "HSAs Offers Tax-Advantaged Savings", fill in the tax deduction you'll get from contributing to an HSA (the amount of your HSA contribution).**

   If the numbers in the Difference boxes are positive, a high-deductible plan may save you money.

Negotiating with Health Care Providers

With health care costs rising so rapidly, it makes sense to negotiate for better rates on the health care services you receive, especially if you're paying for your own care. Here's how to figure out what services you need, if they're covered, how much they cost, and how to negotiate the best price:

1. **Identify the care you need.**

   You need to know exactly what health care services you need. Ask your doctor for the code for any test or service she performed. Make sure you spell the test or service correctly.

2. **Find out if you're covered.**

   Ask your insurance company if the test or service is covered.

 In reality, it isn't easy to control your health-care costs, although you can reduce them by comparing what doctors, hospitals, and other services charge, and then choosing a less-expensive provider.

3. **If the test or service isn't covered, check online for price ranges.**

   Websites like HealthcareBluebook.com (*http://tinyurl.com/yh4x8z5*), OutofPocket.com (*http://tinyurl.com/yzox45y*), as well as some state health department websites provide price data. These sites aren't comprehensive, but they're a place to start, as you can see below. Pricedoc.com shows doctors with fixed fees for services and procedures. Coverage is spotty, especially for smaller cities and rural areas.

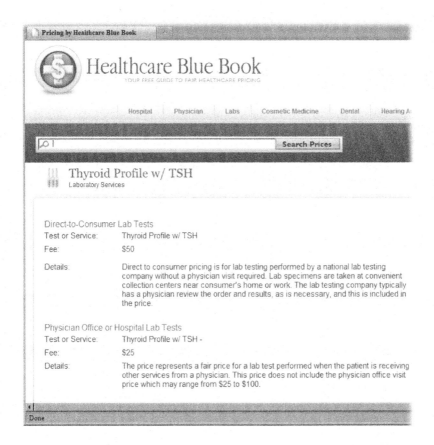

4. **Get quotes in writing.**

   Call health care providers in your area. Tell the billing office you're paying for the service yourself. Ask if there are any related costs that aren't included in that price. Ask for the quote in writing, either via email or fax. HealthcareBlueBook.com has a printable pricing agreement form you can print, which is available on their search result page.

   Tip If you've already had a procedure, try to negotiate a discount after the fact. Speak to someone in billing, and explain that you're paying yourself. Ask for a discount. For large bills, ask for a payment plan to pay over several months.

Paying for Long-Term Care

You don't know how long you're going to live or what your health will be like as you get older. What is certain is that long-term care will cost a bundle should you require it decades from now (page 16). Medicare doesn't cover those costs, which is why so many financial advisors recommend long-term care insurance, which covers nursing homes, assisted living, and in-home care.

Long-term care insurance premiums depend on how old you are, your health, and the policy's benefits. AARP provides a calculator to help you figure out your costs (*http://tinyurl.com/5t96mn*). Get quotes on long-term care insurance at LongTermCareInsuranceTree.com (*http://tinyurl.com/5t96mn*).

Index

Symbols

spending savings for, **209–212**
types of accounts for, **200**
Uniform Gifts to Minors Act (UGMA),
  200, **204**
commodity funds, **78**
companies. *See also* small businesses
  accounts payable of, evaluating, **126**
  assets of, evaluating, **126**
  balance sheet, **106–108**
  cash flow statement, **108**
  cash of, evaluating, **126**
  debt of, analyzing, **112–115**, **126**
  earnings per share (EPS), **126**
  growth of, evaluating, **108–111**
  income statement, **105–106**
  inventory of, evaluating, **126**
  management effectiveness of,
    115–118
  price ratios for, **120–124**
  profitability of, **118–120**
  quality of, evaluating, **111–120**
  return on assets (ROA), **116**
  return on equity (ROE), **115–116**
  revenues of, **125**
  shareholders' equity, **108**
  turnover ratios of, **117–118**
  value of, evaluating, **120–125**
company size
  categories of, **80**, **83**
  diversification by, **162**
compound annual growth rate, **110**
compounding
  benefits of, for investing, **16–20**
  of inflation, **15–16**
convertible bonds, **135**
co-pays, **215**
cost of goods sold, **106**
Couch Potato Portfolio, **168**
coupon rate for bonds, **128**, **129**, **133**,
  134–135
Coverdell education savings account,
  67, **200**, **203–204**
credit cards, **41–43**
credit quality
  of bond funds, **81**
  of bonds, **131–133**

Ctrl+clicking, how to, **7**
currency risk, **159**
current ratio of a company, **114**
current yield of bonds, **137**

D

day traders, **104**
debts, company, **112–115**, **126**
debts, personal
  buying stock on margin, **43**
  good reasons for, **40**
  high-interest, getting rid of, **41–43**
  paying off before retiring, **27**
debt-to-equity ratio, **113**
defined-benefit plans, **29**
defined-contribution plans, **30**
diversification. *See* asset allocation
dividend reinvestment plan (DRIP), **111**
dividends, **158**
  from mutual funds, **63**
  reinvesting, **158**
  from REITs, **62**, **142–143**, **145**, **148**
  from stock, **56**, **58**, **124**
dividend yield, **124**
dollar cost averaging, **4**, **178**
double-clicking, as used in this book, **6**
dragging, as used in this book, **6**
DRIP (dividend reinvestment plan), **111**

E

earnings per share (EPS), **126**
economic risk, **158**
efficient market theory, **120**
ego, excessive, **51**
eHealthInsurance.com website, **216**
employer-sponsored insurance plans,
  215–216
employer's stock, risks of investing in,
  47, **157**
EPS (earnings per share), **126**
equity, for a company, **108**
equity REITs, **143–144**
equity risk, **159**
estate plans for parents, **35**
Estimating Your Retirement Needs
  worksheet, **25–27**

exchange-traded funds (ETFs), **61**, **72**, **75–76**. *See also* mutual funds
choosing, **92–93**
expenses of, **76**
in lazy portfolio, **167**
REIT ETFs, **62**
tax issues regarding, **68**
trading volume of, **93**
value of, when calculated, **72**, **75**
expense ratio, **90**, **91**
expenses and fees. *See also* college expenses; debts, personal; health care
during retirement, **25–27**, **177**
for ETFs, **76**
for 401(k) plans, **179**
for 403(b) plans, **179**
for index funds, **60**
for mutual funds, **61**, **74**, **90–92**, **98**
12b-1 fees, **91**
expenses, company, **106**

F

face amount of bonds. *See* principal of bonds
federal Stafford loans, **210**
fees. *See* expenses and fees
FFO (funds from operations), **147**
financial advisor, **48**, **52**
financial goals. *See* goals
529 college prepaid plan, **67**, **200**, **202–203**
529 college savings plan, **67**, **200–202**, **204–208**
Flexible Spending Accounts (FSAs), **216**
followers (type of investor), **46**, **48–49**
foreign funds, **80**
401(k) plans, **178–181**
advantages of, **178–179**
choosing investments in, **100–101**
disadvantages of, **179–180**
fees for, **179**
maximum contribution for, **30**, **65**
for small businesses, **187**
tax issues regarding, **65**, **178**

403(b) plans, **178–181**
advantages of, **178–179**
choosing investments in, **100**
disadvantages of, **179–180**
fees for, **179**
maximum contribution for, **65**
tax issues regarding, **65**, **178**
front-end loads, **92**
FSAs (Flexible Spending Accounts), **216**
fundamental analysis, **104**
fund brokerage commissions, **91**
funds, **59–61**, **71**. *See also* exchange-traded funds (ETFs); index funds; mutual funds
funds from operations (FFO), **147**

G

gender differences in investing habits and results, **46**
geography, diversification by, **162**
Gilbertson, Kevin (TinyURL website), **7**
global funds, **80**
goals. *See also* college expenses; health care; retirement
contributions required to achieve, **31–33**, **37–38**, **43**
determining, **3**, **21–23**
enjoyable pursuits, **36**
inheritance, leaving, **36**
second home, **35**
short-term, **14**
versions of, based on likelihood of accomplishing, **22**
Graham, Benjamin (stock advice by), **111**
gross margin for a company, **119**
gross profit, **106**
growth funds, **79**
growth of company, evaluating, **108–111**

H

health care, **33–34**
cost of, **27**, **224**
employer-sponsored insurance plans, **215–216**

investment objective of a fund, 77
investment returns, **156–159**. *See also* dividends
average, **17**, **19**
compared to inflation rate, **17**
compounding's effect on, **17–19**
realistic expectations for, **44–45**
versus risk, **156**
investments. *See also* bonds; mutual funds; real estate investment funds; stocks
asset allocation for, **153–154**, **159–167**
buying and selling frequently, **50**
current, attachment to, **47**
distributing according to how accounts are taxed, **67–70**
in employer's stock, risks of, **47**, **157**
fees associated with. *See* expenses and fees
managing, **99–102**, **154–155**, **188–191**
rebalancing, **170–172**
reviewing, **155**, **169–170**
investment style categories, **79**
investors
followers, **46**, **48–49**
gender differences in habits and results of, **46**
leaders, **46**, **49–51**
power players, **46**, **51–52**
protectors, **46**, **46–48**
psychological pitfalls of, **45–52**
IRAs, **181–183**
catch-up contribution, **181**
converting to Roth IRAs, **183–187**
inherited IRAs, **66**, **183**
rollover IRAs, **65**, **180**
Roth IRAs, **66**, **182–187**
SEP-IRAs, **66**, **187**
traditional IRAs, **65**, **181–182**, **183–187**
issuer of bonds, **58**, **129**

K

Keogh plans, **187**
keyboard shortcuts, **7**

L

large-cap stocks, **80**
lazy portfolio, **166–168**
leaders (type of investor), **46**, **49–51**
level loads, **92**
liabilities, for a company, **107**
life insurance, **33**, **188**
living wills, **35**
load-adjusted returns, **89**
loans. *See* debts; mortgage
long-term bonds, **134**
long-term capital gains, **63**
LongTermCareInsuranceTree.com website, **226**
long-term care (LTC), **33–34**, **226**
losses
discounting as out of your control, **50**
dislike of, **47**
forgetting about, **51**
ignoring, **48**
offsetting with gains, **70**, **99**
LTC (long-term care), **33–34**, **226**

M

management effectiveness of a company, **115–118**
market index, **60**
marketing and distribution expenses, **91**
market risk, **158**
maturity
of bond funds, **81**
of bonds, **58**, **129**, **133–134**
medical expenses. *See* health care
medical savings account (MSA), **67**
medium-term bonds, **134**
menus, how to use, **7–8**
mergers of mutual funds, **98**
micro-company stocks, **159**
mid-cap stocks, **80**
Missing CD website, **9**, **15**
mistakes in investing, **48**
money market funds, **78**
Morningstar website, **79–90**, **95**, **121**, **147**, **150–152**

profit margin for a company, **118**
prospectus
  for bonds, **132**
  for funds, **77, 82, 89, 92**
protectors (type of investor), **46, 46–48**
PSR (price/sales ratio), **124**
psychological pitfalls in investing, **45–52**

Q

quality of company, evaluating, **111–120**
quick ratio of a company, **115**

R

rational price of a stock, **122**
real estate investment trusts (REITs),
    61–62, 141–143
  cash reinvested by, **145**
  choosing, **144–152**
  depreciation affecting, **147**
  dividends from, **62, 142–143, 145, 148**
  profits of, **146**
  screening, **149–152**
  tax issues regarding, **63, 69, 142**
  types of, **143–144**
receivables turnover ratio, **118**
redemption fees, **91**
red zone, **189–191**
reinvesting dividends, **158**
reinvestment risk, **159**
REIT ETFs, **62**
REIT mutual funds, **62, 150–152**
REITs. *See* real estate investment trusts
required minimum distributions (RMDs),
    180
resources. *See* books; website resources
retirement. *See also* 401(k) plans; 403(b)
    plans; IRAs; Roth IRAs
  accounts for, **177–187**
  alone, **25**
  average amount Americans have
    saved for, **28**
  cash reserve during, **195–196**
  contributions required for, **31–33**
  cost of, determining, **25–27, 177**
  life insurance for, **33, 188**

living off investment income during,
    30
managing investments prior to,
    188–191
postponing, **172, 191**
principal, withdrawing, **30, 194**
priority of, **23, 177**
red zone prior to, **189–191**
small business plans for, **187**
Social Security for, **191–193**
sources of income for, **28–30**
when to begin, **24–25, 176**
withdrawing money during, **194–196**
working during, **30**
Retirement_Plan.xls worksheet, **25–27,**
    31–33, 37
return on assets (ROA), **116**
return on equity (ROE), **115–116**
returns. *See* investment returns
revenues of company, **125**
revenue statement. *See* income
    statement, company
right-clicking, how to, **6**
risk, **156–159**
  with bonds, **59**
  phases of life determining, **163**
  reducing as goals near, **188**
  reducing, bonds for, **128**
  with stock, **57**
  tolerance of, **3–5, 46, 154, 160**
RMDs (required minimum distributions),
    180
ROA (return on assets), **116**
ROE (return on equity), **115–116**
rolling returns, **88**
rollover IRAs, **65, 180**
Roth 401(k) plans, **180**
Roth, Allan (certified financial planner),
    168
Roth conversion, **66**
Roth IRAs, **66, 182–187**
Rutgers University website, **160**

S

salary. *See* wages
Savingforcollege.com website, **206**

savings accounts, 2
saving toward financial goals, 31–33, 37–38, 43
The Second-Grader Portfolio, 168
second home, 35
SEC (Securities and Exchange Commission) website, 161
Section 529 college prepaid plan, 67, 200, 202–203
Section 529 college savings plan, 67, 200–202, 204–208
sector, diversification by, 162
secured bonds, 131
Securities and Exchange Commission (SEC) website, 161
senior bonds, 132
SEP-IRAs, 66, 187
shareholders' equity. See equity
share price of bonds, 139
shares of stock. See stock
Sharpe ratio, 95
Shift+clicking, how to, 7
short-term bonds, 134
short-term capital gains, 63
short-term successes, desire for, 45
simple interest, 18
SIMPLE IRAs, 187
small businesses. See also companies
   retirement plans for, 187
   SEP-IRAs for, 66
   starting, loan for, 40
small-cap stocks, 80
SmartMoney's One Asset Allocation System, 165
Social Security, 28–29, 191–193
   benefits calculator for, 28
   benefits from, based on retirement age, 25, 29
   benefits from, delaying, 192–193
   eligibility for, 28, 192
   full retirement age, 29, 192
   history of, 24
   how long it will be around, 29
   life expectancy and, 193
   Wage Index website, 16
   working while receiving benefits from, 193

speculative bonds, 132, 159
spending, guidelines for, 43–44, 194–196
spread, of bond prices, 139
Stafford loans, 210
stepped-up basis, for stock inheritances, 68
stock, 56–58, 103. See also companies
   advice regarding
      by Benjamin Graham, 111
      by Warren Buffet, 103
   buying on margin, 43
   capital gains from, 56
   day traders of, 104
   dividends from, 56, 58, 124
   employer's, risks of investing in, 47, 157
   fundamental analysis of, 104
   inheriting on stepped-up basis, 68
   micro-company stocks, 159
   rational price of, 122
   returns from, 156–157
   reviewing, 170
   risk of, 57
   tax issues regarding, 63, 68
   technical analysis of, 103
   trends in, evaluating, 125–126
stock funds, 78
subordinated bonds, 132
Swensen, David (author), 169

T

target date funds, 77
taxable accounts, 62
   bonds in, issues regarding, 130
   managing, 69–70
   types of investments to hold in, 68–69
tax-adjusted returns, 89
tax-advantaged accounts, 62, 64–67, 68–69, 100
tax-deferred accounts, 64–67
taxes, 62–70
   bonds and, 63, 69, 130
   calculator for, 99
   during retirement, 27

Get even more for your money.

Join the O'Reilly Community, and register the O'Reilly books you own. It's free, and you'll get:

- $4.99 ebook upgrade offer
- 40% upgrade offer on O'Reilly print books
- Membership discounts on books and events
- Free lifetime updates to ebooks and videos
- Multiple ebook formats, DRM FREE
- Participation in the O'Reilly community
- Newsletters
- Account management
- 100% Satisfaction Guarantee

Signing up is easy:

1. Go to: oreilly.com/go/register
2. Create an O'Reilly login.
3. Provide your address.
4. Register your books.

Note: English-language books only

To order books online:
oreilly.com/store

For questions about products or an order:
orders@oreilly.com

To sign up to get topic-specific email announcements and/or news about upcoming books, conferences, special offers, and new technologies:
elists@oreilly.com

For technical questions about book content:
booktech@oreilly.com

To submit new book proposals to our editors:
proposals@oreilly.com

O'Reilly books are available in multiple DRM-free ebook formats. For more information:
oreilly.com/ebooks

O'REILLY®

Have it your way.

O'Reilly eBooks

- Lifetime access to the book when you buy through oreilly.com
- Provided in up to four DRM-free file formats, for use on the devices of your choice: PDF, .epub, Kindle-compatible .mobi, and Android .apk
- Fully searchable, with copy-and-paste and print functionality
- Alerts when files are updated with corrections and additions

oreilly.com/ebooks/

Safari Books Online

- Access the contents and quickly search over 7000 books on technology, business, and certification guides
- Learn from expert video tutorials, and explore thousands of hours of video on technology and design topics
- Download whole books or chapters in PDF format, at no extra cost, to print or read on the go
- Get early access to books as they're being written
- Interact directly with authors of upcoming books
- Save up to 35% on O'Reilly print books

See the complete Safari Library at safari.oreilly.com

O'REILLY®

Personal Investing

THE MISSING CD

There's no CD with this book; you just saved $5.00.

Instead, every single Web address, practice file, and piece of downloadable software mentioned in this book is available at www.missingmanuals.com (click the Missing CD icon). There you'll find a tidy list of links, organized by chapter.

Don't miss a thing!
Sign up for the free Missing Manual email announcement list at www.missingmanuals.com. We'll let you know when we release new titles, make free sample chapters available, and update the features and articles on the Missing Manual Web site.

CPSIA information can be obtained
at www.ICGtesting.com
Printed in the USA
BVOW03s1002091216
470322BV00012B/131/P

9 781449 381783

Personal Investing

THE MISSING CD

There's no CD with this book; you just saved $5.00.

Instead, every single Web address, practice file, and piece of downloadable software mentioned in this book is available at www.missingmanuals.com (click the Missing CD icon). There you'll find a tidy list of links, organized by chapter.

Don't miss a thing!
Sign up for the free Missing Manual email announcement list at www.missingmanuals.com. We'll let you know when we release new titles, make free sample chapters available, and update the features and articles on the Missing Manual Web site.

CPSIA information can be obtained
at www.ICGtesting.com
Printed in the USA
BVOW03s1002091216
470322BV00012B/131/P